Beyond the Protest Square

Protest, Media and Culture

Series Editors: Ruth Sanz Sabido is Reader in Media and Social Inequality at Canterbury Christ Church University, UK; Stuart Price is Professor of Media and Political Discourse and Chair of the Media Discourse Group at De Montfort University, UK

Protest, Media and Culture publishes edited collections and monographs dedicated to the study and analysis of an irrepressible phenomenon: the worldwide resurgence of social, cultural, political and economic discontent.

Sites of Protest
Edited by Stuart Price and Ruth Sanz Sabido

Protest Campaigns, Media and Political Opportunities
Jonathan Cable

The Pink Tide: Media Access and Political Power in Latin America
Edited by Lee Artz

artWORK: Art, Labour and Activism
Edited by Alberto Cossu, Jessica Holtaway and Paula Serafini

Songs of Social Protest: International Perspectives
Edited by Aileen Dillane, Martin J Power, Eoin Devereux, and Amanda Haynes

Beyond the Protest Square: Digital Media and Augmented Dissent
Tetyana Lokot

Beyond the Protest Square

Digital Media and Augmented Dissent

Tetyana Lokot

ROWMAN & LITTLEFIELD

London • New York

Rowman & Littlefield International Ltd. is an affiliate of Rowman & Littlefield
4501 Forbes Boulevard, Suite 200, Lanham, Maryland 20706, USA
With additional offices in Boulder, New York, Toronto (Canada), and Plymouth (UK)
www.rowman.com

British Library Cataloguing in Publication Data

A catalogue record for this book is available from the British Library

Library of Congress Cataloging-in-Publication Data

Names: Lokot, Tetyana, 1981- author.
Title: Beyond the protest square : digital media and augmented dissent / Tetyana Lokot.
Other titles: Augmented dissent
Description: London ; New York : Rowman & Littlefield, [2021] |
    Series: Protest, media and culture | Revision of author's thesis (doctoral)—University
    of Maryland at College Park, 2016, titled Augmented dissent : the affordances
    of ICTs for citizen protest (a case study of the Ukraine Euromaidan protests of
    2013-2014). | Includes bibliographical references and index. | Summary: "The book
    provides an overview of existing theoretical discussions and field research on the role
    of digital technology, the internet, and social media in social transformations, civic
    culture, and protests"— Provided by publisher.
Identifiers: LCCN 2020054132 (print) | LCCN 2020054133 (ebook) |
    ISBN 9781786605962 (cloth) | ISBN 9781786605979 (epub)
    ISBN 9781538181225 (pbk)
Subjects: LCSH: Digital media--Political aspects--Case studies. | Protest
    movements in mass media—Case studies. | Digital media—Political
    aspects—Ukraine. | Digital media—Political aspects—Russia
    (Federation) | Protest movements—Ukraine—History—21st century. |
    Protest movements--Russia (Federation)—History—21st century. |
    Ukraine—History—Euromaidan Protests, 2013-2014. | Ukraine—Politics
    and government—1991- | Russia (Federation)—Politics and government—1991-
Classification: LCC HM851 .L655 2021 (print) | LCC HM851 (ebook) |
    DDC 302.23/1—dc23
LC record available at https://lccn.loc.gov/2020054132
LC ebook record available at https://lccn.loc.gov/2020054133

Contents

List of Figures   vii

List of Tables   ix

Acknowledgments   xi

1 Introduction   1

2 Digital Media and Society in Ukraine and Russia   15

3 Euromaidan Protesters: A Snapshot   29

4 Space, Distance, and Digital Media   49

5 Socially Mediated Visibility and Protest Witnessing   69

6 Protest Organizing and Networked Communities   89

7 Information Sharing and Protest Frames   117

8 Russia: Protest in the Age of Networked Authoritarianism   141

9 Conclusion: Beyond the Protest Square   157

Notes   171

References   173

Index   187

About the Author   199

List of Figures

Figure 3.1   Map of Ukraine, CIA Factbook   32
Figure 6.1   The Galas Website as Captured on February 8, 2014   109
Figure 6.2   Leaflet Produced by Galas, Mapping Key Protest
             Locations and Resources   112

List of Tables

Table 3.1   Summary of Information about Interview Participants   30
Table 3.2   Device Use and Internet Access among Interview
            Participants   34

Acknowledgments

There are many people who contributed to making this research and this book possible. From protesters and activists to select academics who (like me) spend too much time on Twitter, I want to thank everyone who helped me think, question, investigate, triangulate, understand, and write. Many of you probably had no idea you were helping, but you were!

My cherished mentor and friend Sarah Oates has been a source of inspiration, knowledge, wisdom, and enthusiasm about academic work and research for many years, and her support and guidance have made me the scholar I am today. She guided me through the start of my academic adventures and supervised my dissertation which forms the basis of this book. She continues to inspire me to ask difficult, but interesting, questions. For that, I am always grateful.

I would not be where I am in academia today were it not for my Ukrainian alma mater, the Kyiv-Mohyla Academy. My deepest thanks go to Serhiy Kvit, who was my dean and who first believed in me as a teacher and a scholar.

I want to thank my fellow academics at the Philip Merrill College of Journalism and others at the University of Maryland, who have challenged my thinking and offered unwavering support, critique and advice in my time there. Linda Steiner, Kalyani Chadha, Nick Diakopoulos, Sahar Khamis, Micha Koliska, Joanna Nurmis, Klive Oh, Saranaz Barforoush, Boya Xu, Rob Wells—thank you so much.

The *Global Voices* community has been a part of my life since 2013 and has continuously inspired my research on Ukraine, Russia, and the power of networks and civic mobilization. I am immensely thankful to Kevin Rothrock, Ivan Sigal, Arzu Geybullayeva, Ellery Biddle, Abir Ghattas, and so many others.

My colleagues at the School of Communications at Dublin City University, Trish Morgan, Dónal Mulligan, and Declan Fahy deserve special praise for endless cups of coffee and supportive conversation in the final stages of this book.

Laura Portwood-Stacer, a wonderful academic-turned-developmental-editor, helped me see the story behind the research and offered a lot of useful advice about academic book writing along the way. Thanks, Laura!

The research for this book was made possible with generous funding from the University of Maryland, the ZEIT-Stiftung Ebelin und Gerd Bucerius Trajectories of Change Fellowship, and from the Faculty of Humanities and Social Sciences at Dublin City University. I am also thankful to all of my research participants and to many other people in Ukraine and Russia who helped me make this book a reality.

I am forever grateful to my Mom and Dad, Nina and Michael, who brought me up to love books and reading and to be curious about the world, but gave me complete freedom to choose my way. Thanks also go to my brother Vasya for always being there for me. My cats, Luna and Masyan, have been a source of comfort and comic relief.

Most of all, I want to thank my husband, Pasha, who has supported me through this wild ride. His constant presence has been an anchor in turbulent times, and his love of life has kept me sane—as has our shared passion for words and his excellent taste in music.

Finally, I am grateful to the series editors, Ruth Sanz Sabido and Stuart Price, for enabling me to write this book, and to everyone at Rowman & Littlefield International who helped make it possible. Thank you all so much!

Chapter 1

Introduction

A Facebook post by a Ukrainian-Afghani journalist Mustafa Nayyem is often credited with sparking the Euromaidan protests that took over Ukraine in late autumn 2013. On November 21, after news appeared that then-President Viktor Yanukovych would refuse to sign the EU Association Agreement, Nayyem posted on Facebook:

> Come on guys, let's be serious. If you really want to do something, don't just "like" this post. Write that you are ready, and we can try to start something.

Then he posted again:

> Let's meet at 10:30 p.m. near the monument to independence in the middle of the Maidan. (Nayyem 2014b)

The posts are a cornerstone of the popular mythology of the Ukrainian Euromaidan protest. But, as Nayyem himself admitted, "no one person can claim credit for starting this uprising" (Nayyem 2014b). Nor can any one Facebook post be credited with making the uprising into the massive protest event that it turned out to be. But the internet and social media did play an important role in how the protest took off, how it unfolded, and what its final shape turned out to be. Equally important were the perceptions of the protest participants about the opportunities and limitations for protest action afforded to them by digital technology. This book is about all of these and more.

The research presented in this book has two goals. The first one is to understand what affordances of digital media were perceived and used by citizens to participate in the recent protests in Ukraine and to analyze in detail how these affordances may enable or limit protest action depending on the political and social context, the participating actors, and the technology used in each case. The second, loftier goal is to build on this in-depth examination of affordances of digital media to develop the concept of *augmented dissent* as a useful way to explain how protest happens in the hybrid spaces where material and digital elements of reality are closely entangled.

I argue that a nuanced understanding of how digital media can augment protest action and of the factors that determine possibilities or limits for participation in discontent can inform how we make decisions about creating, regulating, and using networked technologies in the context of political and civic agency. The book contributes to this understanding and so is valuable in this regard, but it also demonstrates that protest affordances of digital media can be contentious. In some cases, they can empower protesters and provide them with expansive opportunities for action and experimentation. In others, depending on how states and governments recognize and seek to make use of or police these affordances, the space for online and offline protest can be severely diminished as part of general restrictions on online expression and political freedom. An example of this is found toward the end of the book, when findings from Ukraine are applied to more recent protest events in Russia.

The book's core argument is that protesters in Ukraine and Russia perceive digital media as affording them a qualitatively different experience of protest. When protest activity is augmented by the fusing together of offline and online structures and mechanisms, it offers individuals a variety of modes of participation and makes the potentialities for action accessible to a diverse range of players. This variety and diversity, however, are shaped by the context in which protest activity happens. We already know that factors such as the absence or presence of strong democratic institutions, independent media or a mature civil society and experienced activist organizations influence the possibility, scale, and outcomes of protest in general. But there is an emerging connection between these traditional factors and the status of internet freedom and habitual digital media use, as well as levels of state control, censorship, and surveillance in the digital sphere. When these factors combine, the resulting environment, augmented by the unique mix of digital and material aspects, influences how activists in a given society perceive the internet and social media, and what possibilities they see in using these technologies for achieving protest-related goals. The book concludes that, in the case of Ukraine and Russia, these contexts differed significantly, so the opportunities and limitations of digital technologies and networks for augmented protest in each country took on very different shapes.

PROTEST AND DIGITAL MEDIA
IN THE HYBRID REALITY

This book is inspired by ongoing interest in the role of information and communication technologies in social movements and protest activity, specifically in the post-Soviet space. The last decade or so has seen an increase in mass protest events in the region, with protests erupting in Russia, Belarus, Georgia, Ukraine, Armenia, and elsewhere. From the 2004 Orange Revolution in Ukraine to the Bolotnaya rallies of 2011–2012 in Moscow to the Euromaidan protests in Ukraine in 2013–2014 and the Electric Yerevan rallies in Armenia in 2015, a gradual increase in the use of digital technologies and social media platforms by citizens has become evident (Goldstein 2007; Oates and Lokot 2013; Onuch 2015).

Unlike the so-called "Arab Spring" protests in the Middle East and North Africa region that became a popular focus of academic and media attention, there have been significantly fewer studies of the use of internet and social media in protest events in the former Soviet states and Eastern Europe. Similarly, Western protest events such as the Occupy movement and the more recent anti-Trump movement have received overwhelming attention in the English-language scholarly writing. This book is aimed at filling this gap in scholarship on internet and society in Eastern Europe, as well as contributing to the broader field of digital media and protest scholarship. It expands the traditional area studies perspective by drawing on a range of different disciplines, including media and communication studies, social movement studies, and internet studies. This allows the book to present an innovative interdisciplinary inquiry into the role of digital media in protest activity that is enriched by its geographic and political contextualization.

The contribution of this book is significant because, unlike other existing studies of protests in Eastern Europe, it frames the broader political and social transformations through a narrow focus on digital media practices and their potential to augment or limit the power of grassroots discontent. Using the concept of communicative affordances of technology, an emerging strand of thinking about technology, digital media, and power, the book focuses less on the success or failure of protests, but more on how the practices of dissent are shaped variously by networked technologies, the people using them, and the local political, cultural, and social contexts.

Public debates about the growing role of digital media in human lives, both in everyday life and in moments of upheaval, continue. Though the focus might move from the democratizing potential of the internet to the power of social media platforms and the critiques of algorithms and artificial intelligence, these issues are hotly contested and discussed. It is thus important to understand how protest organizers and participants conceive of networked technologies and their potential; how they experience protest in spaces that are augmented by digital media; and how they, in turn, extend and subvert the affordances of these networked technologies and platforms in creative and often unexpected ways. Using fieldwork findings from the Euromaidan protest in Ukraine and applying them to the more recent 2017 anti-corruption protests in Russia, the book demonstrates that technology use in protest events is highly context-dependent and heavily influenced by citizens' perceptions of the affordances of networked media for organizing, mobilization, self-expression and claims-making. At the same time, the book argues that despite the limitations of local contexts and power structures, digital media have become an intrinsic part of the protest experience and can enable various forms of dissent, albeit through wildly divergent means.

The book employs the theoretical framework of affordances of digital media to understand how digital media augmented citizens' protest opportunities and how they afforded new possibilities for dissent or limited them. Increasingly, scholars focusing on the internet and its growing embeddedness in our social and political lives argue that technologies are socially constructed, yet possess some power to shape various aspects of human existence, including communication in networked spaces, the formation of networked publics (boyd 2010), and internet-mediated activism (Earl and Kimport 2011). The book draws on the concept of affordances (boyd 2010; Gibson 1979; Majchrzak et al. 2013) to argue that the possibilities for (and limitations of) dissent-related action emerge from the complex connections between protest participants, the digital media devices and platforms available to them, and the political, cultural, and social context around them.

An affordance in a broader sense refers to the "mutuality of actor intentions and technology capabilities that provide the potential for a particular action" (Majchrzak et al. 2013, 39). This means using a particular networked technology can result in multiple action possibilities for different actors in different environments. This approach to understanding technology allows for framing the possibilities and limitations of protest action involving it in contextual terms, since cues for affordances are drawn from the environment around the individual, often at or just before the moment of action. Importantly, because technological affordances are derived from the negotiation of an individual's subjective perception of utility and the objective qualities of a particular technology (Gibson 1979), it is crucial to recognize the role of human imagination in how digital media are perceived in the context of protest. Nagy and Neff (2015) suggest the term "imagined affordances" to describe expectations of technology that may not be fully structurally or rationally realized, but are nonetheless present in sociotechnical systems, emerging in specific contexts and under specific circumstances. Such affordances are never static and are dependent on both human action and the actions of platforms and devices

(Nagy and Neff 2015), and as the book demonstrates, they play an important role in enabling creative expression and ad hoc activity during the protest events.

Elaborating the concept of augmented dissent, where affordances for protest action emerge from a combination of material and digital elements, the book engages with Chadwick's idea of the hybrid media system (2017) and posits that in a protest's media system, new and old media logics coexist, collide, and interpenetrate in complex ways. The hybrid ontology, Chadwick and his coauthors argue, "draws attention to boundaries, to flux, to in-betweenness, and it concerns how practices intermesh and coevolve" (Chadwick, Dennis, and Smith 2016, 9). In a similar attempt to find a comprehensive approach to examining the interconnections between old and new, mainstream and citizen media, Hoskins and O'Loughlin suggest the concept of a "new media ecology" to explain how existing traditional and new digital media technologies can be understood and studied as existing in a complex set of interrelationships within a specific context (Hoskins and O'Loughlin 2010). Similarly, this book argues that both the material and the digital elements of a protest's hybrid reality make up the protest event, and that it is impossible to separate them, to argue that one is more real than the other. Instead, it suggests that the most productive way to understand the experience of protest with digital media is to view it as *augmented dissent*, wherein the atoms and bits of protest activity enmesh and extend into each other. This augmentation is, of course, context-dependent, and the book presents a variety of observations about how this augmented dissent manifests in protests in Ukraine and later, in Russia. The idea of augmentation suggests that older and newer logics, offline and online activities, forms of participation and protest tactics exist simultaneously, and extend into each other in complicated ways instead of simply replacing one another.

Building on these key theoretical debates, the book uses the case of the 2013–2014 Euromaidan mass protest in Ukraine to examine the affordances of the internet and social media for dissent in this unique context. It examines in great detail the various contextual variables that influenced or limited the possibilities for action afforded by technology, such as the level of media freedom, digital literacy, and internet penetration; the relevant protest and activism experience and the location of protest participants; the likelihood of government threats, censorship, or crackdowns; and the stakes and aims of the protest (mobilizing citizens, raising awareness of brutality, or regime change). It highlights several specific affordances of digital media that emerged as key in the Ukrainian protest, including ephemerality, flexibility, visibility, scalability, and persistence. These findings are then applied to the case of more recent anti-corruption protests in Russia in 2017 to show how differences in national and political contexts can significantly reshape the possibilities for augmented dissent. The book also discusses how, once these affordances emerge in one protest, they can offer or limit action possibilities depending on who and how recognizes, uses, or seeks to co-opt them.

CASE STUDIES: FOCUSING ON UKRAINE (AND RUSSIA)

While most of the scholarly attention has been centered on protest movements in Western Europe and North America (and, more recently, in the MENA region), protest events in former Soviet countries have been much less researched. This is likely due to the geographic and lingual proximity of the events to key centers of scholarship in the former case, and the prominent nature and the scale of the MENA protests, where governments have been toppled and dictators removed from power, in the latter.

Before Ukraine's Euromaidan drew the world's attention in 2013, there were only a handful of recent studies looking at countries such as Georgia, Ukraine, and other former Soviet republics where "revolutions" of sorts have occurred (Rose Revolution in Georgia in 2003, Orange Revolution in Ukraine in 2004, among others), as well as Russia, where that has not happened. This scarcity emerges as an additional reason to study digital media and protests in Ukraine and its neighborhood in more depth, and the research in this book contributes to the wider academic debate about digital media, politics, and society in other countries in the region.

The Euromaidan protest in Ukraine presents a case that is interesting in many respects: a grassroots movement sparked in the fall of 2013 by a relatively small group of protesters opposing a sudden decision by then-President Viktor Yanukovych to sign the EU Association Agreement met with police brutality and turned into a much broader and larger mass protest against government corruption and for human rights and dignity. The Euromaidan protests ended in more police violence and significant pushback from the protesters and resulted in the exile of the president and the removal of the government. Social media contributed to initial protest mobilization, and the protest action was documented in live-streamed videos and Instagram photos, and reported on Twitter and Facebook networks stretching across country borders. At every stage of the protest, digital media played an important part in how Euromaidan happened, how it was witnessed, and how it was perceived.

Scholars have examined some of the more general aspects of Euromaidan, such as why people initially rose up, who the protesters were, and how the protest developed. However, few have investigated in detail the uses and perceptions of digital technologies by Euromaidan participants beyond essentially noting that social media were indeed used by some protesters as "tools" for mobilization and information dissemination.

Ukraine and Russia are not only entangled in a problematic historical and cultural past and a tense political present but also share a growing segment of the Cyrillic web. Their political spheres and civil societies are undeniably connected. A number of scholars (e.g., Greene 2014) have focused on recent Russian protest events, but most have adopted a historical or political lens to do so. On the other hand, there is a growing focus on the role of the internet and digital media in Russian political and civic life (see Oates 2013), including its role in the viability and outcomes of mass protests in Russia. This book suggests that the events of Ukrainian Euromaidan offer interesting parallels to how the affordances of the internet and digital media for protest come to be perceived by both the Russian state and by Russian activists. To this end, it applies the findings from Ukraine to the most recent protest-related activity and anti-corruption protests in Russia in 2017 to establish whether tactical diffusion and conceptual cross-pollination between the two countries' networked publics have occurred and whether the Russian protesters have interpreted the affordances of digital media in their unique way, as contextualized by the Russian political and social context.

The emergence of the Euromaidan movement and the ensuing turmoil in Ukraine has drawn increased attention to the region's evolving civic and political context. It may be too early to say what the long-term impact of the Ukrainian protest will be, given that the unrest of 2013–2014 has turned into an ongoing geopolitical conflict with Russia. In Russia itself, opposition activists find themselves operating under increasing constraints, and their future is also uncertain. Still, there is significant value in analyzing how and why protesters and governments have used digital media to shape these protest events, as this analysis can inform broader understanding of the place of networked technologies in contested democratic societies.

METHODS AND DATA USED

The material for this book was collected through a multimodal ethnographic approach employed by multiple scholars of social movements and protest events (e.g., Barassi 2013; Mattoni and Treré 2014). The multimodal ethnography includes multiple interviews with Euromaidan protest participants conducted in person during the protest in Kyiv, Ukraine, in the winter of 2013–2014 and after the protest in Kyiv, other Ukrainian cities and outside of Ukraine. The interviews were complemented by a virtual ethnography of online protest and activist communities, conducted in December 2013 to February 2014; and two weeks of ethnographic observation of the central protest camp in downtown Kyiv and in other locations around the city in December 2013 and January 2014. Virtual ethnography of Russian activist and protest groups between August 2016 and August 2017 generated additional research material for the book. This multipronged data collection strategy was used to capture the assemblage of emergent and often ephemeral practices that together represent the variously mediated and spatially diverse protest initiatives. Employing interdisciplinary data gathering methods was necessary to capture the perceptions and uses of digital media by protesters and to describe the full range of protesters' practices in a broader context of the protest as a highly networked space where the material and the digital entwine, and where bodies, technology, and places augment each other.

During the interview phases, participants were asked to explain how they used digital media during the protest period; to discuss how these media fit into their tactical and strategic protest decisions (especially around information and media issues); and to describe what having recourse to these technologies and media platforms meant to them. The semi-structured, open-ended interview scheme was designed to achieve an immersive, in-depth understanding of the perceptions of protest participants of the role of digital media in protest activity and to relate these perceptions with their overall ideas about civic and political participation and their understanding of the place of digital media in everyday life.

The primary purpose of conducting virtual ethnographic observation on Euromaidan-related social media communities was to observe how participants were using these platforms, what kind of materials and media they were publishing and sharing, and what perceptions and opinions of digital media and their role in protest activity were being expressed. Considering these publicly available sources was important in order to triangulate interviewees' responses with the digitally mediated activity of the Euromaidan networks. This data also provided additional evidence reflecting the connections and tensions between citizens' perceptions of digital media and the visible practices of augmented dissent.

During the second virtual ethnography phase, focused on the Russian protests, I conducted ethnographic observation of a range of public online practices of Russian opposition activists. Examining their strategies, tactics, and content shared online allowed me to draw conclusions about their understanding of the affordances of digital media for activism and dissent. The extant data was collected from publicly available opposition websites, Twitter feeds, YouTube channels, and key activist Telegram channels and groups. Because of temporal limitations and the scope of the research project, the observation was constrained to the period between August 2016 and August 2017. This time period included several significant anti-corruption protest rallies that took place in multiple locations across Russia. The results of the observation were then triangulated with findings from the Euromaidan research to reveal similarities and differences in the perceptions of affordances of digital media for protest activity and in the contexts in which they emerged.

The research in this book provides in-depth insights into how networked technologies were used and perceived by protest participants, and what opportunities and limitations these technologies afforded for protest participation. The comparison between rich data from Ukraine and more recent events in Russia, coupled with historical information about the context for dissent and the digital media environment in each country meant I could examine the results through the prism of the communicative affordances framework, and draw conclusions about participants' perceptions of the role of networked technologies in protest activity as well as the complex intertwining of their online and offline lives.

CONTEXTUALIZING THE RESEARCHER

One of the challenges of doing research on protests in Ukraine and Russia is that as a researcher, I am inextricably embedded into the events, processes, and transformations happening in these countries. As with citizens of most former Soviet states, including Ukrainians, my identity is complex and reflective of the historic, national, and social transformations the region and its people have undergone. I grew up in eastern Ukraine during the last decade of the Soviet Union in a largely Russian-speaking environment, but learned Ukrainian as my second language in my early years. My family has mixed Russian, Ukrainian, Belarusian, and Polish roots. Such multifaceted histories and nuanced identities are indicative of the multiplicity and complexity of how most Ukrainians identify themselves within the post-Soviet and the global context. While my personal and professional connections inform my choices for designing and conducting research for this book, there is also an opportunity for greater reflexivity and deeper understanding of the situation exactly because I am so intimately concerned about and embedded in much of what was happening during and after these protests. As many of my research participants, I have both experienced being at the center of the protest in Kyiv and used social media to follow protest news and to engage with other participants of the protests in Ukraine and in Russia.

OVERVIEW OF THE BOOK

A protest is best understood as a puzzle of many pieces, interlocked in complex configurations. How protesters perceive digital media and the possibilities they offer, and what they do with these technologies, is only one piece of this puzzle. The book goes into a detailed examination of the affordances of digital media for protest participation and the factors that shaped them in the protests in Ukraine and later, in Russia. To understand where power is situated and how it is contested within mediated spaces is key to understanding the role of digital media in protesters' activity.

This book consists of nine chapters. Following this introduction, chapter 2 discusses the development of the internet and digital media in Ukraine and Russia amid historical, political, civic, and cultural transformations of the post-Soviet space leading up to the recent protests. Here, I consider the key similarities and differences between the two countries, including the evolution of their forms of state governance, their media systems, and their networked infrastructure. Tracing the diverging paths of the two states after the collapse of the Soviet Union, this chapter provides the necessary context for understanding the broader role of networked technologies in the political and social lives of Ukrainians and Russians today. I argue that elements of the overall country context, such as geopolitical orientations, the status of media freedom and free expression, internet regulation, and the development of civil society and grassroots activism shape the affordances of digital media available to actors in both Ukraine and Russia. Reflecting on these different environments, this chapter sets the scene for the more in-depth study of digital media uses and perceptions in protest activity that follows.

Chapters 3 and 4 sketch a detailed portrait of the Ukrainian protesters I interviewed and single out key factors that shaped them as protest actors. Chapter 3 provides general demographic information and other relevant characteristics of my interviewees. I then focus on their media consumption habits and digital media use patterns, analyzing how these shifted during the protest. The chapter delineates several key distinctions within the protester sample: that between more and less politically and civically engaged individuals; that between experienced protest participants and those for whom protest participation was novel; and that between the more moderate and more intense digital media users.

Chapter 4 focuses on how location, space, and distance shape augmented protest participation. I consider how the various locations of the Euromaidan protesters and their corresponding distance from the protest square in Kyiv modified their perceptions of digital media and their usefulness in protest participation. I find that protesters used digital media to create a variety of flexible participation scenarios, depending on their location. The internet and social media were also instrumental in augmenting their perceptions of the space and boundaries of protest events, as well as their feeling of copresence.

Chapters 5, 6, and 7 discuss the findings of the research from the Euromaidan protest in Ukraine, focusing on the key perceived affordances of digital media for protest activity and the key modes of protest participation they made possible. Chapter 5 deals with the changing notions of visibility and witnessing in protest events augmented by mobile technology and social media. It examines widespread practices of visual and textual documentation during the protest, such as live streaming, real-time image sharing, live tweeting, and blogging. The chapter finds that visibility is seen as a key affordance of digital media by protesters and that such visibility is often used strategically to achieve protest aims. As one of the consequences, highly visible hybrid protest activity also changes participants' experience of witnessing, giving them the ability to be part of the protest, to witness its events and to bear witness to the testimonies of others simultaneously, using a combination of physical and digital means. These augmented experiences in turn impact how participants make meaning and memories of the protest events, as well as how they experience the aftermath of the protest.

Chapter 6 focuses on participants' experiences of digitally mediated protest organizing and connective action. It provides an overall context for these experiences during Euromaidan, while also discussing a specific case of a group of protest participants, a collective called Galas, that played a role in streamlining and managing the logistics of the Ukrainian protest. I find that protesters relied on the ephemeral connections afforded by social media to build networked communities of volunteers, manage social capital, and verify credibility through a combination of strong and weak ties. The flexible temporalities of digital media connections also afforded a variety of meaningful participatory scenarios, including part-time and long-distance protest engagement.

Chapter 7 centers on the affordances of networked platforms for information sharing, mediated event framing, narrative construction and information diffusion within the Euromaidan protest. The chapter details the choices the protesters made about their messaging and argues that they not only exploited the scalability and persistence of social media but also relied on socially mediated visibility, as well as the fleeting trends and adaptable vernaculars of social media platforms to draw attention to the events of Euromaidan and to create stronger affective connections within the protest community. The research documented in chapters 5, 6, and 7 finds that the internet and social media afford protest participants different opportunities for action depending on civic activism experience, distance from the physical center of the protest, and the overall level of engagement. At the same time, these chapters also reveal that, despite these differences, digital media afford protesters a variety of opportunities for protest engagement and offer a broad, inclusive set of modes of participation.

Chapter 8 analyzes the more recent anti-government protests in Russia and the use of networked technologies by Russian activists in light of the affordances of digital media for protest emerging from the Euromaidan field-work in Ukraine. The Russian state, alarmed by the 2011–2012 Bolotnaya protests against election falsifications, and taken aback by the regime change that followed Euromaidan in Ukraine, now sees the internet and social media as a crucial element of the struggle for power and control. As the Kremlin attempts to curb and restrict internet activity through the means of censorship, draconian laws, and pervasive surveillance, Russian opposition activists and protesters embrace the affordances of digital media not only to claw back opportunities for alternative expression and to make visible government cor-ruption and human rights abuses but also as means of practicing conspicuous security and radical transparency in the face of increasingly invasive state pressure and restrictive internet regulations and protest laws. They adopt the affordances of ephemerality, flexibility, scalability, and strategic visibility, but reimagine them to counteract government censorship and surveillance and to contest the state's monopoly on political expression, civic mobilization and, increasingly, on the digital public sphere as a whole.

The final chapter concludes with a discussion of how understanding the affordances of digital media for protest in Ukraine and Russia helps shape the concept of augmented dissent, complicating the notion of protest that meshes together offline and online elements into a single reality. This chapter also discusses how the findings in the book contribute to further research on dissent in hybrid media systems and how the concept of augmented protest can inform a broader understanding of the convergence of digital rights and the right to protest.

UNDERSTANDING AUGMENTED DISSENT

Being a "cyberoptimist" has fallen out of fashion: the idea of the democ-ratizing potential of digital media has suffered a slow death in the wake of irresponsible data mining practices and data breaches, mass surveillance, algorithmic abuse, and disinformation wars. Being a "cyberpessimist," how-ever, also seems like intellectual laziness. Instead, this book argues that digi-tal media are best understood as part of the augmented reality of protest—a single reality that goes beyond the bodies, the tents, and the cobblestones in the protest square, incorporating live streams, different time zones, encrypted conversations, and simultaneous translation of protest updates into different languages. In this complex, polyphonous environment, a critical examination of exactly how the digital and the physical augment each other, how bodies and technologies resonate, is the only way forward.

This book offers a glimpse of the reality of augmented dissent through the prism of two different, but interlinked contexts. It suggests that the affordances of digital media for protest in an environment with free internet and dysfunctional state power can contribute to an experience that is exploratory, bridging, and expansive, as was the case in Ukraine. The very same affordances, however, can also make the experience of augmented dissent strategic, survival-oriented, and one of contestation. This happens when they emerge in a networked authoritarian environment such as Russia and are available to the state seeking control over all spheres of life as well as to activists fighting for a modicum of agency and a space for resistance.

Chapter 2

Digital Media and Society
in Ukraine and Russia

To understand the current relationship between mass protest and digital media in Ukraine and its neighborhood, it is useful to track the developments during the almost three decades since the fall of the Soviet Union in 1991. Though the common Soviet legacy has some implications for how countries in the region are governed and for the political and civic sensibilities of their citizens, we also have to account for the divergent paths they have taken in terms of shaping their political and media systems, as well as their social contracts. It is also worthwhile to compare how both the state and the citizens in Ukraine and Russia (as its most influential post-Soviet neighbor) conceive of the role of media and information more broadly, and the internet more specifically, in the negotiation of power and agency in their societies. These country-specific contexts, informed by shared histories and contrasting aspirations, are a necessary part of the equation that produces the protest-related affordances of digital media, the central theme of this book. This chapter, therefore, delves into the contexts shaping the opportunities and limitations for protest actors and networked technologies in Ukraine and Russia.

INFORMATION, INTERNET, AND DEMOCRACY

There is an ongoing scholarly debate around the democratizing potential of the internet and the possibility of pinpointing the inherent nature of digital technologies as neutral, democratic, or authoritarian. In particular, scholars present various arguments about whether networked technologies enable grassroots dissent and under what conditions, and whether they can also be used to stifle expressions of discontent. It's worth noting that in many countries, the internet and social media platforms in and of themselves have

15

become highly contested political spaces in which both the state and civil society operate. Both MacKinnon (2012) and Howard (2010) note that the internet in particular has become both the site and the means for protest activity and social movement formation. This dualist nature of networked technologies has altered the dynamics of political communication in all kinds of states, including authoritarian, democratic, and hybrid regimes. In various ways, social movement and protest leaders have been able to use digital media to organize mass protest activities, mobilize the public, bring their demands to higher levels of the national or global agendas and, in some cases, even challenge regimes (Howard 2010). However, scholars such as Morozov (2011) and Gunitsky (2015) have cautioned that internet and social media are not by default built to be a platform for protests and revolutions, and that there are many conditions which might influence a protest organized with digital media (such as the ease of performing a required action, the popularity of a given platform in a country, etc.). Goldstein, in his report "The Role of Digital Networked Technologies in the Ukrainian Orange Revolution" (2007) stresses the importance of avoiding "cyberutopianism"—the notion that internet and digital technology will always lead to a more inclusive political climate and a more democratic state. In fact, other academic research has shown that in some cases, repressive governments are able to exploit the networked nature of the internet, algorithmic social media feeds, and technologies such as facial recognition to limit access to independent media, stifle dissent, and sanction citizen agency.

Increasingly, scholars focusing on the internet and its growing embeddedness in our social and political lives argue that technologies are socially constructed, yet possess some power to shape various aspects of human existence, including communication in networked spaces, the formation of networked publics (boyd 2010), and internet-mediated activism (Earl and Kimport 2011). These critical debates demonstrate that, while technologies themselves may be imbued with certain values by their creators, they can be used both for and against democratic or liberal aims, depending on existing structures of power and the levels of digital media literacy among citizens or adoption of certain technologies by governments.

STATE, MEDIA, AND SOCIETY IN UKRAINE

Ukraine gained its independence in 1991 after the dissolution of the Soviet Union. As Wilson (2016) notes, for Ukraine, there was no real revolution, and those who came to power at the helm of a newly independent country were the same Communist and nomenklatura officials who ran the republic before. It took the Ukrainian political elites and civil society years more to begin rebuilding toward a more democratic model of governance, so Wilson astutely calls the protests of 2004 and 2014 the two "catch-up revolutions" that came fairly late in the process.

Kiryukhin (2015) observes that after the country gained independence, identity problems turned out to be more important for Ukraine than the problem of establishing democratic institutions—yet another factor in its comparatively unhurried democratic development in Russia's influential shadow. This focus on rebuilding a national identity has also meant that the discourse prevalent among political and intellectual elites in Ukraine has mostly focused on debates about the nation's self-determination between the West and the East, national memory, history, religion, and culture—but not human rights or democratic values.

Because most of the power structures in newly independent Ukraine were inherited from the Soviet hierarchy, they also reshaped the new elites and networks in their own interests. In mid-2000s, Ukraine was a state with a weak rule of law, no independent judiciary, and little room for the chaos of the early 1990s, having organized it into a neatly autocratic system with only the token signs of democracy, among them elected institutions such as a president and an ineffective parliament. By this point, most of the important economic assets had been corruptly privatized under President Leonid Kuchma (who ran Ukraine in 1994–2005), and the country was, in practical terms, run by oligarchic clans, most of them reporting to the chief "manager"—the president.

As the political opposition at the time was weak, independent journalists in early to mid-2000s found themselves central to the effort of challenging Kuchma's regime and battling the non-free mainstream media environment where most media companies and newsrooms were either managed from above or resorted to self-censorship to avoid additional pressure. A pivotal moment that put the Ukrainian society on a new track toward political and civic change was the 2000 murder of opposition journalist Georgiy Gongadze, who founded one of the first independent news websites in Ukraine, *Ukrainska Pravda* (*The Ukrainian Truth*) in April 2000. The website was created specifically "to circumvent the authorities' repressive crackdown on free speech" (Goldstein 2007), published anti-corruption investigations, and quickly became popular among the independent elites, opposition supporters, and intellectuals. In September 2000, Gongadze mysteriously disappeared. Two months later, a headless body alleged to be his was found in a forest outside of Kyiv. Opposition politicians accused President Kuchma of orchestrating the murder of the journalist, who had previously been investigating an arms sale Ukraine had approved. The murder investigation went on for years, and several persons have been charged with performing the murder and jailed. Gongadze's body was finally buried in Ukraine in March 2016.

The Gongadze case marked not only the emergence of the Ukraine Without Kuchma protest movement but also a broader awareness of the internet as an alternative platform for news, investigative journalism, and uncensored public discourse (Goldstein 2007). This recognition was still quite modest, since the majority of Ukrainians, especially outside of the capital, had little to no internet access (the percentage of internet penetration in the 48-million-strong country at the time is estimated to have been in the single digits), but the resonance around the Gongadze affair certainly created some momentum around overall interest in online media platforms and related technology as spaces where dissent could occur. Kyj found that *Ukrainska Pravda*'s popularity inspired opposition groups to develop their own political action websites during the 2004 presidential elections, and contributed to the burgeoning online presence of political and civic activist collectives such as Pora and Maidan.org.ua (Kyj 2006) that went on to play important roles in the Orange Revolution and subsequent political developments.

Although pro-Western Viktor Yushchenko emerged as the likely opposition candidate in the 2004 elections, Kuchma's regime was also challenged by eastern Ukraine powerhouse Viktor Yanukovych's candidacy. Because the electoral support for the incumbent political forces was divided, Yanukovych ended up with fewer votes than expected. Yanukovych's crude attempts to fix the vote and deny Yushchenko the presidency led to the mass protests dubbed the "Orange Revolution" in 2004 (Orange was the main color of Yushchenko's Our Ukraine party logo and branding).

While some researchers, such as Goldstein (2007), claim that citizen journalism and the internet played a decisive role in the Orange Revolution, it was probably less decisive than claimed, due to low internet penetration (*Ukrainska Pravda* 2012) and the way protest mobilization was initially organized from the top down by opposition parties cooperating with an emerging civic sector nurtured by international donor support. However, Goldstein (2007) also notes that the Orange Revolution marked an important moment for the convergence of rapid political change and the availability and emergence of information and communication networks that were largely open and independent. In his overview of digital technology use in the 2004 protest, Goldstein underscores the important roles of the emerging Ukrainian online media outlets in providing faithful reporting on election fraud and the ensuing protest activity, the growing ubiquity of mobile communications and text messaging, and their use for coordination of activist efforts, and the growing Ukrainian segment of the online blogosphere which played host to many discussions, and sharing of practices among civil society groups, though fell short of reaching the public in broader ways.

For the Orange Revolution, which was very much a political protest orchestrated by a small cluster of political activists and civic organizers allied with the opposition parties, the internet was instrumental in allowing for the creation of a space for dissenting opinions and independent reporting in an otherwise controlled and self-censored media environment. The activists at the heart of the protest also used emerging online platforms such as blogs (mostly LiveJournal) and mobile connectivity to coordinate their discourse and mobilization efforts, as well as elections monitoring and protest activity. But for the average protest participant in 2004, the internet mattered very little, and average Ukrainians still largely relied on traditional media and word of mouth for their news and crisis updates (Kyj 2006). Since social media as we know it today was mostly nonexistent and the available digital platforms were mostly the tool of political elites and select civil society organizations (Goldstein 2007), those using them simply could not afford to have very much public influence.

The increasingly rapid growth of cellular connectivity and internet penetration in Ukraine—from 3 to 4 percent of internet users among the adult population in 2004–2005 to 29 percent in 2010, and almost 40 percent in 2013 (*Ukrainska Pravda* 2012)—coincided between 2004 and 2014 with a series of changes in the country's political climate.

Although the participants expressed a range of frustrations and demands within the framework of the protest, the Orange Revolution, however momentous, was largely only about righting the wrong of an illegally fixed election. Yushchenko duly took office after a repeat vote, and the protesters went home. What followed in the wake of the protest was not a true democratic breakthrough: without real unity in the former opposition camp and its various factions vying for positions of power, Yushchenko proved to be an ineffective president, embarking on a presidency largely filled with drawn-out speeches and cultural diplomacy. In particular, he failed to manage the new political coalition and to address entrenched corruption and weak respect for the rule of law (Kubicek 2009).

Between 2005 and 2010, the "orange" party camp lost their political dividends gained during the protest, and subsequently, Yushchenko lost the 2010 presidential election to his nemesis Viktor Yanukovych. Despite Yanukovych's loss of face in 2004, he had continued to be politically active. After becoming president, Yanukovych overturned Yushchenko's constitutional reforms (that in 2005 gave more power to parliament and less to the presidential office) and rapidly restored a traditional presidential monopoly of power. Initially, Yanukovych had all the hallmarks of a "strong leader," and proclaimed a pragmatic approach to the country's economic and political development. In practice, though, this meant a hyper-centralization of power, the tightening of the reins on the state apparatus, installing people close to him in all key positions throughout the government and at any points where graft or enrichment could be possible within the state, such as the state procurement system and the energy sector.

The turn to nepotism and pervasive corruption also meant a shrinking of the space for media freedom and dissent. Among other things, Yanukovych's state machine and the power-friendly oligarchs, most of whom hold media assets in their business portfolios (Ryabinska 2011), were intent on controlling the mainstream media. At the time, the majority of national TV channels were owned by media holdings either belonging to or tied to Yanukovych-friendly business owners. This meant that news coverage of key government figures was plentiful, but sanitized. Any investigative or expository reporting mostly had to move to the handful of opposition-leaning mainstream media, including TV, print, and online outlets.

Given the general repressive and co-opted climate of the media sphere in Ukraine, it might come as a surprise that the online media managed to blossom under the circumstances. This is mainly due to the fact that the Ukrainian legal system considers the internet to be a personal communication tool rather than a mass media platform (International Business Publications 2008). This meant that while online journalists did not enjoy many of the privileges of their mainstream colleagues (such as being accredited to attend government meetings), they also were free from the threat of defamation or libel charges and viewed the internet as a platform for uncensored and objective information (Semetko and Krasnoboka 2003). Exactly because the status of online journalists and bloggers was amorphous, the state could not decide how to deal with them or how to silence them, beyond direct action and brute force (as happened in Gongadze's case). The government's lack of sophistication in the area of digital technology and online communication also explains why the internet remained a relatively free space for journalism, political debate, and public discourse despite an otherwise repressive atmosphere in society (Dyczok and Gaman-Golutvina 2009).

Though in the 2000s Ukrainian legislation governing the internet and access to information was relatively liberal, a number of legislative initiatives introduced in 2011 aimed to control electronic media, monitor internet activity on ethical grounds, and limit certain "undesirable" content (*Ukrainska Pravda* 2011). Anonymous distributed denial-of-service (DDoS) attacks against civic initiatives online were scarce. Political parties and the government also used the internet as a tool for political competition, engaging in legitimate forms of communication such as social media use and blogging, as well as more manipulative techniques such as trolling and astroturfing. These efforts point to the weak potential for state-imposed limitations on the online public sphere.

The availability of a free and open internet and a growing number of easy-to-use tools and platforms for public deliberation, discussions, and organizing was a factor in the development of civil society and political activism in Ukraine in the decade after 2004. By 2007–2008, urban activism was blossoming in Ukraine, with activists blogging about their efforts to oppose illegal construction and destruction of historic buildings in Ukrainian cities. The "Save Old Kyiv" movement, for instance, actively used LiveJournal to generate support for their civic activity and protest events (Bohdanova 2011), and later built their own website to catalogue illegal construction attempts around the capital. The web was also used by anti-corruption activists who started posting their investigative reports online, sustained by media development grants. Election monitoring was another kind of activity that utilized the affordances of digital technology (Lysenko and Desouza 2014), using a combination of crowdsourced reporting by observers, journalists, and volunteers (through text messages, emails, and submissions through a web form) and an interactive online map that publicized and tracked election violations in 2010 and 2012 (Lokot 2015a). All of these instances, coupled with a diminishing trust in the government (*Interfax-Ukraine* 2011), pointed to a growing understanding among civil society actors that they simply could not rely on the political elites to conduct reforms necessary for democratic development. Moreover, their job as citizens was to use any means possible, including digital media and technology, to hold the authorities accountable for their actions and to shine a light on the increasingly corrupt system of personal favors and connections that had permeated the Ukrainian government and parliament.

STATE, MEDIA, AND SOCIETY IN RUSSIA

For Russia, the 1991 collapse of the Soviet Union was as momentous as it was a case of "more of the same": the country remained a diverse nation-state occupying a huge land mass, but had lost direct political and economic influence on the neighboring republics. Boris Yeltsin, who became President in 1991, and his cadre of politicians who came to run newly independent Russia, all came from the Soviet political system. There were attempts at political and economic reform, including the widespread (and somewhat chaotic) privatization (Adachi 2006), and the emergence of underdeveloped political parties and gradually maturing opposition (Gel'man 2008). But overall, Russia found it hard to move on from the Cold War era, and to redefine itself as a newly democratic state that eschewed centralized control and political nepotism. When Vladimir Putin stepped in as Yeltsin's successor at the start of the 2000s, he inherited a country that was searching for meaning, as well as for economic stability. So he and his colleagues got to work on both. With Putin's reign virtually uninterrupted since then (apart from a brief stint as Prime Minister in 2008–2012 when Dmitry Medvedev served as President), Russians have seen a tightening of state control over all spheres of life, growing exclusion of opposition actors from mainstream politics, and the emergence of a system consistently dominated by the ruling United Russia party that some scholars refer to as managed democracy (Lipman and McFaul 2001), and others designate as a consolidated authoritarian regime ("Nations in Transit 2013: Russia" 2013).

In its struggles to rebuild its identity after the fall of the Soviet Union, Russia has attempted to construct new shared meanings of past, present, and future by crafting new strategic narratives about its history, its nationhood, and its citizens. Since the time of Putin's first coming to power at the start of 2000, the dominant self-identity of the Russian state's strategic narrative has been one of a great power and a strong, sovereign state (Szostek 2017). That has been coupled with a fear of political and civil unrest as a result of Western interference (tied to the "color revolutions" in neighboring states, including Ukraine). This has led to what Snyder describes as a "politics of eternity," in which the national self-identity relies on a continuous cycle of Russia's perceived victimhood at the hands of Western states and a conviction that "government cannot aid society as a whole but can guard against threats" (Snyder 2018, 8). In this narrative, citizens emerge as securitized subjects that should be manipulated into emotional states of elation or fear. Such manipulation is exercised by political actors not only through mainstream media channels but also through digital media. Importantly, active citizens, who engage in politics through activism, protest, and advocacy, are also seen as part of the existential threat to Russia's autonomy and security.

Throughout Russian history, issues of state security have often taken precedence over individual freedoms and rights of citizens. This approach is also evident in Russia's modern-day national narrative. The conditional rhetoric of national security is quite pervasive: it is visible in domestic politics and the state's perception of opposition forces, foreign policy threats, defense of social norms, and "traditional" cultural values. This logic can also be traced in Russia's ongoing crackdown on internet freedoms through a series of increasingly restrictive laws and regulations.

Centralized state control over citizens' communications was a foundation of Soviet governance and one of the main tools of influence upon Soviet dissident movements, and today's Russia has readily embraced this legacy. This control was achieved through censorship of mainstream media, foreign publications, and literary works; restrictions on ownership and use of technology such as photocopiers (Hanson 2008); and through pervasive wiretapping and surveillance of citizen communications (Soldatov and Borogan 2015). Russian media, encouraged by the Soviet policy of glasnost in late 1980s to promote critical debate, were instrumental in the dissolution of the USSR (Oates 2013) and continued to be influential in the Russian public sphere in the 1990s and 2000s. Still, the Soviet legacy and Putin's own intelligence background meant that media were viewed by the state as instruments of power, and therefore establishing control over the media sphere was a matter of national security.

Technically, the Russian constitution guarantees freedom of speech and press freedom, but the state apparatus has abused the country's politicized judiciary system to harass independent journalists and civil society activists documenting widespread abuses by the authorities. Russian law also contains a broad definition of extremism that Russian officials have been increasingly using to silence government critics, including journalists and protesters. The enforcement of this and other restrictive legal measures has encouraged self-censorship among media professionals and, increasingly, internet users.

By the start of 2010s, Russia remained a country where some information networks retained their freedom, yet key political structures such as the ruling party were focused on retaining long-term control and self-enrichment, and social movements and civic activity were thin on the ground. Though there was comparative media diversity, the media system overall was not free, with a large proportion of national mainstream media channels owned or co-opted by the state. The Russian state continues to place a high value on controlling information flows in mainstream and digital media and managing or curtailing any expressions of dissent within the country's public social life. To achieve this, Russian authorities have employed an evolving system of what Deibert et al. (2010) refer to as "information controls"—a broad constellation of techniques, practices, and regulations that circumscribe the kinds of information technology, media channels, and electronic communications available to citizens. Such an ecosystem of controls works at many levels and may include technical means such as "filtering, distributed denial of service attacks, electronic surveillance, malware, or other computer-based means of denying, shaping, and monitoring information," as well as more opaque measures such as "laws, social understandings of 'inappropriate' content, media licensing, content removal, defamation policies, slander laws, secretive sharing of data between public and private bodies, or strategic lawsuit actions" ("Citizen Lab Summer Institute" 2015). State surveillance and censorship, along with restrictive and arbitrarily applied laws, have been the central tenets of Russia's evolving information controls mechanism.

December 2011 became a pivotal moment for Russian political and social life, as it saw the start of the largest mass protests since the early 1990s. The flawed parliamentary elections that paved the way for Vladimir Putin's return to the presidency in March 2012 pushed the growing discontent of the Russian population onto the streets and into the online public sphere. Russian opposition forces and some of the intellectual elites were able to mobilize large rallies in Moscow on December 10 and 24, 2011, backed by smaller protests scattered across the country, where participants decried the electoral abuses and called for an end to Putin's corrupt and ongoing tenure.

While not all those who showed up to protest were mobilized online, survey data shows that those who were more engaged online tended to be more politically active and more likely to support the liberal opposition in Russia (Greene 2012b).

Shut out by the mainstream media, the organizers of the "winter of discontent" turned to comparatively unobstructed online networks and channels to boost engagement, spread protest messages, and legitimize protest claims. The internet-based independent media outlets and social media platforms were used to coordinate protest rallies and provide evidence of protest numbers, which the state tended to downplay. More importantly, a "war of frames" emerged between state-controlled media and independent sources around whether the protests really enjoyed widespread grassroots support and were a genuine threat to Russian political leaders (Oates and Lokot 2013). While state-run news channels admitted only that citizens were dissatisfied with the political process, most commercial media and internet-based sources were far more critical of the regime.

The protest rallies lasted well into 2012, and the regime began to crack down on protest leaders and participants with physical attacks, detentions, and later, arrests, fines, and jail sentences for the Bolotnaya prisoners.[1] At the same time, the Russian authorities, spooked by the unrest and seeing in it an echo of the "color revolutions" in other post-Soviet states, quickly approved a series of repressive regulations aimed at further restricting freedom of the media, curtailing civic agency, and stifling free speech and expression online. Criminal defamation was reintroduced in a law adopted in July 2012, providing for large fines or weeks of forced labor as punishments. Other new regulatory measures included thousandfold fine increases for participation in unsanctioned rallies (from a maximum of 300 rubles to 300,000 rubles) and a law requiring civil society organizations who benefited from foreign funding to register with the Justice Ministry as "foreign agents" ("Freedom of the Press 2013: Russia" 2013).

Another restrictive law that was adopted in July 2012 and came into force that November granted unprecedented blocking powers to Russian telecommunications regulator Roskomnadzor and other state bodies. Federal Law #139-FZ mandated the creation of a "blacklist"[2] registry of websites that internet service providers (ISPs) within Russia were required to block (Rothrock 2012). The law, intended to curtail access to illegal or otherwise harmful material on the internet, complemented the growing list of banned content on the RuNet, which at that point already included a government-maintained list of "extremist materials." Websites could be added to the blacklist extrajudicially, and many critics of the new measures claimed they could be used to directly censor online content and impede the growing role of the internet as an alternative source of news and a space for debate.

POLITICAL CHANGE AND INTERNET
REGULATION: DIVERGING PATHS

By 2013, Ukraine saw a deterioration of democratic developments, hindered by the continuing oligarchic takeover of key state power institutions, but its media and information space remained relatively diverse and included a number of independent outlets. Moreover, the internet in Ukraine remained largely free (Freedom House's *Freedom on the Net* report designated the country as "Free" in 2013)[3] and the number of internet users was growing quickly, with penetration going from 33.7 percent in 2012 to nearly 42 percent in 2013, according to the International Telecommunications Union ("Percentage of Individuals Using the Internet" 2013).

Though the use of the internet and digital media in the Euromaidan protest, discussed in great detail in the following chapters, concerned the Yanukovych-era officials enough to warrant the notorious "anti-protest laws" adopted in January 2014 ("Freedom on the Net 2014: Ukraine" 2014), this crackdown on internet use and civic freedom was short-lived, and the laws were eventually repealed. Since then, the post-Euromaidan government and parliament have endeavored to introduce tighter internet regulation in the name of cybersecurity, citing the ongoing Russia-Ukraine conflict in the East and South of the country, with partial success. The popular Russian social media networks, VKontakte and Odnoklassniki, were officially blocked in Ukraine in 2017 (Morton 2017), alongside other Russian websites labeled as sources of disinformation or propaganda. Several attempts have been made by lawmakers to introduce carbon copies of Russian internet legislation, for example, requiring bloggers to identify themselves to the state (Lokot 2015b) or give the government extrajudicial powers to shut down media outlets and block websites (Reporters Without Borders 2014), but they have been largely unsuccessful, meeting with backlash and criticism from internet users, journalists, and human rights activists. While these developments are worrying and will certainly have implications for digital freedom in Ukraine in the near future, the case remains that in terms of the affordances of digital media for (domestic) protest, the Ukrainian political, regulatory, and social context remains a mostly free one. Still, the subtle shifts toward more control over the Ukrainian online environment have warranted the country's slide from "Free" to "Partly Free" in the *Freedom on the Net* report rankings in 2014, where it remains to this day.

At the same time, the Russian state has continued to view control of information flows and restricting expressions of dissent as key to retaining its power. Moreover, control over technologically mediated communications has become part of the national governance and security agenda. Some scholars argue that the regime can best be described as "networked authoritarianism"

(Maréchal 2017; Greene 2012a), as the state aspires to control all spheres of mediated social life while investing in high-tech networked infrastructure and developing connectivity. With mainstream media largely run or co-opted by the state, the Russian internet has until recently been a relatively free, if contested space for alternative opinions and debate (Oates 2013). However, the authorities, alarmed by the unrest of 2011–2012 and the protests and regime change in several neighboring countries, including Ukraine, have sought to systematically restrict online freedom and curtail the rights of Russian internet users. Russia's *Freedom on the Net* ranking, which remained in the Partly Free category since the first report in 2009, showed annual decreases in the three main categories of indicators, including obstacles to access, limits on content, and violations of user rights. It finally tipped over into the "Not Free" category in mid-2015 ("Freedom on the Net 2015: Russia" 2015), and remains there, thanks to an endless stream of new regulatory measures and extra-legal abuses that represent an escalating crackdown on free speech and dissenting opinions online. Social media content is regularly deleted or blocked on the grounds of intolerance or disrespect toward government officials, and users are regularly fined and even jailed for posting, sharing, or even liking content deemed to contain calls to extremism or mass disorder. Russia's Supreme Court estimates that convictions under the extremism charge have more than tripled between 2012 and 2017 (*The Moscow Times* 2018b), and human rights organizations note a large number of these are for online activity (Gainutdinov and Chikov 2018). The latest wave of protests in 2017–2019 has also seen more convictions for promoting illegal rallies or documenting (and therefore participating in) protests on social media. In May 2018, dozens of Russian anti-corruption activists were charged with "inciting mass riots" for retweeting information about an opposition protest and jailed for up to thirty days (*Runet Echo* 2018). In June 2018, a liberal opposition activist was handed a two-year suspended sentence, allegedly on extremism charges, for posts critical of President Vladimir Putin (*The Moscow Times* 2018a).

Ukraine and Russia's paths with regard to political and societal developments, civic freedoms, and internet governance are unquestionably connected, conditioned by geographic proximity, tangled geopolitical, energy-related, and oligarchic interests, overlapping online public spheres and telecommunications infrastructures. But increasingly, these paths are diverging.

The Ukrainian government, in its corrupt and repressive period before and during the Euromaidan protest in 2013–2014, saw no real threat from the networked publics and only attempted to suppress internet and media freedom and bring them under state control in line with the country's economic and political structures when the discontent grew to epic proportions. The post-Euromaidan Ukrainian state, torn between European integration and the ongoing conflict with Russia, is now attempting to balance democratic standards of free speech with issues of cybersecurity and information manipulation. Throughout these tumultuous times, the internet in Ukraine has remained a predominantly free space for public debate and alternative opinions. Though digital media have become an integral part of everyday life, they manage to remain independent of the state apparatus, owing to a decentralized internet infrastructure, a vibrant independent media sector, and a lively and diverse civil society.

In Russia, the state has come to a growing realization of the centrality of the online public sphere in Russian political and civic life. As with independent media, the Russian authorities saw the networked publics and the opportunities for action open to them as an existential threat to the strategic narrative of the great sovereign state. In the past decade, the Kremlin has been methodically re-engineering the structural, social, and cultural norms around internet use in Russia to achieve greater control over the digital media environment. Through a host of new laws impacting everything from content to anonymity and privacy, and through co-opting internet infrastructure and ownership of key native social media platforms, Putin's government has shown that it is fully on board with viewing the internet—and its affordances for dissent—as part of "real life." As such, it must be made part of the national security and state sovereignty machine, and that means Russians' private digital communications are fair game for law enforcement, encryption, and VPNs are virtually outlawed, and users can go to prison for retweets of a protest march announcement.

CONCLUSION

The affordances and limitations of digital media for protest are inevitably informed by the context or environment in which they arise. Factors such as the possibility of political pluralism or regime change in the country, as well as the maturity of civil society and social movement histories, impact the levels of internet freedom and free expression, as well as the reach of state control, surveillance, and censorship. This influences how activists perceive the internet and social media and how they are able to use them for protest. The Russian context is very different from the Ukrainian one, and so it informs the choices of Russian activists and protesters, as they consider the opportunities and limitations of digital technologies and networks for organizing, mobilization, activism, and dissent.

Are digital media an integral part of citizens' lives and, with few limits on access or concerns about censorship, a natural element of protest activity? In that case, as in Ukraine, protesters can focus on other threats, for example,

physical ones, and can creatively negotiate various communicative and organizational challenges through the use of connected devices and social media.
Or are digital networks seen as a necessary measure used to avoid state surveillance and bypass controlled mainstream media in an attempt to reach as
many eyeballs as possible and generate at least some debate about contentious
issues? Then, as in Russia, the protest affordances of the internet and social
media will be shaped as much by the existing restrictions and limitations
placed by the state on the digital public sphere, as by the clever strategies of
opposition activists, digital rights advocates, and protest participants to carve
out a space for any dissent at all. In both Ukraine and Russia, the political and
social realities of each country fuse with the adoption of networked media
platforms by the state and the citizens, resulting in a structure of protest
opportunities that is made up of both atoms and bits, differently configured.
These different possibilities of what a protest could look like suggest that
augmented dissent is a complex construct exactly because the protest square
could be variously augmented, depending on who and how gets to access the
networked technologies and the capabilities for action they contain.

The next several chapters offer an in-depth look at the "who and how" of
the Euromaidan protest in Ukraine, exploring the key characteristics of the
protest actors from my interviews, and the main affordances of digital media
for protest that were perceived by these protest participants.

Chapter 3

Euromaidan Protesters

A Snapshot

As we've seen from chapter 2, the affordances of social media and networked technologies for protest do not exist in a vacuum. Instead, they emerge as opportunities or limitations from the coming together of technologies and actors in a particular context. Chapter 2 provided an overview of the social, political, and technological circumstances in Ukraine and Russia that circumscribe how citizens perceive the role of digital media in society and how they think about the usefulness or uselessness of certain aspects of internet-enabled networks for civic and political activity. No context is complete, however, without an in-depth look at the actors coming into contact with the networked tools and platforms. This chapter and the next one, therefore, focus on the Euromaidan protesters who participated in the interviews I conducted during and after the protest.

Beyond demographic profiles, several factors emerge as key to how protesters perceived and used digital media, as reported by the interviewees. These factors include overall media consumption and internet use patterns; prior levels of political and civic engagement; prior experience of activism, organizing, or protest activity. These variables modulated the affordances of the internet and social media for dissent in various ways, resulting in a spectrum of perceptions and opinions ranging from skepticism to enthusiasm. Interviewees spoke especially keenly of experiencing the shift between their everyday internet and social media use and the "extraordinary" mode their use patterns transformed into as they began to participate in Euromaidan. Media use habits, protest experience, and level of political interest combined to inform a multiplicity of ways in which technology was seen as empowering or limiting one's participation. Analyzing these variables and placing them into the political, civic, and technological context of the 2013–2014 protest activity in Ukraine provides further support for the core argument of the book: that social media was seen by protesters who used it as a conduit to a qualitatively different protest experience and as offering a variety of diverse modes of participation, augmented by the joining together of offline and online structures and networks.

MY INTERVIEW SUBJECTS

We cannot begin to understand the relationship between dissent and technology without in-depth conversations with people who participate in the protest and who use technology about this relationship. While network analysis and content mining of social media can tell us a lot, they almost never reveal the whole story. To really understand this relationship, and to contextualize this understanding, it is necessary to conduct work in the field, and to employ ethnographic methods to do so.

I conducted a total of fifty-nine semi-structured, open-ended interviews during my fieldwork research on Euromaidan. The interviews were held in three waves throughout the period between the winter of 2013 and the autumn of 2015. Table 3.1 presents a summary of information about the three waves of interviews.

The initial pilot interviews (12) took place in Kyiv (the capital of Ukraine) during the Euromaidan protests in December 2013 and January 2014, with participants purposively sampled from various active Euromaidan groups and initiatives to represent a spectrum of ages, civic activism experience, and digital literacy. A second wave of interviews (10) was conducted in the period from March 2014 to May 2014, shortly after the end of the Euromaidan protest and the beginning of the Russian-orchestrated conflict in Ukraine. The interviews took place in the Washington, DC, area with individuals who identified as Ukrainians living in the United States and as having participated in Euromaidan. Participants were recruited from several key

Table 3.1   Summary of Information about Interview Participants

Interview wave	Time period	Location	Number of interviews	Breakdown by gender (female/male)
Wave 1. Ukraine	December 2013– January 2014	Kyiv, Ukraine	12	4 f, 8 m
Wave 2. United States	March 2014– May 2014	Washington, DC, USA	10	6 f, 4 m
Wave 3. Ukraine	August 2015– December 2015	Kyiv, Kharkiv, Odesa, Ukraine	37	16 f, 21 m

Ukrainian communities and groups in the Washington, DC, area, using their public Facebook pages to place recruitment ads and then sampled randomly from the pool of those who agreed to participate in the study. Finally, a third wave of interviews (37) was conducted in the summer and autumn of 2015 (between the months of August and December) in Ukraine, with participants initially recruited from several still operational Euromaidan communities and groups, using their Facebook community pages to place recruitment ads as well as through snowball sampling stemming from the pilot interview series participants, the third-wave interviewees, and their networks. These interviews were conducted in Kyiv; in Kharkiv,[1] a large city in eastern Ukraine which saw some fairly active Euromaidan action during the protest; and in Odesa, a port city in the south of Ukraine that was also one of the key sites of Euromaidan action, though to a lesser extent than Kyiv and Kharkiv (see map in figure 3.1).

The interview participants' ages ranged from twenty-three to forty-nine years: the median age was thirty-four years and the mode for age was thirty-one. Most participants said they resided in or near urban areas. Almost 95 percent of the respondents held a bachelor's, master's or a higher postgraduate degree, with the remaining 5 percent in the process of completing their higher education. All participants were either employed, self-employed, freelance workers, or students, and a number of those who self-reported as students also said they worked part-time.

MEDIA HABITS AND INTERNET USE

In terms of media consumption and engagement, my interviewees named television and online media as their most frequent sources of information and news, with print and radio lagging far behind (although it's worth noting that many of the online websites named were those of print publications). A number of interviewees who said they watched television news, current affairs programs, and talk shows, shared a habit of "channel browsing," or switching between news bulletins to compare how certain events were being reported on. As one participant from Kyiv remarked, "the actual truth is usually somewhere in the middle, so it's useful to see what everyone is saying—and not saying."

While residents of Ukraine relied more heavily on a mix of Ukrainian (both Ukrainian- and Russian-language) and Russian news media outlets, those living in Washington, DC, consumed a more varied diet of Ukrainian, Russian, and Western media content, citing the need for more nuanced news about their homeland. As one marketing manager at an international company put it:

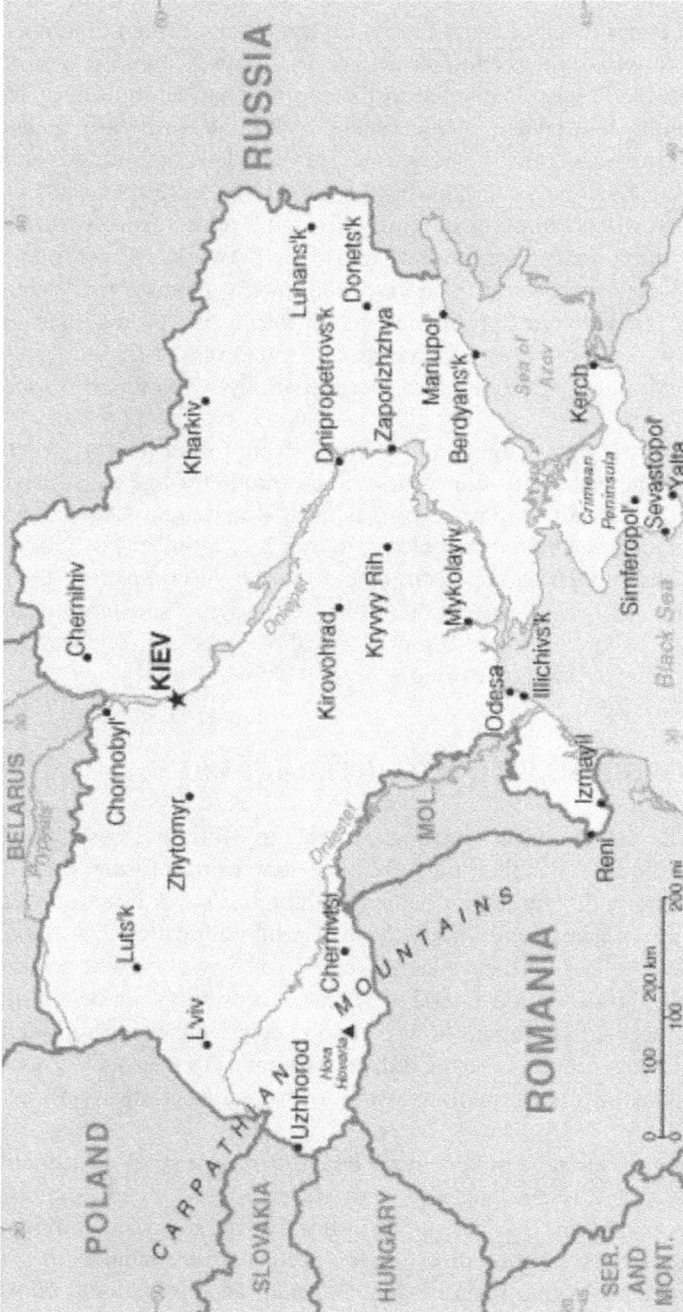

Figure 3.1 Map of Ukraine, CIA Factbook. Public Domain, https://commons.wikimedia.org/w/index.php?curid=89586.

If you only watch American channels or read *The New York Times*, *The Post* or *BuzzFeed*, there's just not enough coverage of Ukraine or the region in general. And if there is it's mostly geopolitics and Putin. So I almost have to also find local (Ukrainian) content to supplement that.

A participant from Kharkiv unknowingly echoed this sentiment describing how Ukraine was portrayed in the international media:

It's often annoying how Ukraine is either mentioned [in international media] when something bad happens, or in repetitive, stale, predictable contexts: Chernobyl, Orange Revolution, Russia's little neighbor . . . [. . .] It's like they're not even trying.

A number of respondents said they relied on their social network for the latest news and interesting feature stories and opinions. A graduate student interviewed in Washington, DC, said she mostly read what news crossed her Facebook feed and attributed this habit to convenience as well as a lack of time:

I follow enough people that there's regularly something to read, some link to follow or a video to watch that's relevant. With all of my academic work, I honestly don't have the time to explore news websites. Maybe that's narrow-minded, but the Facebook links are right there, and I can see which ones come recommended.

In terms of information and communication technology use, 100 percent of respondents reported owning a personal computer, whether laptop, desktop, or both. Eighty-eight percent reported owning a smartphone, and the remaining 12 percent said they used a simple cell phone, mostly for calls and text messages. A little over 30 percent reported owning a tablet (Apple iPad, an Android-based model, or a Windows Surface). In addition, 40 percent said they owned and regularly used a photo or video camera (these figures are summarized in table 3.2).

Ninety percent of respondents said they had internet access at home, and the remaining ones said they accessed the web at work or at school. Almost 80 percent said they accessed the internet daily, with the rest accessing it a few times a week. One of the more active participants, a student in Kyiv, said she had a hard time thinking of her internet use as "going" online, since her smartphone was always connected and she checked messages and social media feeds throughout the day. When talking about their internet use, practically all participants said they had used social networks prior to Euromaidan,

Table 3.2   Device Use and Internet Access among Interview Participants

Type of device or connection	Percentage of interview participants using (N=59)
Personal computer (laptop/desktop)	100%
Smartphone	88%
Other (non-smartphone) mobile phone	12%
Tablet	32%
Photo or video camera	40%
Internet access at home (broadband or mobile)	90%

as well as visiting news sites, photo and video platforms. They also reported using the internet for banking, travel, and health information search needs, among other use scenarios.

The majority of protesters I spoke with stressed that their internet use became more frequent and more prolonged during the Euromaidan protests. An interviewee in Kyiv recalled "constantly following the news" online during Euromaidan and being "hyperaware" of the different goings on. An interviewee in Odesa, a law student, said she started following the events "through posts from Kyiv-based protest participants on Facebook" and simultaneously scanning mainstream media reports, but quickly gave up on traditional media sources as it became clear that they were "not keeping up with the mad pace at which things were developing." Several of the Washington, DC-based participants said they monitored Euromaidan news on Twitter and Facebook, as well as on Ukrainian mainstream media platforms, and often ended up going to bed at odd hours because of the time difference (seven hours between Kyiv and Washington, DC, time zones).

EXPERIENCE: FROM SEASONED ACTIVISTS TO NOVICE PROTESTERS

When they spoke about their civic engagement, experience with social or political activism, and volunteering, participants seemed to fall into two broad groups, which could be designated as having experience of and/or being new to civic activism in the context of the Euromaidan protest. Saunders et al. (2012) similarly suggest distinguishing protest participants between "novices" (those with little or no past protest or activism experience) and "returners" (those with some protest or activism experience). The words "old" and "new" were actually used in their interviews by quite a number of the more experienced participants, who used them to differentiate between those who had been involved with civic movements, nonprofit organizations or similar institutions before Euromaidan, and those for whom Euromaidan was the first such experience, or at least the first large-scale civic uprising or protest. Those who fell into the "new" group usually did not call themselves that, but insisted their interest in civic life and political activism had been minimal prior to Euromaidan, and even if they had done some volunteer or charity work, it was never framed in terms of activism or political activity. The "old"/ "new" distinction provides a useful frame for understanding how prior protest experience shaped interviewees' Euromaidan involvement overall, as well as how they saw the possibilities for action and limitations afforded by the internet and social media within the protest context.

The distribution of participants between the two extremes was uneven, with roughly one-third of the respondents falling into the "old," experienced civic activist camp, and about two-thirds falling into the group that was "new" to civic activism and mass protests. Each of the groups certainly had a spectrum of experience in terms of their history of civic activity or lack thereof, but their self-assessment as belonging to one or the other group, reflected in how they described themselves, their histories, and their actions in the interviews, came across clearly.

A data journalist from Kyiv was the first person I interviewed during the pilot phase of the interviews, and he immediately used the "old" and "new" references, reluctantly putting himself in with the "old guard." He also remarked that a number of those who were involved in civic activism during the 2004 Ukrainian Orange Revolution protests and earlier were no longer active as civil society members.

> Right now, there are both old and new people in Euromaidan networks, but there are lots of new people. Some of the old people are there, but most have gone away from activism. I have some experience, but I haven't been too involved in these older networks. I'm much more interested in what's happening right now.

Another interviewee from Kyiv, involved with one of the groups coordinating anything from information exchange to housing options within Euromaidan, said he also considered himself part of the "experienced" civic activists camp, but stressed that he and other people he knew from before the protest were not necessarily in leading roles during the Orange Revolution, since the leadership at that point was fairly small and insular.

> In 2004 people were much more interested in just street protests, and no one wanted to do organising or planning. I liked working in the field, I can also help connect people, solve some problems, but I wasn't in the coordinating councils.

The same respondent noted that the grassroots organizing during Euromaidan did not necessarily rely exclusively on the "returner" individuals, communities, and networks, and said he was pleasantly surprised at how well some of the "novice" groups and communities within Euromaidan were able to self-organize with little to no civic activism experience.

> There is very little hierarchy in all these communities, maybe in some of the older ones, the veterans, but it's still very flat, though. But the organization where I'm involved has a very flat structure, with a handful of coordinators, three times that number of permanent volunteers, and ten times more people who join for one-time actions or campaigns.

Those within the interview pool who were new to civic activity often relied on their other experience, such as their professional skills or academic service and charitable work to inform their Euromaidan engagement and decision-making. An IT manager I spoke to in Kyiv recalled how he first realized he was eager to do something and found a niche within Euromaidan to work:

> The Saturday after the riot police beat and dispersed the students, I came to the Mykhaylivska square and saw how much stuff people were bringing, and how there was plenty of some things, but others were still lacking. I got the idea that it would be good to coordinate these resources. And since I'm an IT guy, the idea of using the internet for this was kind of self-evident.

The manager then described how he not only used his experience in managing IT projects and worked with other people such as designers and programmers to find a solution but also relied on personal connections to do so.

> While I was mulling over this idea with colleagues, I remembered that a friend of ours, when there were freak snowfalls in spring of 2013, he launched an Ushahidi-based website for something similar. . . And we just came to the office, sat down and spent the evening working into the night to put the website together. So it's not like we even had time to come up with something or decide on the best options, it just happened.

A respondent in Odesa, who spent several months in Kyiv at the time of Euromaidan, said her human resource management skills also came in handy when she joined one of the heterogeneous groups attempting to organize within the larger protest movement. Her collective monitored the injured, wounded and later, those killed during the protests, as well as keeping track of the people who disappeared or went missing. She referred to her work during the protest as "managing an amorphous structure in a stressful situation under time constraints" and said quite a lot of the effort went into managing small crises and networking with other groups and communities, all with varying levels of organization or chaos.

> Since I work in management, as a skill I think I've improved it, I've tried this different kind, a kind of crisis management, and it has enriched my experience—both as a professional and as a citizen.

Describing her engagement with Euromaidan from Washington, DC, an interviewee working for a marketing agency said she had to adapt her copywriting and analytical skills to producing "regular reports on what was going right and what was going wrong" in Kyiv and other protest locations in Ukraine, and then work together with other local protesters to disseminate reports to influential individuals and the local Ukrainian diaspora community in Washington, DC, as well as those in other American cities.

> This was basically two-three hours per day of monitoring, checking, verifying, contextualizing and explaining. Then we compiled the report into a neat little PDF file and off it went: to our email list, to Facebook, to be printed and taken to cultural clubs, churches, and anywhere it was wanted.

Two of the interviewees in Ukraine were involved as volunteers in producing a similar online digest of Euromaidan news and events for the English-speaking audience, and said it was a grueling job that required them not only to use their skills (as journalist and academic writer, respectively) daily but also to learn on the job. One of them, a former journalist for a web portal, said they often had "heated arguments" with some of the more experienced activists in their project team about what worked and what did not for their product.

> They had civil society work and experience on their side, of course. They maybe knew how to frame unrest, injustice, human rights. [. . .] But I had my own years of experience, and my gut, and my intuition about what would draw the reader in and how to cover certain claims or actions. Honestly, we were all on a very short fuse, so I learned that civic activism and producing a citizen media product is as much about patience and working while stressed as it is about evocative writing.

The distinction between protesters who were either "returners" or "novices" to civic activism and organizing proved to be one of the key dimensions in the interview pool that impacted the various aspects of participating in the Euromaidan protest and informed the respondent's narratives of their own engagement, perception of, and use of digital media. At the same time, daily internet use habits and routines also contributed to protesters' modes of participation, often undergoing drastic changes in the process.

EVERYDAY DIGITAL MEDIA USE

One of the key themes that emerged from the interviews was the subtle transformation in how Euromaidan participants perceived digital media and how their modes of use shifted in a crisis. These distinctions between routine and extraordinary uses and perceptions of digital technology as articulated by the interviewees are illuminating as they point to certain affordances of digital media specific to protest activity.

Certainly, there is not a clear line that can be drawn between routine and crisis uses of the internet and social media by citizens. It is rather a continuum or a scale along which behavior and perception may shift. The norm might be different for different individuals, depending on factors such as their ease of access to the internet in general, their media consumption habits, their interest in political or civic life, and their preferred mode of political engagement. Since, as Kendall (1999) notes, interactions and activity online "cannot be divorced from the offline social and political contexts within which participants live their daily lives," there is a close correlation between the national, local, and individual social and political contexts and what users see as the norm for routine digital media use.

Everyday use of internet and social media tools can include consuming news and information online, engaging with the information by commenting on posts and sharing links, personal communication with friends and family, and using various utilitarian online services. Most importantly, going online to seek out news and information can contribute toward building the knowledge required to engage in civic and political life. Couldry et al. (2007) note the important role of communication technologies in mediating everyday thoughts, conversation, and activities that may, under certain conditions, help bridge the mundane and the extraordinary. Dahlgren (2003) ties regular new media use with his notion of civic culture as the key concept underlying the daily experience of citizenship.

An increasing number of studies find that in countries where traditional systems of economic and social welfare are corrupt or dysfunctional, and the independent media is weak or co-opted by the state for its own ends, citizens turn to the internet-enabled tools to manage their "everyday rights." The term is used broadly to include not only more fundamental human rights such as freedom of speech or expression or gender equality, but also more mundane things like healthcare, childcare, social security, access to justice and legal assistance, among others (Oates 2013). This shift can occur not only in failed states or authoritarian regimes but also in developing and even stable democracies, where citizens have not given up on democratic values but rather lost trust in the traditional means through which they are delivered (Norris 1999).

As citizens discover new spaces and venues for achieving their rights and freedoms, however mundane, they are reinterpreting and complicating the meaning of political activism and political issues, as well as the very answer to the question "what is political?" In post-Soviet states such as Russia and Ukraine, the new understanding of political action enabled by the new media tools has been augmented by the understanding of the internet as a liberator, a platform alternative to traditional media co-opted by political or business elites promoting their own agenda and interests (Fossato, Lloyd, and Verkhovsky 2008). With the dearth of independent traditional media able to hold the government accountable, citizens increasingly shift to various online platforms, from blogging websites like LiveJournal to the later-in-the-game social networks such as Facebook and Twitter. They use these online platforms for debates, deliberation, complaining, expressing their civic and political position as well as seeking out like-minded individuals to engage in these discussions and, potentially, to create ephemeral communities targeted at achieving specific social and political goals, however small or large.

While digital media seem to imbue the ordinary citizens with greater agency, Gunitsky (2015) notes that active citizen participation in social media does not inherently signal regime weakness, and may actually "enhance regime strength and adaptability," as state actors learn to use the tools for their own ends. Still, the affordances of online media for providing alternative outlets for citizen claims and calls to action and for enabling organization for such action create a qualitatively new civic and political context, made especially visible in societies where independent media and free speech are restricted or put under pressure.

In her 2013 study of the role of the internet and digital media in the Russian political and social life, Oates found compelling evidence that the web and possibilities for everyday action that it offers can change the fundamental nature of politics in the country, affording citizens the power to articulate their grievances and successfully demand change (Oates 2013). These findings relate first and foremost to the everyday rights context, describing cases of chronically ill patients and parents with sick children organizing and fighting for their rights to health care and medication online, as well as environmental activists raising awareness of illegal construction endangering a forest in Russia. None of these cases were revolutionary, nor did these citizens seek to overthrow the government or change the regime. Instead, these activities reflect how their everyday discussions and seeking advice or help online can shift into crisis mode and gain more urgency when the situation calls for it, providing opportunities for acts such as open letters to officials, online petitions, collecting testimonies and complaints, organizing pickets, challenging the mainstream media, and such. Moreover, these case studies of successful use of the internet to defend everyday rights push us to question whether citizens will be empowered and inspired by such "everyday" victories and small-scale change to attempt to use the same tools to organize, communicate, and act in a crisis, including demands for large-scale political and social change.

PRE-EUROMAIDAN ROUTINES

The theme of differences in internet and social media use during ordinary moments and during the Euromaidan protest was a continuous thread throughout the interviews conducted at various times during and after the protest activity took place. Although participants' definitions of what constitutes normal or ordinary internet use differed, virtually everyone noted that how they used the internet and social media changed during the protest period. The changes reported dealt with intensity of use, the number and the choice of sources of information online, certain habits and behavior on social media, and kinds of activity, purpose of activity, or reasons for activity that citizens found themselves engaging in online. These are described in more detail below.

Most respondents reported some level of mundane internet activity prior to the protest events in the form of occasional social media use to consume and share information and keep in touch with close friends and family, as well as visiting media websites and other sources of information, entertainment, or useful online services. The intensity of online activity varied, with the most active users joking about "checking Facebook messenger every five minutes," and the least active describing social media such as Facebook or Twitter as "useless" and "mostly distracting."

Those who used social media specifically for interpersonal communication more often cited "staying in touch" with family members and close friends, as well as "networking with industry colleagues," "job searching," "keeping up with the office gossip," and "arranging outings or weekend plans" as their main reasons. Most of these were done through Facebook (with a lean toward more international, as well as local connections) or VKontakte, the Russian-language internet's Facebook lookalike, popular in many post-Soviet countries, including Ukraine.

On the contrary, casual use of the microblogging service Twitter seemed to be less widespread: most of the respondents who used it professed being more tech-savvy or even "internet addicts," and the majority used it on their smartphones. The main uses of Twitter amounted to "following news in Ukraine and abroad," "peeking at celebrity feeds (on Twitter as well as Instagram)", and tweeting and retweeting "cool or useful links." Several of those who said they had Twitter accounts admitted they had started them as part of the over-all fad around 2009–2010, and were mostly rebroadcasting what they posted on Facebook, using an automated function. The position of those who said they did not use Twitter is best summed up by one respondent, a magazine designer from Odesa:

> I've never understood what the use of it [Twitter] was. It just didn't make sense to me. Why limit yourself to 140 characters, when you can write as much as your heart desires on Facebook or VK [VKontakte]? Plus, all my pals are already there [on Facebook and VKontakte], so yet another reason to stick to it.

Quite a few respondents observed that social media had become their start-ing point when they consumed or searched for latest news, and said they were forgoing visiting the main pages of news websites in favor of reading their stories or articles via their social media feeds, whether by following the official pages of their preferred media outlets or by seeing news shared by their friend network. There were some discrepancies in terms of what such news consumption choices meant, with part of the respondent pool admitting they felt like they were limiting their exposure to different viewpoints due to filtering their information stream online. One respondent, a museum curator based in Kyiv, said she often felt like "seeing the same names, locations and viewpoints" rolling across her Facebook page daily.

Yet others noted that they were actually discovering new stories and sources of information because of the breadth of the selection their friends were choosing to share on their own feeds. This aligns with earlier findings by scholars that point to a positive relationship between consuming informa-tion and being active on social media and political engagement (Boulianne 2016; Skoric et al. 2016). A protest participant from Kharkiv, a computer science student, confessed he "relied upon his Twitter feed to bring stuff" he "wouldn't normally see on his RSS feeds reader," which he had set up to aggregate mostly tech and IT news.

In terms of other online activities, the perceptions of what amounts to everyday civic or political engagement were closely tied to participants' overall understanding of what political or civic activism means. When first questioned, most identified only traditional kinds of political activity, such as voting, as explicitly political, but when asked about their civic engagement, human rights interests, or community involvement, practically all respon-dents admitted they had convictions, wanted to change things in Ukrainian society, and felt their involvement in some kind of activism or charity work could result in such a change. Several respondents suggested being politically active also meant, in the words of one interviewee, "to voice my opinion, to be active in convincing others of a certain course of action." Another respondent said political participation generally meant "taking part in things that you think are important and relevant to you, and to your country." Examples of civic and community activities which could be construed as political included protests, pickets, talking to the media, social network activity, and signing online petitions. A few interviewees said they had volunteered in charity work or organized community initiatives, like English-language clubs, environmental campaigns, or animal rescue.

When probed further, respondents described quite a few different kinds of activity they casually engaged in online, including sharing and signing online petitions, retweeting or reposting calls for help (such as fundraising to help sick friends or acquaintances) or posts raising awareness of third-party activist efforts, and changing their Facebook avatars to support a cause. A significant number of participants recalled joining a Facebook or VKontakte group of an initiative or a cause they supported offline, to show their affiliation or solidarity: examples of these included a feminist group, a campaign to get Ukraine's capital Kyiv to build more and better bike lanes, a student-run documentary film festival, and a page to support an animal shelter that was being evicted from their current building.

Though they rarely described these acts as political, most of those who did engage in them agreed that these represented some expression of their agency as citizens and allowed them to enact change in small, but meaningful ways. As one woman in Kyiv, who said she used social networks mostly to keep up with friends and family, admitted,

> For me, it's just pressing "like" or "share" on a post about a cute cat up for adoption, I don't even think about this as a significant act, since things like this pop up in my feed all the time. But what if it's not a cat, but a sick child who needs a blood donor? I guess, if enough of us do it, it can really change someone's life.

Admittedly, several of the interviewees said they were skeptical of the potential of likes and shares to enable meaningful change. One respondent, a financial analyst who moved to the United States from Ukraine in 2008 for a graduate degree and stayed to work, said he was predisposed "to actually go do something, like give blood" or donate funds if the situation called for it and if he knew who he was helping, and added that he thought "it was easy to add a +1" to someone's request for help, but that "the statistical likelihood" of that +1 actually making a difference "was next to nothing."

On the other hand, many of the respondents who did acknowledge using the internet to engage in some form of civic activity, volunteer initiatives, charity projects and other kinds of activism, pointed out that online platforms and their affordances for easily aggregating attention and making things go viral were helpful in boosting awareness of a cause or campaign, even if they did so temporarily. An IT manager from Kyiv described how an initiative set up online by one of his friends during a freak snowstorm in the spring of 2013, when the adverse weather led to traffic jams and car accidents in the capital, had easily found its target audience.

> By the time K. (the friend) thought to set up some kind of centralized crowd-sourcing effort on a dedicated website, there was already a Twitter and Facebook hashtag, #kyivsnow, which people started using to post calls for help or useful information. [. . .] Click the hashtag—and there you have a stream of drivers stuck in snowdrifts and Kyivites offering hot tea and food to those caught on the road. K. just set up a map and shared it with the [same] hashtag.

A number of more seasoned Euromaidan participants, who had some experience in civic organizing and activism, noted the potential of blogs and social media to stimulate public debate around a contested issue and to gain proponents to join a cause that was deemed "publicly important" or "worthy," though not necessarily political. One Kyiv resident described her experience of helping to campaign against illegal construction projects in Kyiv's historic Podil district and using LiveJournal as the platform to generate discussion around the issue.

> We knew that not everyone [on LiveJournal] was interested in the corruption allegations behind the construction, so we tried to find alternative motivations. One of these was pushing the fact that the [old] building was a historical landmark and had sentimental value. To many in Kyiv, it was unimaginable that it would be torn down or rebuilt into a shopping mall. So we stressed that, found some archival pictures [. . .] to win more people to our side. And, as always on LJ, people came armed with opinions.

DIGITAL MEDIA USE DURING EUROMAIDAN: A SHIFT TO THE EXTRAORDINARY

Most of my interviewees found out about the dropping of the EU Association Agreement by President Yanukovych through Ukrainian news media. But over two-thirds of respondents, regardless of their location or other factors, reported first hearing about protest activity on social media. Facebook was overwhelmingly the source where they learned about the start of the protests in November 2013, with a number of people citing influential

Afghani-Ukrainian journalist Mustafa Nayyem and his call to protest on Facebook or reposts of his post as their key sources. One interviewee from Kyiv recalled:

> I was following the association agreement prep quite closely, so I knew people were unhappy, and then somewhere I saw reports that Mustafa (Nayyem) called to gather on Facebook.

Once they started following the Euromaidan protest or engaging with it in some way, most users reported a shift in the intensity of their social media use and the time they spent online. Regardless of their previous level of social media engagement or news consumption online, every respondent noted that they started spending more time online and engaging with the various information and communication tools differently. One Kharkiv respondent called his new internet use pattern "almost neurotic" when he described constantly checking his social media feeds and monitoring news headlines on his smartphone. Another respondent, an activist in Kyiv who was coordinating publicity and media relations for one of Euromaidan's grassroots groups, said she was "regularly overwhelmed" by the amount of information appearing online, and added that making sense of what was important required "enormous effort and patience." An IT manager whom I interviewed in Kyiv said his emotional state was impacted by the constant barrage of news and information generated by protest participants and observers online.

> The information field, background influenced me very heavily, I constantly followed the news, and that really hypes you up.

Though during ordinary times most social media active respondents said they could afford to make their communication and information consumption online asynchronous, the protest atmosphere created a temporal shift for them. Especially those who were actively involved in a logistical, monitoring, or media-related role in Euromaidan said they felt it necessary to attempt to keep up with protest events in real time, which also led to an increase in the intensity of internet use.

However, even for those who were physically far from the events on the ground in Kyiv (and later in other large Ukrainian cities), the pressure to follow news as it happened was great. While the difference in time (seven hours with the EST time zone for Washington, DC, for instance) made it difficult to always keep up, multiple protest participants among the group of Ukrainians interviewed in the United States said they were still keyed into the protest news and updates streams. Some attributed it to the "24-hour news cycle" that the protesters occupying the center of the Ukrainian capital and their online support circle created, while others said the kinds of media available online, like video live streams and quickly established protest hashtags (the main one, #euromaidan, used in English, Russian, and Ukrainian) made it easy for them to fall into "the vicious circle of constantly consuming information" and to join scores of other internet users in liking, retweeting and sharing links, videos, photos, and updates. One interviewee, a graduate student in Washington, DC, said that being online and following the Euromaidan news was "like a drug" and added that "the fear of missing something crucial, like another attack by riot police" had made her keep her phone by her person at all times, even when going to bed at night.

Another notable shift in how participants used social media and the internet during the protest period was the change in the number of sources of information or opinions that people followed online or the criteria for selecting such sources to include in their daily information streams. Several people suggested that in order to broaden their knowledge and awareness they started following new users and new groups on social media. For some participants, this was a rather serendipitous process: they saw a post that resonated with them that a friend of theirs had shared and followed the post's author, or were directed to a community page for a protest initiative that they found aligned with their interests and followed or liked it.

For several interviewees, however, these choices were more rational and based on digging deeper into who a person was and where they came from before they chose to add them to their friend list. A journalist I spoke with in Kyiv said that she was more inclined to start following someone new during Euromaidan if "someone I knew commented on their post" or recommended it while resharing. Overall, almost every interviewee reported a growth in the number of accounts, whether personal or community-based, that they were following on social media.

Curiously, there were several mentions during interviews of protest participants deciding to unfollow someone who was previously part of their Facebook feed or Twitter stream. Most of these cases had to do with a difference of opinion regarding the protests, their essence, and the forces behind them. A respondent from Odesa, who works at a public library there, shared this story of unfollowing one of her colleagues on Facebook and the fallout from their disagreement, both online and offline:

> She was dismissive of the Euromaidan movement and the protesters' motivations from the start, but towards the New Year [mid-protest] her posts got really scathing. The worst thing was, she absolutely refused to discuss anything rationally. Once her opinions got really vitriolic, and I got tired of trying to reason with her, I had to unfollow her on Facebook. Let's just say that working together and even being in the same office was very awkward after that.

Respondents also noted that switching into a "protest use mode" for social media led to changes in their usual habits and behavior on the platforms. Those protest participants who dealt with organizing things such as medical help or fundraising, as well as those who coordinated logistics and resources, said social media was a key ingredient is assessing people's trustworthiness and reputation. This meant that they spent more time exploring the online networks and content posted by people who were in responsible positions in the protest community or wanted to occupy such positions. Suddenly, weak ties became important, and finding someone you knew and trusted on the list of "mutual friends" with a person who was suggested as useful was an indication of "good standing," as one respondent put it. Another participant, a Ukrainian public relations manager based in Washington, DC, said that the professional social network LinkedIn, usually despised by most casual users for incessant reminders and notifications, became unexpectedly useful for assessing professionals in a particular area (such as lobbying, management, or medicine) and determining how reliable they were. "If you had connections in common, you could go to those people and ask them: is X really a decent person with good networks? Can we trust them?" the PR manager explained.

Other digital media habits that were remade by the protest reality included constantly keeping all communication devices charged and carrying chargers or power banks everywhere. This was especially important for Euromaidan participants on the ground in Kyiv or elsewhere in Ukraine, who relied on mobile internet and smartphones for coordinating their work and staying abreast of the latest happenings. One protester interviewed in Kyiv during the Euromaidan protests in December 2013, laughingly showed me his backpack, which contained two phones (a smartphone "for internet and social media" and a simple cell phone "for emergency calls," multiple cables, chargers and power banks, a laptop, and an external hard drive "for backups in case the laptop gets smashed."

Despite these extra measures taken to stay in contact with people and get the latest news, none of the activists on the ground reported taking any precautions in terms of digital security. No one reported using two-step authentication on their emails or social media accounts or using VPN for anonymous browsing. Though these were not specifically discussed during the interviews, the lack of change in these cybersecurity habits was likely due to the general lax climate in regards to how unafraid activists in Ukraine generally were in 2013–2014 of government or law enforcement surveillance. Throughout the protest, there was sporadic indication of surveillance, and most of it had to do with tracking the mobile phones of certain activists, several of whom were ambushed and kidnapped by government-sponsored thugs during the later stages of Euromaidan. These physical hazards were perceived by protesters to be much more dangerous than any threat of digital surveillance.

A pivotal moment that made some activists think about the government's potential for technical threats was a day in late January 2014 when those present in the vicinity of the Maidan (Independence Square) in downtown Kyiv received an unsolicited mass text message on their phones saying, "Dear subscriber, you have been registered as a participant of a mass protest" (EuroMaydan 2014). One interviewee, a landscape architect in Kyiv, recalled:

It really jolted me, when that text popped up, and I thought, could they be watching us? But the overall mood was so upbeat at the time, that people immediately started laughing about it, saying "they can't arrest us all." At that point, there were thousands in the square, so they probably couldn't.

A key change in mode of use during protest time that many participants noted related to using certain apps, tools, and features as means of documenting, recording, or witnessing the events that occurred. While witnessing as a key affordance of social media and the internet during moments of crisis in protest will be discussed in more detail further on in this book, it is important to note that quite a few respondents indicated this particular shift in their use of new media specifically. The instances of shifting use included using existing apps, such as Facebook or Twitter, to record verbal and visual reports of daily life as well as critical moments in protest locations, or to record participants' own reactions to what had occurred. One interviewee in Kharkiv, a student who had gone to Kyiv to participate in the protest, and later returned to his own city to manage the protest camp there, said that on some days, especially if something significant had happened, like an attack by riot police or an especially poignant speech, "you could see dozens of people posting descriptions of the same moment, sharing the same photo." He said, "it created a feeling of solidarity, of belonging to the same group in this one moment."

Another shift in feature selection was that some of the respondents, whose activity on social media was previously primarily private or protected, made their accounts public during the protest, for the sake of better coordination and visibility. An activist in Kyiv, an international nonprofit employee who served as a volunteer medic during the protest, summed it up thusly:

It was uncomfortable at first, opening my Facebook up, and making my thoughts available to so many new people, but I think, ultimately, it was productive, and not just because of better coordination (for the volunteer medics). I like to think that my posts may, along the way, have turned around a few users who were doubtful about the protest's goals and its participants' credibility.

Activists working on the ground in Ukraine reported an increased use of specific apps by certain communities: the AutoMaidan drivers who were active in helping transport people and resources started using a walkie-talkie app called Zello to coordinate their locations and warn about threats and roadblocks, while citizen journalists installed and made use of smartphone and tablet live streaming apps such as UStream, to broadcast what was happening in different locations to thousands of viewers. Many of the Euromaidan participants who were located abroad said the live streams were a key element of their daily social media diet. The live streamed videos were then archived, some of them capturing key clashes and loss of civilian life, later emerging as important historical documents and even going on to become evidence in criminal investigations, many of them still ongoing.

CONCLUSION

Mainstream and social media routines, prior activism and protest experience, and preexisting interest in political engagement emerge as key factors circumscribing the perceptions of my interviewees about the opportunities and limitations of digital media for protest participation. More than anything, this chapter demonstrates the diversity of the protest community, encompassing seasoned activists and protest novices, digital enthusiasts, and conservative internet users. More importantly, these factors were also mitigated by the capabilities of technology, affording people a variety of participation scenarios: full-time and part-time ones, real-time and delayed ones, limited by lack of experience and elevated by simplified engagement mechanisms, supported by both strong and weak ties.

The book's core argument—that the affordances of digital media contribute to a qualitatively different experience of protest—finds support in protest participants' reflections on how their use of the internet and social media changed during Euromaidan events. The shifts in intensity and temporality of social media use, in the choice of sources of information and networks of connections, and, ultimately, in overall habits of social media use, reflect a transition between the routine capabilities of digital technology and the extraordinary affordances that emerge in the context of mass dissent.

The discussion of factors predicating these protest affordances would be incomplete without focusing on the relationship between the variables discussed above and another central factor—that of the location of protesters with respect to the physical and digital space of the protest. The next chapter considers the role of distance and place in Euromaidan protesters' understanding of digitally mediated participation.

Chapter 4

Space, Distance, and Digital Media

On November 21, 2013, I happened to be in New York, where I was delivering a guest lecture on the internet and media in Ukraine in my colleague's class at Columbia University's School of International and Public Affairs. The day after the lecture, my colleague posted a snapshot of me in class to Facebook. Our mutual friend in Kyiv commented on the post that night: "Hey, we have a revolution going on here!" to which I replied: "Yep, we're already watching the livestreams." Indeed, we've done nothing but, glued to our laptops and taking in updates, photos, and videos. My first experience of Euromaidan was a long-distance one.

Later in the winter of 2013, I spent time at the protest camp in Independence Square in Kyiv, weaving between people and tents, inhaling the cold air and the smell of smoke from the cooking fires and listening to the sounds of the protest. Yet every evening, when I got back to my apartment, I kept checking the social media feeds and my email, following the news and updates on Euromaidan action, arranging interviews, marveling at photos capturing parts of the action I wasn't able to see in person. The space of the protest, it seemed, extended far beyond the city square, but the locations of its participants modified their experience of Euromaidan and their opportunities for engagement, resulting in a multiplicity of protest experiences.

As with protesters' previous experience of civic activism and their levels of political engagement and digital media use, the location of individuals and communities, as well as their distance from protest events on the ground in Ukraine, was a defining factor that circumscribed their perceptions of how they could engage in dissent and how digital media came into their tactical and strategic choices.

One of the key concepts in understanding the affordances of digital media for protest movements and civic activism more broadly is the idea of a networked society, in which the dynamics of domination and resistance rely on forming networks and network strategies of offense and defense (Castells 2009). As social movements today often rely on digital networks for diffusion of information, communication, and coordination, the transition toward networked culture becomes not merely technological but deeply tied into societal changes, as networks become ways to be, rather than ways to do. This networked perception of distance from the center of the protest emerged in participants' interview responses focusing on the different ways they dealt with the various distances from the action on the ground. A key theme here was that physical or geographic distance did not preclude them from engaging with the protest activity or community. Rather, the internet and social media offered my interviewees different opportunities for action and allowed them to conceive of themselves as participants of the protest in various ways, depending on how far they were from the main square in Kyiv.

Because the internet is a global network that connects people across borders and jurisdictions, it is important to consider the transnational nature of many recent protest movements and what that might mean for their outcome and for the role distance and space play in these cross-border activities. In many cases, organizing transnationally has become more necessary for protest movements: as political and economic decisions are shifting to an international level (Walgrave et al. 2012), movements increasingly need to target international or transnational bodies with their claims and actions. Due to rapid developments in digital and mobile technology, transnational protests are also becoming easier to organize than they previously were (Della Porta and Tarrow 2005). At the same time, the online platforms themselves are often global in nature (van Dijck and Poell 2015), and that forces all societal actors—state agencies, mass media, and civil society organizations—to reconsider and recalibrate their position in this global public, political, economic, and cultural space.

The Euromaidan protest embraced transborder networks and connections, comprising individuals and groups from within and beyond Ukraine, and its claims and messages were translated to and broadcast in many languages and to many eyes and ears globally. However, the initial motivation of the protest movement was as much about internal Ukrainian affairs (human rights issues, corruption, and abuse of power) as it was about transborder diplomacy and international politics (i.e., the EU Association Agreement). This twofold agenda developed into a complicated set of meanings and messages that Euromaidan protesters at various locations in relation to the protest epicenter had to negotiate in their activity. But such a broad mandate for dissent also meant individuals and communities could come into the action on their own terms, with their own motivations and ideas for tactics and strategy. The dual local/global nature of Euromaidan also meant that engaging participants not just inside but also outside Ukraine was important.

Within analyses of the role of internet platforms and social media websites in sustaining global networks, a consistent theme is the potential for these tools to enable cross-border flows of information that could empower pro-democracy movements. However, in some cases (though not always), meaningful discourse and political debate on social media tend to be associated with inside-country networks. Though transnational services like Facebook and Twitter are important outlets for political expression, Gunitsky (2015) notes the less well-studied, country-specific social media outlets, such as China's WeChat or Russia's VKontakte, are also becoming both a source of citizen participation and a tool for repressions by nondemocratic governments that co-opt control of the internal communication and digital infrastructure.

In Ukraine, however, there is a unique case in which there are no significant native country-specific social media platforms: instead, the largest shares of social media activity online are on Russian VKontakte and on Facebook. While on both platforms the networks are deeply embedded into the local context, there is no evidence that they are insular: VKontakte networks most of the former USSR, while on Facebook the Ukrainian community has strong international ties due to strong Ukrainian diasporas abroad and a history of educational exchanges. Additionally, the Ukrainian Facebook contingent exhibits far more political activity and discourse, since VKontakte has effectively been co-opted by the Russian state (Toor 2014) and its audience is overall younger and less mature than that of Facebook.

SELECTION OF INTERVIEW LOCATIONS

In terms of location and distance, the interview participants within this research project fall into three distinct groups: those closest to the physical central hub of the protest located in the capital city of Kyiv; those in other Ukrainian cities where coordinated protest activity also took place; and Ukrainians living abroad who consider themselves to be Euromaidan participants. In interviews, representatives of each group discussed their perception of space, location, and distance within the framework of the protest, and reflected on the interplay between using digital media and their relative distance or proximity to the protest camp on the ground as the physical epicenter of the action.

The initial decision to conduct a pilot round of interviews in Kyiv was motivated by the fact that the city was the epicenter of the initial protest movement and the locus of most of the activity. Additionally, a large number of protesters from other cities were also in Kyiv at the time (December 2013–January 2014).

The Washington, DC, metro area was chosen not only because of its sizeable Ukrainian diaspora but also because it is an interesting part of the United States, with a high concentration of government offices, state agencies, and international organizations as well as a diverse international population. Indeed, most of the respondents from this wave worked for international organizations (in the area of finance, law, or governance), and most have also completed or are completing a graduate or postgraduate degree at a university in the area.

For the third wave of interviews, in addition to Kyiv, two other cities, Kharkiv and Odesa, were selected as locations for interview, due to a critical mass of protest participants from the two locations who volunteered to be interviewed and funding limitations for conducting the research. Both cities also emerged as active sites of protest action during Euromaidan and subsequent hubs of volunteer activity after the protests.

KYIV: THE PROTEST SQUARE AND NEARBY

Although the initial calls to react to President Yanukovych's decision not to sign the EU Association Agreement appeared online around November 21–22, 2013, the mobilization and physical occupation of the center of Kyiv by Euromaidan protesters didn't really take off until a few days later. Onuch (2015) found that several different variables, including structural opportunities of historic anniversaries (namely the Holodomor famine),[1] the illegitimate use of extreme violence by the regime against the peaceful protesters (starting with the first instance of riot police brutality on November 30, 2013), and the protesters' ability to disseminate and access information on the internet, helped solidify the initial protest community and lay the foundations for its rapid expansion and entrenchment.

The central Independence Square (Maidan Nezalezhnosti) and surrounding areas in Kyiv became the de facto center of the protest for several reasons: first, it had historically been the space where similar protests, including the Orange Revolution, had taken place; second, the location was in close proximity to government buildings, including the Presidential Administration, the Cabinet of Ministers, the Parliament, and the Kyiv city hall; and third, both the Independence Square and the nearby European Square, where the action also spread, had symbolic value as iconic representations of Ukraine and Kyiv, but were also intersections of key transport lines and routes in the city, so blocking and occupying them had a disruptive effect on "normal life" as a whole.

Varnelis and Friedberg (2008) note that the networked society changes our understanding of the concept of place, transforming our sense of proximity and distance, turning place and space into deeply contested processes of transformation. In these circumstances, Castells (2010) claims that networks facilitate not only a culture of endless deconstruction and reconstruction but also a multilateral discourse field for activists and protest participants enabled by the networked communications structure. This flexibility allows citizens to engage in dissent in various forms and to various degrees, as technology augments perceptions of protest spaces and the boundaries of places where protest events occur, and mitigates the varying distances at which participants are located from each other and from any physical loci of dissent. While the internet and the tools it offers are often said to "close" or "bridge" the distance between individuals and groups, being physically close to or remote from the protest activity that is occurring in a particular location is still a factor that modulates the affordances and limitations of digital technology for protest engagement that different activists and activist communities perceive.

The protest participants among the interviewees who were in Kyiv during the Euromaidan protest mentioned that their proximity to the gathering civic "firestorm" was as much of a driver to join the protest as the posts and discussions by their connections and friends on social networks. A respondent in Kyiv who joined the protest fairly early on summarized his motivations in the following list:

> There were several motivating factors for me: first, the very fact of the change of course [by Yanukovych] made me very mad; and just general anger at what was going on in the country, the ignorance, incompetence, unethical behavior of the authorities—this was gathering over time, and I guess this was the last drop which made me want to take some action. Then there were several "speeches" (posts online) by people I know and respect, personally or in general, apolitical people, intellectuals, who called to action, to do something, and I wanted to support them. That was the second impulse. And then, just the fact that this [the protest] was so close by, and wasn't that much of an effort to get there.

Several Kyiv-based activists said they were greatly influenced by the growing size of the crowd in Independence Square and the adjoining areas. Curiously, the volume of people in the physical protest space was an influence both on those who saw it directly when they came to downtown Kyiv and on those who saw its mediated representations through images, videos, and textual reports posted on social networks. One protester, a graduate student, recalled her amazement at seeing the gathering grow so quickly:

[The first time] when I actually did go out to the square and protest properly was the weekend when the largest Maidan came together [at the start of December]. Before that, I came a few times shortly to the smaller protests, out of curiosity mostly, but the weekend when they [officials] didn't sign [the agreement] and the first big group came together, I was out of Kyiv, and I was sorry I had left when I saw the photos of the huge crowd posted online. And the week after that I came and became an active participant.

For many of the Kyiv-based participants, their online activity and presence was as much a part of their protest activity as actually being in the physical center of the dissent. Koliska and Roberts (2015), for instance, theorize self-photography or "selfies" as visual interaction between the person and the space they are in that helps produce meaning and perform a particular identity that is informed by both the space and the self. Several interviewees reported regularly posting selfies and photos of their surroundings on Instagram, and updates of daily activities on Facebook and other platforms, "not just as proof that I was there, but because that was what everyone was doing," as one respondent put it. Another participant, an advertising executive, pointed out that documenting their presence at the protest in Maidan was "a normal part of everyday life":

> because we're so used to snapping shots of whatever we do, but this time, there was actually something exciting to share, something extraordinary that we're doing and that we are present for. How could you not want to share that?

Some Kyivites actually saw the location-enabled social media platforms such as Foursquare, Facebook, Twitter, and Instagram, which allow users to mark their geographic location when posting, as affording them the possibility to create a feeling of "strength in numbers." Not everyone was able to spend whole days (or nights) in the protest camp, so a fairly large amount of people reported there after their day jobs or did shifts when they could, including over the weekend, bringing supplies, water, food, chargers, or simply coming to join the crowds in the square. The ability to mark themselves as present at the center of the action created what one respondent referred to as "a certain sense of solidarity, especially when you looked at all the other people marked as being in the same location." An IT manager who spent most of the first half of the Euromaidan period working from his office, recalls the feeling of almost sport-like desire to "bridge the distance" between the protest epicenter and his location, an office building five blocks away.

> Of course, I was able to do helpful stuff even sitting in my office, like put-ting people in touch with each other via Facebook Messenger and making

phone calls. But we would still run down to Khreshchatyk [Kyiv's main street that brackets the central square] after work just to add another check-in on Foursquare to the protest event there, to boost the numbers.

A few of the more experienced activists interviewed in Kyiv reported a certain lack of organization during the first several weeks of Euromaidan protests, but said it looked like that didn't diminish the enthusiasm of those who came to the physical protest site. A human resources manager who had ample civic organizing experience recalled her initial impression of seeing the growing crowd on Independence Square:

> Since I've been a civic activist for a while, I was actually pretty skeptical about Euromaidan at first, and my skepticism wasn't wholly unfounded, because things were kind of chaotic. Despite the fact that there were all these people gathering there [in Maidan], very few really knew what to do beyond Facebook posts asking more people to make [protest] signs and to come join.

While many of the Kyiv-based interviewees agreed that the physical occupation of the center of the city was important in symbolic terms as a statement of intent and a visual reminder of disagreement with the authorities and their decision, they stressed that doing things beyond simply being in the square (whether physically or via location statuses on social media) was also important, pointing to a reconfiguration of the notion of public and protest space (van Dijck and Poell 2015) and of the very sense of proximity to protest events (Varnelis and Friedberg 2008) within the new context of networked communication. Another experienced activist, the data journalist I interviewed in Kyiv during Euromaidan, was similarly critical of the protesters' initial approach to organizing, and said he had used both direct contact and conversations with people in the physical epicenter of the action and outreach through his networks of social media connections to attempt to determine what it was the protesters were trying to achieve, what was necessary in terms of organization, human resources, and other support, and then to communicate all this to the people present in the downtown protest location and to those who were not there yet but were considering joining.

> Physically I came out, and talked to people, and said you can stand here or you can also go and do something. And then we figured out collectively—online, offline—what needed to get done.

As Euromaidan grew in size and awareness of the protest spread through word of mouth, social media and, gradually, mainstream media, the attention directed at the protest and the engagement of people with it increased simultaneously offline and online. More people accumulated in the center of the Ukrainian capital, and even more citizens were following the protest activity via mediated means: Facebook posts, Twitter hashtags, and live video streams. This meant that people at varying distances from the center of the protest engaged in its significant digital and physical components, working together to produce what Wanenchak (2013) refers to as a "single movement reality." In this reality of protest, the physical and digital sometimes augmented each other in unexpected ways. One of the activists who ended up coordinating logistics and human resources as part of one of the newly formed civic communities within Euromaidan told me that she found it quite ironic that, with such a large concentration of people in one place, it was actually quite difficult to manage information and activity on the ground.

> One's of Maidan's peculiarities in terms of information reach was that, despite the huge stage and constant flow of speakers there, and broadcasting of stuff from there, there were tons of people who had no idea what was happening and would come up to tents or booths and ask "What's happening? What's going on?" So, despite them physically being in the square, there was this desperate need to coordinate information.

Many of the activists interviewed, who had spent large amounts of time in the protest camp, also recognized that it was often difficult to know what was happening beyond the immediate visual perimeter: though the camp was concentrated in just one part of town, it quickly became a sprawling, vast thing. As one respondent, who at one point worked as a protest camp guard, put it,

> It really was like a small city in itself, and often it was easier to just call or message someone on the other end of the camp than troop all the way there to find out if they needed tea or gasoline. And once the attacks by [government] thugs and riot police started happening, one end of the camp often had no idea anything was amiss until they saw it on Facebook or someone managed to call and tell us to find our shields and take positions.

In that regard, those who were in charge of coordinating information posit that a combination of face-to-face meetings, phone calls and texts, email, and social media platforms were the most efficient way of getting across news, distributing tasks and managing people and resources. Because the participant make up was so varied and because some people were always at the protest camp, others only came occasionally, and still others worked elsewhere in the city, coordination often required multiple means of communication and keeping records in several places. An interviewee who helped out at a medical supplies point described their practices to me this way:

You've got protesters in the camp who are sick, so we need a physical list of medicines they need, and it's hanging right by our table in the [Trade Union] building, but we also have to give it to someone to put online, as there are people on Facebook who are asking what they should buy and bring to us. At the same time, we already have a huge overflowing bin of various drugs and supplies, and someone has to sort through that to figure out what we have plenty of, and what we are lacking severely. So that's another list, and it also has to go on our wall, and then we make copies to give to other hubs in the Maidan, and to put that on Facebook as well.

Once the protest movement spread to other cities in Ukraine, local activists in Kyiv found themselves making new connections with protesters in the regions to share advice, to coordinate protest frames, messages, and tactics, and also to learn from local experience in some of the other cities. This is in line with Earl and Kimport's suggested affordance of networked social media for tactical diffusion that requires less physical copresence to share activism-related knowledge and replicate organization and action patterns (Earl and Kimport 2011). A Kyiv-based activist who coordinated information outreach for one of the groups that grew out of Euromaidan said digital media played a big part in establishing and maintaining the regional networks, and stressed that regional outposts helped build a broader informal, horizontal structure for their particular protest community.

Communicating with regions and regional coordinators was a big part of the work, because at first, we were so overloaded that we couldn't get around to it, and it is so important. There is less structure there, people have less information, and they're less protected, so we need to help. We didn't want them to rely on random stuff they see coming out from Euromaidan on social media, because there are rumours, scaremongering, speculations—so we had to find time to set up regular communications, share what we were doing, what mistakes we'd made, how we'd managed to be productive. [. . .] Group Skype calls were particularly helpful as they saved time. And it was also helpful just to share verified information about what was happening in Kyiv, which was hard to come by in this chaos even for us, even though we were right there.

OUTSIDE KYIV: KHARKIV AND ODESA

Because Kyiv and the Independence Square were the site of the most visible protest activity during the Euromaidan protests and saw the most government-directed violent repressions, they became synonymous with the protest itself in international media frames (Zelinska 2015) and in the overall perception of those who experienced the events in mediated ways. But the protest activity spread far beyond Kyiv and virtually every regional seat (with 26 regions in Ukraine overall) and many smaller towns saw protesters setting up tents, occupying government buildings, and building protest communities on the ground. Those researchers who have to date studied the Euromaidan protest movement rarely mention locations of the protests that took place outside of Kyiv (Pishchikova and Ogryzko 2014). Onuch (2014), for instance, names several of them, including Dnipropetrovsk, Donetsk, Kharkiv, Kherson, Lviv, Odesa, and parts of Crimea. Local opinion polls report that about 20 percent of Ukrainians participated in the Euromaidan protest in some way, with 5 percent of those in Kyiv, 6 percent protesting in other cities and villages, and 9 percent saying they supported the protesters with money, food, or other resources (Ilko Kucheriv Democratic Initiatives Foundation 2014).

Regional Euromaidan participants interviewed for this research study reported varying motivations for engaging in protest activity in their local context. Among the motivations were disappointment with Yanukovych's decision not to sign the EU Association Agreement; general disillusionment with the state of political, economic, and civic freedoms in the country; pervasive corruption, abuse of power, and lack of access to justice. Along with these more abstract grievances, many respondents noted that they had specific issues to raise with their local authorities, including mismanagement of local funds, nepotism in municipal appointments, abuse of power by local law enforcement, and other problems. As a Kharkiv-based programmer told me:

> We wanted to join the big protest that was for European values and human rights and dignity, but we also wanted to stick it to The Man locally, because so many of the problems came from the politicians here, who stuffed their pockets and held on to their seats, often with the blessing of the central authorities.

Nineteen out of twenty-one interviewees in this group said they followed the Kyiv protests on mainstream news channels and social media platforms and relied on their personal networks mediated by digital technology to get reliable information about what was happening. Several interviewees noted that without proper context, it was often hard to make sense of the flood of information coming out about Euromaidan: one respondent in Odesa said she had to spend some time "sorting through sources on Facebook, VKontakte, and Twitter" to figure out "who was the most informed." Another interviewee, a journalism student in Kharkiv, said she felt overwhelmed by the amount of information and live reports:

> I expected there to be media coverage, but what we got was ordinary people with phones and tablets going into the fray and streaming video of stones being

thrown at riot police, activists beaten. It was hard to believe this was happening in Kyiv, it seemed at once very close—the phone camera was right up in people's faces—and very far. And it was non-stop.

Of the twenty-one participants interviewed in Kharkiv and Odesa (twelve in Kharkiv and nine in Odesa), six people reported that they had travelled to Kyiv during the initial stage of the Euromaidan protest and participated in some protest activity there for a period of time, before returning home. Others said they connected with people they knew who were involved in organizing in Kyiv or found useful contacts they didn't have before through seeing who was publicly organizing on Facebook. The public protest communities such as the mega-popular "EuroMaydan" that accumulated hundreds of thousands of followers and the smaller more targeted communities such as "EvromaidanSOS" proved to be useful as hubs of information, connecting regional participants to those in Kyiv and, importantly, to each other. A Kharkiv respondent who was part of a group that worked on covering protest events and news in the city online said it was both inspiring and useful to see what people were doing in other cities:

> [It was] good for morale because our activists could see that other cities were doing the same high-risk things like blocking entrances to local government buildings and putting up stages and tents in downtown. But also, it was a handy way to learn from them, to see how they organized, how they reacted to law enforcement, what they planned to protect their protesters and how they promoted their agenda [. . .] to others who weren't involved yet.

Regional protest communities also set up their own online communities and hashtags, such as "Euromaidan Kharkiv" or "Euromaidan Donetsk," to mobilize other citizens locally and provide targeted information on local protest activity. Each of these groups essentially reflected many of the same structural challenges that the Kyiv hub experienced (managing requests and available resources, distributing individual and group tasks, fundraising), but as these protests were smaller in scope, there was comparatively less communication chaos, according to one Odesa interviewee, the owner of a local handmade store who joined the protest activity:

> By the time we started to actively use our Facebook group and our WhatsApp messenger chats and put together lists of useful people on the ground, we'd already seen how it went down in Kyiv, so we were able to replicate some of what worked, and not step on the rake that they'd already stepped on [a Russian-language expression meaning not repeating someone else's mistakes].

A Kharkiv activist who had gone to Kyiv for a time to participate in the Euromaidan action there first-hand also said that the comparatively smaller

local protests made it easier to set up communications, including mobile connections and online chats.

> When I was in Kyiv it was shocking how many people were out of sync and
> often the same thing that needed to get done would be done by three different
> groups, and some other need, like firewood, would be unfulfilled. Or we'd have
> firewood, but nothing to light it with. Here [in Kharkiv], it was much easier to
> divvy up work and know who is in charge of what, as there's just not as many
> people.

Another protester in Odesa noted that it seemed to him like local communities
on social networks were more tightly knit and that allowed for more expedi-
ent construction of trustworthy hubs of activity, where people spent less time
verifying if they could put their faith in someone.

> Facebook was convenient not only because so many people use it, but also
> because you really do know most of these people in everyday life as well, so it's
> not too much of a headache to find someone who has a specific skill or can drive
> a generator to the city centre for you. And also, because the guy is someone's
> cousin or school buddy, you don't feel ashamed asking them to do it. It's almost
> like they're family.

In her examination of the fifty-seven local "maidans"[2] across twenty
Ukrainian regions through the framework of contentious politics, Zelinska
(2015) notes that, among other kinds of activity, the local communities
expressed their political protest by issuing a number of resolutions containing
demands addressed to national and local authorities, as well as the protesters' plans for future action. These documents were harder to cross-reference
than protest tactics and organizational structure, and though the overall tone
of them was similar, they often differed significantly in their content between
each other and compared to Kyiv's claims. Zelinska found that, especially
when it came to identifying their actions, regional protesters chose a variety
of explanations (from simply "engaging in protests" to "implementing direct
governance" and fulfilling "a historical mission").

Interview respondents in Kharkiv and Odesa confirmed that distance from
the epicenter of the protest, both geographical and ideological, made it harder
to coordinate the programmatic component of the protests and to build long-
term strategy into the everyday life of the protest community on the ground.
While some groups managed to find ways to strategize with Kyiv-based
counterparts (such as the Kyiv-based group mentioned in the previous section
above that held semiregular Skype calls with regional coordinators), other
groups had difficulty following the programmatic debates in the capital. One

Kharkiv interviewee, a physicist at a local research institute, lamented the lack of a coherent countrywide narrative:

> I'm no political scientist, but I found it exasperating that there were so many different messages flying out of Kyiv: on stage, on live streams, on Facebook pages, blogs . . . [. . .] I know this protest is praised for being self-organized, and that was great, but the discordant notes from Kyiv were very confusing as we tried to make sense of what we were doing on the ground.

Several of the interviewees in both Kharkiv and Odesa said that while online communication tools and mobile phones were very useful for organizing on the ground and for watching the action in Kyiv at a distance happen in real time, they were less useful for deliberating on joint protest claims or negotiating a common strategy in the long-term context. An Odesa-based history student offered this explanation:

> I think the internet erased that barrier of location: we saw what's happening in Kyiv, and we could immediately react here. If something bad happened here, we got attacked, we had live streams here or someone tweeting, so it got out and Kyiv and everyone else knew about it too. And it was helpful in the here and now, but we can't rely on technology or media to make sense of the future. We might all want to change things, and some of them are different and personal, and some are the same. Figuring out the common ground and making that change large-scale and long lasting is a challenge, and I don't think that's something technology or live streams can help with.

OUTSIDE UKRAINE: WASHINGTON, DC, UNITED STATES

All of the interviewees I spoke with in the United States reported that they followed Ukrainian news media after the initial news of President Yanukovych's refusal to sign the EU Association Agreement. This changed when Facebook became the main source of information about the ensuing protests in late November 2013. Several interviewees again mentioned journalist Mustafa Nayyem and his call to protest on Facebook and several similar popular online figures as their key sources. One interviewee, a financial analyst in an international company, said Facebook was her first means of getting wind of the events in the Ukrainian capital and seeing visual evidence of the protest:

> I was not following Mustafa Nayyem, I only started following him later. . . .
> But I think it was some of my friends who were posting, the friends who are

currently in Kyiv. They were posting about them going to Maidan and reposting his message. I think it was Thursday, but then on the weekend it was a whole bunch of [new] updates, and you saw a lot of people who were posting photos of themselves protesting.

Another interviewee in Washington, DC, a graduate student, said Facebook was also her choice of platform to not only receive updates about the association agreement fallout but also discuss this news with her network.

Facebook was how I first found out, and then just talking to the friends there, discussing the news that our government decided not to sign the association agreement. Of course, we also talked offline about it here, how could we not. But the first one was Facebook.

Although a few of the respondents were catalyzed to connect with other Ukrainians in the United States and act as soon as the first Ukraine Euromaidan protests started on November 21, 2013, for most others, it was the first burst of violence, when students were beaten by riot police on Maidan in Kyiv on November 30, 2013, that made them decide to engage. A Ukrainian expat who works in the banking sector recalled:

It was late at night in Kyiv, but here it was afternoon, so I was just getting off work and saw these photos of people beaten to a bloody pulp come across my Facebook feed. And then someone shared a video. . . . It was shocking, for something this graphic, this brutal to happen and to be shared by people online. I don't think anyone expected this, and that only made it more shocking to see.

Further engagement was also boosted by ongoing conflicts between protesters and government forces, including the shootings and brutality in Kyiv in January and February 2014, which took the lives of over a hundred people. Each of these attacks was meticulously documented by those on the ground in Kyiv, and the records were then shared online, with many of them translated and saved in multiple locations to preserve information.

Personal networks, augmented by the opportunities for engagement with the transborder protest community offered by social media, were the means of choice for first connections with other Ukrainians in the Washington, DC, metropolitan area, in other American cities, and in Ukraine. In the words of one female interviewee,

It was just me and a couple of other friends, and we decided we'd go and protest in front of the [Ukrainian] Embassy. We filed for a permit. None of us had done this before, but we did it in a matter of a day. First, we just spread the message around our friends, it was about twenty people who said that they'd come, and we posted a Facebook post with an event, and people signed up. I think the first time about 50 or 70 people came there.

All the interviewees based in the United States said they first used their personal connections, augmented by Facebook, email, or Twitter, to get in touch with other Ukrainians and to engage in any protest-related activity. Some underscored that personal ties remained important and helped create an atmosphere of trust in the network, which was important for sensitive issues like fundraising and making financial decisions once the money was raised to help activists in Ukraine.

On the other hand, several respondents acknowledged that having wider networks on social media (e.g., friends of friends) afforded them the opportunity to amplify their messages and achieve increased awareness about the protests and the activists' needs. We already know that social media platforms can be instrumental in converting casual connections into weak ties that could have more longevity and be useful in protest networks (Ellison, Steinfield, and Lampe 2011). The "weak ties" networks also allowed Euromaidan participants in the United States to gain access to a wider pool of expertise needed for various tasks during the protests and seek out people such as designers, translators, investigative reporters and analysts, fundraisers, and other professionals. One interviewee, a graduate student, enumerated some of the opportunities his extended network on Facebook and LinkedIn provided him with:

A lot of it, it started just as protests, pickets and things like that, but later on . . . this thing had gone on for three months . . . probably after a month of the protest activity, we decided that it's not that effective, so me and a couple of other friends, who have also been very active, we started seeking out people to start doing fundraising, we started writing letters to the senators, the congresspeople.

Valenzuela, Park, and Kee (2009) have found that, in a civic engagement context, social networks can generate and cement interpersonal interaction and broaden social ties, opening access to new, potentially useful connections in a network. Another interviewee, a financial analyst, said she connected with a group of people possessing very specific skills, and they then used LinkedIn to find other professionals, verifying their trustworthiness through checking in with common connections on the network:

Professionally I do [financial] investigations, so I became part of the group who was doing investigations on, like, the lobbyists of Ukrainian authorities here or investigations on some of the members of the [then-ruling] Party of Regions and then got connected with investigative journalists in Kyiv, started helping them with the things they needed to be covered in America. Our team here had a very special skill-set and it was good to find we could use it to help the Euromaidan.

Digital social movement studies have indicated that the global nature of networked communications has meant that transnational protests are also becoming easier to organize (Della Porta and Tarrow 2005). An interviewee from the group who had previously worked in the government sector said establishing transborder contacts with Kyiv-based activists was essential to connect the local, national, and international contexts, and to see how people based in Washington, DC, and elsewhere in the United States could be most useful to the protest movement and to its cause. One example she gave of how social media enabled such a multiplicity of connections was the intricacy of researching lobbying firms used by the Ukrainian government in the United States.

At first, to get people together, to get some information about what we could do, it was mostly Facebook and personal contacts . . . [. . .] To find information, we just used open source, it's all public, so for example, to do the research on lobbyists, you just look at all of the media coverage that was done, look at the lobbyist disclosure records, look at the letters, who funds them. . . Also, it's useful knowing people who have been involved in professional arena in some things, so for example, someone who is in one of the closed Ukrainian Facebook community groups suggested not just to send a letter to whoever, to [Senator] John McCain, but to his chief of staff and also his secretary, just to make sure it's gonna get to whoever, gets their attention.

Eight of the ten protest participants interviewed in the United States reported engaging in fundraising for the Euromaidan movement in some form, from simply donating money to organizing drives and coordinating the purchase of medical supplies and protective equipment for protesters in Ukraine. Quite a lot of the fundraising in the United States was done online, not only soliciting funds in Facebook groups, doing public drives on Facebook and Twitter, but also creating Facebook event pages for offline charity events such as art sales, dinners, and concerts. Some activists got even more creative, making it possible to donate to pro-Euromaidan charity organizations through the Amazon Smile program. Most of this activity was closely coordinated with Kyiv-based protest communities who were the end recipients of the funds. Transferring money, as one active fundraiser among the respondents stressed, was very delicate business, and it was important to find trustworthy activists at the epicenter of the protest to establish the flow of funds or whatever they had helped purchase.

In addition to raising some financial support, you also have to figure out who you're giving it to. Mostly through personal contacts, people who've been spending a lot of time on Maidan, mostly living there, we were gathering information on the needs, and then doing targeted fundraising. Like, they would tell us that, for example, "we need a defil . . . defib . . . ." I never can pronounce that, "defibrillator." And so we look around at the market, the costs, is it cheaper to buy here and ship or buy it there, how to arrange the transfer and confirm the receipt. It's a process that takes time and effort.

Public and open groups on social media, mainly Facebook, were also useful tools for organizing and structuring the protest effort within the United States. Several loose networks of Ukrainian Americans that engaged in Euromaidan through local protests, fundraising, media outreach and government and international organization advocacy, solidified into communities and then into nonprofits, with a lot of their coordination and communication done via email and private-or public-facing Facebook pages. Because these communities were spread between Washington, DC, New York, Chicago, and other parts of the United States, having these platforms allowed them to keep their members informed about latest events in Kyiv, coordinate simultaneous fundraising and lobbying efforts, and cross-promote their activities in other similar communities. They also instituted a practice of publishing regular online reports about their fundraising successes, and how the funds were being spent, and sharing these transparency reports widely with their networks. These were, one interviewee in Washington, DC, argued, key to building trust within the local and international protest circles:

> People will only give you so much money based on passion, or if the violence in Kyiv is flaring up and things are bad. But to make it last, to keep the funds flowing, you have to show people they can trust you. And being ultra-transparent is a good way to do that. "Look, here's how much you gave us and here's who got it, and here's a photo of the guy after he recovered from his injury." That makes the protesters in Kyiv risking their lives more real and gets your donors to trust you as the intermediary.

Although networked social media transform our perception of the concepts of place and distance, geographical proximity still has an impact on how protest participants experience the protest as a phenomenon overall. Participants interviewed abroad explicitly said that geographical distance from the events in Ukraine made a difference for how they experienced and perceived Euromaidan as a protest movement and an event. Most talked about a difference in their own protest tactics and discussed things they could and could not do in terms of political activity (e.g., standing on the square in Kyiv or helping in the makeshift hospital versus fundraising or contacting congress-people in Washington, DC). As one activist put it,

> We can't actually go to Euromaidan and occupy the square, so we have to get creative: I still want to express myself as Ukrainian, so I go and stand in front of the White House or the Ukrainian Embassy in Georgetown and protest. Or I see people changing their avatars to Ukrainian flags and I do the same, because that creates some sense of unity. Or . . . when the first people were shot to death in Kyiv, we went to the [Ukrainian] Embassy and staged a lie-down protest, covered ourselves with flags, like dead bodies. The Ambassador called the police, but hey, we had a permit, so US law was on our side!

A few interviewees talked about the difference in the perception of events, suggesting that they had a bigger and more balanced picture of what was going on from afar, although real-time info from social networks and live streams afforded them the same speed of receiving news as the people on the ground, and often the same level of emotional hardship as well. A marketing manager in Washington, DC, said she had trouble concentrating on work and bouts of anxiety during Euromaidan, knowing friends and people she knew in Ukraine were involved in it. She also said she felt guilty discussing how difficult it was for her to follow events online, because she felt like it was much harder for those who were actually involved in the protest in Ukraine:

> When you're just watching this online, it's a dumb feeling of sorts, because you can see it from many angles, see the confrontations, the action, but there's nothing you can do apart from sharing the news online, reposting the videos and live streams, translating what is going on into different languages. And you can't sleep.

One respondent said that she felt "less difference in perception based on geographical distance, and more difference based on political distance" (i.e., people's political persuasions), as she found it hard to discuss the events in a reasoned way with people on the other side of the argument. Many respondents said they joined quite a few of the many protest-related communities on Facebook and Twitter that supplied regular updates about events on the ground, to have access to more information in a few concentrated streams. A few respondents said the Ukrainian events made them reconsider Twitter and find it more useful during breaking-news events and periods of unrest, with one respondent saying he "realized what it was for and how it could be used effectively to follow news in real time."

CONCLUSION

The space of the Euromaidan protest was necessarily a hybrid one, stretching as it did from the protest square in Kyiv to other cities in Ukraine and beyond, across borders, and time zones. Proximity to the protest epicenter and distance between key nodes in the activist network were formative not only for the protest as an event but also for shaping the individual experiences and agency of participants. Digital media in this case did not only serve as "bridging" tools, symbolically reducing the distance between the heart of the protest in Ukraine and other locations. Importantly, they afforded people opportunity to participate in protest in various forms and to various degrees, augmenting their perceptions of the space and boundaries of protest events. Crucially, protesters used digital media to create a variety of flexible participation scenarios and deployed these tools and platforms creatively to get around limitations imposed by location, experience, and level of political engagement.

In the preceding chapters, I have outlined the broader context for analyzing protests and digital media use in Ukraine and Russia. I have also drawn on rich data from my interviews with Ukrainian protesters to examine the specific factors that circumscribed their participation in Euromaidan and their perceptions of opportunities and limitations of digital media for dissent. The next three chapters delve into several specific modalities of participation in the protest that emerged out of the mutuality of actor characteristics and intentions and technological capabilities offered by internet and social media in the Ukrainian context. I show how the Euromaidan protesters conceived of participation in the form of protest witnessing, underpinned by socially mediated visibility; in the form of protest organizing and building networked communities, afforded by the ephemerality and flexibility of networked publics; and in the form of information sharing and protest framing, availing of the scalability, persistence, and adaptability of digital media networks.

Chapter 5

Socially Mediated Visibility and Protest Witnessing

It's dark. The camera is shaking, swiveling wildly from side to side. The shot shows riot police pushing people away from the statue of Independence in the eponymous Square, where several dozen protesters were occupying a central spot that night. As the camera pans, the policemen swing their batons left and right, hitting protesters indiscriminately, blows landing on hands, backs, and heads. In the background, people are screaming. Then the camera jerks, and the person holding it yelps, as they also catch a blow from behind. Suddenly, all we can see is the blurry image of the sky, as the live streamer slips and falls. When they get back up, the video stream becomes a cacophony of sounds and images: shouts of indignation and fear, bloodied faces and cradled limbs, the distant lights of an ambulance, the patter of running feet. The camera is still shaking.

This is how I, and many others, remember November 30, 2013, and the first attack on peaceful Euromaidan protesters by the state. The vast majority of people who share this memory were not in the square that night, but witnessed the attack through a handful of live videos streamed online and shared on Facebook and Twitter. Many of the people I spoke to also recalled graphic photos of injured protesters as one of the first triggers that brought home that a peaceful protest in the city center had been brutally attacked and dispersed, and that this warranted some kind of response. From that first riot police attack on peaceful Euromaidan protesters in November 2013 to the bloodiest days toward the end of the protest in February 2014 when dozens of people were killed, the visibility of protest events, and protesters' actions became crucial. These injustices were made visible online in real-time, witnessed by those who were not copresent, and remain available as records of the events to this day. All of this is important because it illustrates how socially mediated visibility contributed to both the outcomes of the Ukrainian protest and the various experiences of its participants.

The Euromaidan protest was a visually spectacular event that attracted significant media and public attention, in part due to the extensive use of social media by protesters to capture and publicize their experiences. Ukrainian protesters relied on socially mediated visibility for expression, disclosure, and testimony during the protest through widespread practices of visual and textual documentation, such as live streaming, real-time image sharing, live tweeting, and blogging. This visibility also afforded them opportunities to transform their witnessing practices as they were reporting, recording, and sharing stories about the protest. In the highly visible counter-spectacle of Euromaidan, protesters were able to simultaneously participate in the events, bear witness to them, and witness the mediated testimonies of others, with bodies and technologies augmenting each other.

Euromaidan protesters leveraged social media visibility strategically because they expected the event to be witnessed: recorded, broadcast, streamed, and captured by mainstream media and citizen reporters alike. Crucially, socially mediated witnessing of protests like Euromaidan provided for a "bottom-up" making of the event, bypassing official channels and making possible the existence of multiple protest temporalities, narratives, representations, memories, and histories. These augmented experiences in turn impacted how participants made meaning and memories of the protest events, as well as how they experienced the aftermath of the protest. Such distributed agency afforded by social media is vital in societies where access to traditional media and memory-making institutions is limited.

SOCIALLY MEDIATED VISIBILITY

In more recent work on social media affordances, scholars single out visibility as a root affordance of social media and argue that it supersedes other affordances and often helps enable them (Flyverbom et al. 2016; Pearce, Vitak, and Barta 2018). Such a conceptualization of socially mediated visibility helps understand the complex relationship between the role of networked technologies in protest activity, protesters' strategic decisions about how they manage the content and associations visible through social media channels, and the resulting consequences stemming from their visible activity on these platforms.

There are several dimensions to socially mediated visibility that shape how it was leveraged by Euromaidan protest participants. First, such visibility is relational, as it requires both a seer and an object (Brighenti 2010). In the case of Euromaidan, the public protest events and the people participating in them were the objects, but participants were often among the seers as well.

Second, socially mediated visibility is strategic (Brighenti 2010; Pearce, Vitak, and Barta 2018): in Ukraine, it was manipulated to help protesters achieve certain goals, such as greater attention and awareness of the protest. But total control is impossible (Edenborg 2017) as visibility also tends to expose individuals and groups engaging in dissent to risks (Uldam 2018), such as state surveillance and attacks. This was certainly true for Euromaidan participants, who experienced digital and physical threats during the events. This tension between strategic decisions and risks means socially mediated visibility is outcome-driven as it affords various outcomes (Brighenti 2010; Thompson 2005) that come with certain costs, reflecting the complex relationship between visibility and power in hyper-mediated environments.

Euromaidan in particular was a highly visible protest, due in no small part to its concentration in a central urban location, but also to extensive use of social media by protesters. While collecting ethnographic data for this study, I focused not only on interviews with protesters in the field during and after the protest but also on the highly visible aspects of Euromaidan activity such as media use at protest sites, and analysis of social media content from protest groups. What I found was that social media use allowed the protesters to strategically make visible their claims, expression, and disclosure about the protest events. I also found that this distributed visibility strategy, while offering protesters some control over what was made visible, also allowed for a horizontalized experience of protest witnessing. Because social media played host to a number of different live streams, a number of different angles of the events (literally and metaphorically) was made available to participants, allowing them to construct a diverse, comprehensive experience of protest, both as participants and as witnesses.

MEDIATED WITNESSING

In a hyper-mediated world, most of our experiences are acquired in, by, and through the media. Every act of witnessing today essentially implies some kind of mediation: at its most fundamental level, it is putting an experience into language for the benefit of those who were not present for the experience. But every act of mediation also entails a kind of witnessing, particularly when technology is used as a surrogate for an absent or remote audience (Frosh and Pinchevski 2009). In most cases, the process of mediated witnessing involves the agent who bears witness (a social media user), the content of the testimony (digital text, audio, images, and video), and the audience who witnesses the agent delivering testimony (other social media users).

Ellis (2009) suggests that witnessing has become ubiquitous as a generalized mode of how humans relate to the world in the age of pervasive mediation, and participatory social media make it even more so. As we engage in producing and consuming user-generated content, more and more citizens create testimony not only because we can appear *in* media and tell others that we were there and saw what happened but also because we can bear witness *by* media, thanks to the wide availability of mobile phone cameras and internet-connected devices that we carry around with us every day. This ubiquity of media-witnessing devices and their everyday use in routine contexts has also meant that digital media users are able to capture remarkable, and often unexpected or serendipitous events and occurrences, because of a habit of perpetual vigilance (Frosh and Pinchevski 2014), the being ready to record, document, and to bear witness.

Tufekçi asserts that information and communication technologies afford the emergence of spectacular, "statement" movements more easily (Tufekçi 2014)—protests that can express identities, grievances, and claims to an attentive public, but are not necessarily willing or able to connect with the traditional political institutions to exert these things. While this claim about a disconnect with mainstream politics does not allow us to discount the political influence of such movements wholesale, the spectacular nature of such protest movements begs closer scrutiny. This is especially important in order to understand how exactly the internet and social media afford protests to be highly visible spectacles when they become an integral part of the protest fabric and what implications this has on how witnessing of these events happens, and what effect it has on the outcomes of such protests.

Social media augment protest movements and events in several important ways, allowing for distributed organizing, flexible networks of protest communities as well as influential individuals working together across geographic and temporal barriers. In addition, there is a sense of copresence afforded by the emotional and symbolic "common protest language" on social media. With spectacular protests, this augmentation also reaches the performative components of protest and the mechanisms by which it can be witnessed. We speak, then, of an augmented counter-spectacle, wherein the augmentation comes by way of the offline and the online extending into each other and beyond the sum of the two.

Other scholars find that social media in particular help create a kind of "virtual stage," affording the emergence of technologically enabled communicative spaces which provide opportunities for collective storytelling and encourage the development of communities of action (Fayard 2012; Shklovski and Valtysson 2012). Still, I prefer the term "augmented" to the term "virtual" as the latter implies some level of detachment from material reality, while the former alludes to the enmeshed nature of atoms and bits in protest events.

An augmented protest as visible spectacle necessarily has significant digital and physical components, working together to produce a single spectacular reality. Protest events can be conceived of as spectacular moments, which, augmented by the affordance of socially mediated visibility, gain new characteristics. Wanenchak suggests the term "augmented eventfulness," implying the need to recognize that "the dynamics of an event need to be understood in the terms of augmented reality," and that they have a reality that goes beyond the physical (Wanenchak 2013), and thus, new ways in which that spectacular reality can be understood and interpreted. For instance, it means that a protest event can leverage social media visibility strategically because it expects to be witnessed: recorded and broadcast by mainstream media, streamed and captured by citizen reporters or its participants alike. This also requires us to consider a more complex notion of witnessing, affording opportunities to citizens to simultaneously participate in the events, bear witness to them, and witness the testimonies of others. This augmented witnessing and the multiple protest experiences it produces are the main outcomes of strategic use of socially mediated visibility by Euromaidan protesters.

STRATEGIC VISIBILITY IN THE
EUROMAIDAN PROTEST

In interviews, protest participants discussed the spectacular, highly visible nature of Euromaidan as represented in its cultural, symbolic, and visual language. However, they also continually touched upon the act of bearing witness to the protest events, articulated as part of participating in or engaging with the protest itself. In interviews, they mentioned terms such as "seeing it with my own eyes," "being witness to historic events," "witnessing history made live," as well as "seeing events unfold" on their social media feeds, being "glued to my phone" and "preserving" records of "how Ukraine was transformed, along with its people" for posterity.

The protest as a spectacular event aimed at attracting attention and capturing the public imagination, expects to be witnessed, and seeks to become meaningful as a visible symbolic performance staged for its intended audiences. Its intrinsic nature as an event, a moment to be captured, distributed, repeated, and symbolically transformed, is precisely the reason for its occurrence, and social media can play an important role in affording these objectives through creating opportunities for witnessing in, by and through digital media means. As one Kyiv participant pointed out,

> It's part of why we created slogans, why we made posters and memes, why we wanted photos and videos to go online, and the news to talk about us. We wanted people to see, and we wanted them to be captivated by what they saw.

When discussing how social media tools allowed them both to feel copresent with other protest participants within Euromaidan and to feel visible, participants most often discussed various visual and multimedia symbolic markers that anchored their understanding of what it meant to be part of the protest movement. For instance, images of the crowd gathering on Maidan in Kyiv or images of the clashes between protesters and riot police were some of the most common imagery shared by protest participants on social media to signal they were joining the discourse of Euromaidan dissent. By posting or reposting these images in protest-related groups on Facebook or on the #euromaidan hashtag on Twitter, users not only indicated their solidarity with the protest but also made visible key moments of resistance or repression. These visual symbols were also quite commonly cited as the inspiration for more engagement and activity within the protest. A young man from Kyiv who said he was more of an observer of the protests at first, and then joined as a participant later, recalled seeing the video of the first police crackdown on protesters on Facebook and the effect it had on him:

> When on November 30 [2013] . . . when the riot police brutally disbanded the student Maidan, [. . .] in the morning when I saw the video of this horrible event, I was over it, I wanted to do something.

While visuals of violence and conflict were powerful, respondents also cited more positive and inspirational videos as instrumental in creating a sense of belonging and community. A protester from Odesa recalled another video, shot with a drone during one of the more massive gatherings in Kyiv's central square during Euromaidan in mid-December 2013 that was quite popular among social media users:

> Do you remember this amazing footage, shot from above, when Okean Elzy [a popular Ukrainian pop-rock band] played in Maidan? [. . .] It got dark, and so people lit up their phones, thousands of them, and when the camera got up high, all you could see were these tiny lights, a sea of tiny lights. . . . It was really quite a sight, and it made me think "I am a part of that."

AUGMENTED WITNESSING

Socially mediated visibility augments the witnessing practices of protesters because it interacts with other social media affordances to produce new multimodal ways of witnessing protest events. Peters (2009) differentiates between four traditional modalities of witnessing: "being there" (presence in time and space), "live transmission" (presence in time, absence in space), "historicity" (presence in space, absence in time), and "recording" (absence in time and space). To Peters, in that order, these have increasingly lower value as faithful accounts of events witnessed. But the advent of interactive, real-time media with new affordances for visibility, participation, and copresence augments the mechanics of witnessing in protest events, entangling its basic elements in new and complex ways. Even as Ukrainian citizens became protest participants and thus engaged in the event and action through both digital and material means, they also simultaneously bore witness to Euromaidan events themselves in various ways afforded by digital technology: through "being there," through live streaming, through reposting others' content, and through creating records and archival content. Finally, the very same citizens who engaged in protest and bore witness to it from their various vantage points also become the audience reading, hearing, or seeing the testimony of other witness-bearers.

This augmented witnessing in the Euromaidan protests was more complex, combining different modalities and helping redefine absence and presence by means of socially mediated visibility. It also allowed for a greater diversity of what participants qualified as "witnessing" and how they talked about it as a set of practices that allowed them to see, capture, connect with, and make meaning of the visible spectacle of protest.

WITNESSING AS PARTICIPATION

Witnessing protest events as a form of participation took many shapes in Euromaidan, depending on participant roles, their distance from the physical protest camp and their choice of digital media channels. Some participants bore witness by being in the immediate vicinity of the action on the ground and by capturing and sharing visuals on social media. Others witnessed the events of the protest through live streams and images being posted to Twitter in real time, while being in a different time zone thousands of kilometers away. For some, the witnessing was almost constant, while for others, it was fragmented, though no less meaningful. Socially mediated visibility was used by protesters to augment the notion of being present and being a witness by offering digital presence through real-time or delayed visual and textual streams and records.

Protest participants had various ways of how they conceived of their engagement with the protest as witnessing. While protesters in Kyiv and some of those in the regions spoke of the importance of physical presence at the site(s) of the protest, and those in the regions and abroad discussed creating their own physical protest sites to mirror the epicenter of the action, many also said they counted the protest activity made visible by social networks as not just "being there," but "being it [the protest event or action]." The work of mediated visibility, therefore, was intrinsic to constructing the overall protest events and making them available to witnesses in multiple modalities, as well as to making mediated participation in the protest more meaningful.

Live video streams certainly were not pioneered by Euromaidan protesters, but they came to play a central role in the augmented witnessing of the protest. The first live streams were set up by citizen journalists at the very beginning of the Euromaidan protests, and they multiplied after the first bout of police violence on November 30, 2013. A student blogger under the alias Krus Krus (real name Oleksandr Baraboshko) was one of the first to live stream from Maidan, frustrated with the lack of coverage, and his live videos on UStream became immediately popular. Volunteer teams such as Spilno. TV, made up of protest participants, combined live streaming with other protest activities, and were often in the thick of the action. This not only led to multiple injuries for live streamers filming clashes with police but also became a learning experience for streamers, who rapidly acquired helmets, high visibility vests, spare batteries for their cameras and smartphones, and later, gas masks.

Amateur streamers gradually improved their technique, taping their devices to tripods, providing views of the action from different angles, figuring out the best shooting locations once the protest camp was set up, and adding live commentary in different languages, including English. Later, the citizens' live video offerings by individuals and groups like Spilno.TV were supplemented by professional journalists producing live online video for their media outlets (such as Hromadske TV, Radio Svoboda (Radio Liberty), Espreso TV). The growing number of live streams showed key moments of protest-related violence and tension as well as routine life in the protest camp. Typical videos showed activities such as cooking, singing, training security guards, and sometimes featured interviews with participants and public lectures organized for protesters by a group called Free Maidan University. At key moments of contention, numerous Twitter and Facebook users also liveblogged the most heated standoffs and clashes and posted strings of photos, often screen capping the live videos in real time as proof.

In rapid interviews with regional Euromaidan participants, Onuch (2015) found that they viewed live video streams as "easier to consume and understand" than traditional media coverage or Twitter messages, and that they had changed their outlook on the protests and made them more motivated to join in. Regional and Kyiv-based activists perceived live streaming as "direct information for direct action" and as information that was "interactive, real-time, unfiltered, uncensored [and] not politicised" (Onuch 2015). These findings align with how the protest participants I interviewed talked about live video provided by citizen and professional journalists in terms of facilitating feelings of "being in the midst of the action," "seeing it from people's point of view," and "following the clashes [between protesters and riot police] as they happened." At the same time, those protesters who themselves produced the live streams also saw the mobilizing capacity of the videos. One of the Spilno.TV volunteers said in an interview that when they started to live stream in mid-December 2013, the channel had 2,500 viewers, and by the time of real escalation in late January 2014 more than 90,000 people were watching. "The people would start watching, then they would share the links [to the live stream], and then they would come down [to the square] in Kyiv themselves," the volunteer recalled.

Live video streams and nearly real-time coverage of events on Twitter were especially poignant in terms of creating a perception of copresence and of bearing witness for participants outside of Kyiv, including those in the regions of Ukraine and abroad. A banking software specialist whom I interviewed in Washington, DC, said that the temporal aspect of being able to watch coverage from the ground in real-time was, as he put it,

> the closest you could get to being there and living through it without actually being there. I really don't know if I can compare it to anything, this feeling when you're sitting on the edge of your chair watching the crowd in Instytutska[1] engage in a battle for every meter of space with the police, pushing forward and pulling back. [. . .] I felt their fear, and I felt their hope.

Media scholars find that citizen video, especially live streamed footage of events, can encode an extraordinary sense of presence and participation (Andén-Papadopoulos 2013). Regardless of their location, my interviewees noted the importance of live video streams in making them feel as though they were not only observing the protest action, but were directly "in medias res," due to the format of the video streams, which were shot from hand-held devices and often from within the mass of people, allowing those viewing to look at the scene from the position of the person in the crowd. A programmer in Kharkiv recalled watching one of the many live streams from the confrontation between protesters and police in Instytutska Street on December 11, 2013:

> It looked like a video game, in the sense that you could see what was happening at the video streamer's eye level, just like you would if you were standing right there. . . . And though it was shaky and would break up often because the connection wasn't that good, it still felt like I was right there . . . [. . .] I could see steam coming out of people's mouths in the cold, could hear them breathing next to the camera, the tension in the crowd was almost palpable. . . . When I remember it now, I wasn't there pushing against the cops, but it feels like I was.

This augmentation of "being" and "participating" shifted the attention some-what from the physical space of the protest: although mainstream media still centered on the burning tires and barricades and masses of people as their main representations of Euromaidan, there were also reports on the other visible ways of being participants of the protest: reports of live streams and Twitter feeds, screenshots of important protest-related posts from Facebook and hashtag archives—these were all becoming legitimate sources of action and information worth reporting on and worth witnessing.

WITNESSING AS AFFECTIVE CONNECTION

Discussing the importance of bearing witness to the events of the Euromaidan protest, participants stressed that content shared on social media played an important part because it allowed people to see, witness, and emotionally connect with the protesters and their actions on the ground and elsewhere. Significantly, social media and other online tools also offered flexibility and an array of ways to bear witness to the actions of protesters, including pro-viding raw live coverage, publishing posts that could be read later in chrono-logical order, posting photo albums, as well as archiving edited or unedited videos and making them publicly available.

A participant in Kyiv who at one time volunteered as part of the "self-defense" (*samooborona*) security forces in the protest camp said he tried as much as possible to capture details of protest events in photographs, notes he posted on Facebook, and to keep a diary of the days he spent in Euromaidan. He said seeing what was happening in other locations, as well as online, was made possible for him via live reports or online footage he could watch later. He stressed that to him, it was important to witness what was happening in affective terms, and not just in order to know how events were unfolding:

> This wasn't just important to see strategically, to see how they [the police] were acting, and what we would have to learn to protect against. It was also an emotional thing, a connection. I am here, standing guard because that's my task and my place, so I will tell what I saw from here, but I want to see what is happening elsewhere, so that later I can say: look, I was part of this too, and tell the story.

Another Kyiv participant said that live streams and rapid reports of what was happening on Twitter and Facebook were important to him to feel like he was "keyed into" the protest activity and mood so that he could pick up where he left when his next "protest shift" came up.

Because there were so many people, working on so many things, the mood swings were frequent, so it was always good to check on what was going on to be aware and prepared. [. . .] It was quite something to watch how people's emotions and feelings shifted a changed on social media, like this great ocean of joy then despair, then elation again.

A Ukrainian graduate student based in New York (and visiting friends in Washington, DC, when I interviewed her) said that for her, the real-time capabilities of social media were important as they provided an emotional connection to those on the ground, while also allowing protesters in other places around the world to share information with those in Kyiv, to demonstrate solidarity, and create a greater feeling of cohesiveness in the overall movement.

Apart from just watching the streams from Kyiv, which we all did all the time, religiously, we could also stream our own protest rally near the White House on YouTube and [. . .] knowing that someone in Kyiv or in Ukraine might see it and feel we had their back, that there were more people joining the protest, I think that was important to show our support, to show we were together.

Being part of the engaged audience and seeing the live citizen and media reports of the events in Euromaidan was what had moved many interview respondents to become more active within the protest. Especially for "new" activists, seeing the videos and photos of police brutality and repression against "ordinary people," "peaceful protesters" was an emotional experience that played a part in their mobilization and further engagement with the protest movement. An Odesa-based interviewee who lived in Kyiv at the time of the Euromaidan protests recalled seeing the footage from the first police attack on November 30, 2013:

It was wild and wrong on some fundamental level, seeing these helpless people bloodied and bruised, running away from the police in full riot gear. . . . It made me afraid, but it also made me angry. It made me feel helpless, so I knew this was the time to do something more. I think for many people [. . .] seeing these things brought it home that this wasn't about EU or whatever, not anymore. . . . This was about humanity, about dignity, and that was being taken from us.

In addition to emotionally connecting to the protest events and bearing witness to them in affective terms, participants also discussed witnessing in terms of being the audience and seeing and reading what others who bore witness had put online. A point made by several interviewees was that being part of this networked audience felt at once very personal and like "being a part of something big," with one respondent in Washington, DC, saying it gave her a certain feeling of validation:

> Knowing that there were thousands of other people watching these live streams, seeing these photos, scrolling through tweets, just like I was [. . .] felt somehow reassuring, like this wasn't just going to happen and be forgotten, like all of us were watching history being made, watching these brave people and feeling we were part of this history.

COMMEMORATIVE WITNESSING

Preserving and telling the stories of Euromaidan was seen as another important task of those who were bearing witness to the protest. According to interview participants, it was crucial to capture the protest events and their "essence" to make it available to others: "preserving for posterity," "keeping a record," "adding to the collective memory" all came up in the interviewees' narratives. Participants talked about how social media allowed them not only to participate in the moment of witnessing but also to extend the witnessing act beyond the moment, to make it more meaningful and impactful. A bank employee I interviewed in Washington, DC, said it was important for her to have the mediated evidence of the protest available and to add her own to the mix:

> These are unforgettable events, so we will all tell our stories of course, but I think it is important to also have all these public records, available to anyone, that can help us tell the story, add color, add details, make it sharper. This is a record of our history, of how we changed as a people, so it's important to preserve it. We have to remember it.

Another participant in Kyiv, a human resources specialist, said it was important that the content captured by those bearing witness (most of whom were also participants and part of the event) was made publicly available, but that none of the single narratives should be taken as objective or as the indisputable truth:

> I'm glad that there are many videos, many posts. . . . They are each a story of how a person or a group of people perceived or engaged with the movement, but none of them tell the whole story on their own. I think when we try to make sense of these events later, this multitude of voices will be important, and in itself a sign of how grassroots and self-organized this all was.

A student protester from Odesa also spoke positively in his interview of the "multiple histories" and "multiple Maidans" that protesters were able to preserve and make visible through the affordances of social media as they bore witness to the protest events:

> The internet is like a database of Euromaidan histories, and that we are able to search, juxtapose, compare, overlay is a good thing. [. . .] It's not just one, official record, but many records, and that enriches the memories, allows us all to consider that there is more than one way to understand what we went through.

After the Euromaidan protest, the multiple traces of mediated witnessing that were made visible on social media and preserved by participants, became visible in new ways, as they were assembled into collections, timelines, and makeshift memorials. Each such collection tried to make sense of the protest events in its own way and to capture the meaningful experiences of individuals involved in the protest effort.

One such project took the unexpected shape of a physical book, published in November 2014. Titled *"Phantom Pain #maidan,"* the book is made up entirely of over 700 Facebook posts, chronicling the events from November 2013 to June 2014 through the eyes and words of multiple Ukrainian Facebook users. The book's authors, Anastasiia Savytska and Andrey Myrhorodskiy, who were both protest participants, were initially planning to create a photo album with selected text from Facebook posts, but were taken over by the power of the unedited social media content (Lokot 2014a), and spent over two months deciding which posts to include. Though the book is a highly curated collection of Euromaidan experiences, it is a strangely material representation of the socially mediated visibility of the protest, and an example of how digital media can augment physical reality, but also be augmented by it.

Visual memorials aiming to honor those protesters who were killed during the bloodiest days of Euromaidan were created online, combining images, videos, and witness accounts. Multiple Facebook pages and communities devoted to Nebesna Sotnya (the Heavenly Hundred, a collective name for over a 100 protesters who were killed by pro-government forces during Euromaidan) were created in the spring of 2014. Standalone memorial pages, like the Nebesna Sotnya "requiem page" created by news website *Ukrainska Pravda* ("Nebesna Sotnya" 2014), contain photos and brief bios of each of the fallen protesters, along with what is known about them and their time and place of death. Some of the pages also contain quotes from the individuals, and any other crowdsourced images or videos that were captured while they were alive and participating in the protest. These pages, along with dozens of tribute videos on YouTube, afford meaningful postevent witnessing capabilities to both the protesters who were part of the original events, allowing them to relive the experience, and to those who are encountering them for the first time, reducing the affective distance between them and the events of Euromaidan.

MULTIPLE HISTORIES AND
INVESTIGATIVE WITNESSING

The collective yet personal meaning-making as watchers of the content produced by those who bore witness to the protest was compounded for many participants by the affordances of social media for engaging with the content published online more actively, and not just passively consuming it. Several of my interviewees recalled reposting photos and videos during and after Euromaidan and adding their own comments, memories, or stories to them. One participant in Kyiv said she remembered seeing several "videos composed of various user-generated footage and images overlaid with music" as well as some "iconic Euromaidan images" edited by other users to add "inspirational slogans and quotes," resulting in a kind of remix culture appearing around Euromaidan.

For many Euromaidan activists the interactivity and polymedia-heavy nature of Euromaidan witnessing became the basis for a different sort of commemoration. Social media and the ease with which Euromaidan-related content was made visible played an important role in affording witnessing as investigative work. The vast compendium of Euromaidan-related social media content, both tagged and untagged, allowed users to examine the many videos and photos documenting the shootings of protesters, archived on YouTube, Twitter, Facebook, and other platforms. Many of these videos and images were later used in crowdsourced investigations into the deaths of Euromaidan protest participants. Ukrainian social media users were asked to assist in dissecting the footage and examining it closely to reveal new details. A data journalist I interviewed in Kyiv who was engaged in this effort said it was not only a "terrible task" but also "a unique opportunity."

> We have these shots, this footage because someone was brave enough to be there and record it. So we, as viewers, it is our responsibility to make as much as we can out of this content, to see what it is telling us, to squeeze every bit of useful information and data from it that we can.

Another interviewee in Kyiv, who helped crowdsource citizen video footage of the shootings that took place during the last days of the organized protest and left dozens of protesters dead, thought social media and mobile devices were key in uncovering more information about what happened.

> I think the one big difference for me that technology, like smartphones and mobile internet, made was that it made possible to not just see the thing happening if you happened to be right there, but also to capture it as it was happening and then make it public by putting it on YouTube or Facebook. It was made public and it stayed public. Especially when people started getting shot, it was so important to have this footage, these images. [. . .] I think the people who held the camera at those moments even though their hands were shaking were exceedingly brave.

Just as online memorials and tribute videos allow internet users to see the bigger picture of the protests by witnessing the testimonies of others, crowd-sourced investigations ask those willing to bear witness to violence against protesters to participate in collecting relevant material, making sense of it, reconstructing the events of the protest, and verifying key facts and occurrences. This kind of post-protest witnessing work is evidence of how socially mediated visibility augments memory work and the creation of historic records of protests by adding in an investigative component and enabling ordinary citizens to take part in these investigations. Though seemingly aimed at verifying specific facts or acts, this kind of witnessing activity coexists with "multiple histories" of Euromaidan, as it is one of many forms of storytelling about the protest.

In March 2017, the Ukrainian data journalism outlet *Texty.org.ua* published a multimedia long-read called "Three Days in February" ("Three Days in February" 2017). The project, an interactive timeline reconstructing the events of February 18–20, 2014, when dozens of Euromaidan protesters were killed, drew together the videos, images, and textual reports from Ukrainian official sources, social media, and mainstream media to create a highly detailed narrative of what happened over the last three days of the protest. The journalists placed digital media artifacts on a map showing key locations of the protest in Kyiv. It also placed them on a timeline, creating a temporal and geospatial representation of the Euromaidan events and allowing users not only to relive some of them but also to see them in a new context.

The authors of "Three Days in February" explicitly state that their project is "neither an [official] investigation nor an attempt to deliver a judgment" ("Three Days in February" 2017) as the state-run investigation and court proceedings are underway to this day. The investigative slant of the multimedia narrative aimed at reconstructing the killings of protesters and security personnel in precise and horrible detail is joined with the affective power of the crowdsourced content, enabling a new mode of witnessing. Such witnessing is temporally shifted, yet retains the emotional connection to the events as they happened, and allows for new angles of vision and thus, fresh emotional experiences. It also places the "multiple histories" of Euromaidan onto a single timeline, allowing the different bits of factual, geospatial, and visual information to weave together into a rich canvas, underscoring the complex structure of the protest. This kind of post-protest witnessing is what I refer to as augmented, one where the spatial and temporal, visual and textual, digital and material elements all combine into a qualitatively different experience, afforded by socially mediated visibility and other digital media capabilities.

Another useful example of such augmented witnessing is the "Aftermath VR: Euromaidan" project, the brainchild of two photographers who wanted to create a virtual reality experience to reconstruct some of the most poignant events of the protest. Oleksii Furman and Serhiy Polezhaka came up with the initial idea to counterbalance what they saw as fragmented and overly sensationalist coverage of the Ukrainian protest in international mainstream media. In an interview to *Euromaidan Press*, Furman said most of the front-page visuals from the protest camp were "tires, Molotov cocktails, barricades on fire" (Makarenko 2018) and that was just a tiny segment of what was happening at any given time. The authors wanted to use the medium of virtual reality to tell "an immersive, meaningful and cohesive story" of Euromaidan ("Aftermath VR: Euromaidan" 2017) by placing the viewers inside the protest context on a particular day. With initial funding from a Journalism 360 Challenge grant by Google News Lab and the Knight Foundation, and then a Successful Kickstarter campaign in 2018, "Aftermath VR: Euromaidan" formed a larger team and was able to create a virtual representation of Instytutska Street (part of which has been renamed to Heavenly Hundred Heroes Street). The team used photogrammetry to create a three-dimensional model of the street and populated it with archival footage, 360°-video interviews with eyewitnesses and three-dimensional representations of scanned artifacts from the Euromaidan such as shields and helmets. The immersive documentary allows viewers to retrace the paths of protesters on February 20 and to witness some of the events of the day as they happened.

The interactive environment of "Aftermath VR: Euromaidan" is enabled by advanced VR and spatial scanning technology, but it also relies on the images and videos captured by social media users and journalists during the protest. These technologies and content are combined in new ways to create new witnessing experiences, driven by the viewer entering the story as they explore the three-dimensional environment. Though the authors seek to build a faithful recreation of the immediate context of a street in a city in protest, they also rely on socially mediated visibility, augmenting the spatial information with visual traces, interviews, and artifacts. This combination of material and digital elements makes it possible to create a sense of presence, to transport the viewer into the moment of protest, but it also contains the "multiple histories" of Euromaidan, allowing for a self-guided tour complemented by a variety of crowdsourced videos from the day and witness interviews recorded later.

Both "Three Days in February" and "Aftermath VR: Euromaidan" are works in progress, according to their authors. Though the foundational structure exists, the teams are on the lookout for new evidence, and are continuously adding new elements and details to their storylines. This illustrates that augmented witnessing in protest events is an ongoing process: it happens during the events and in their aftermath, and can last as long as someone snaps photos in the protest square, records a live stream from their laptop, seeks out the preserved testimonies of protest participants, comes across them by chance while browsing YouTube, or works to combine these visible traces into a clever geospatial or three-dimensional narrative.

CONCLUSION

In the current reality of mundane internet and social media use to broadcast, record, and make sense of our daily lives, moments of civic and political climaxes find citizens prepared to not only participate in protest events in visible ways but simultaneously bear witness and be the audience that mediated witnessing is directed at. The experience of the event and its story enmesh and become one, complicating the process and phenomenon of witnessing by mixing offline and online components and extending them into each other.

Socially mediated visibility, as a root affordance of social media in protest, was used strategically by Euromaidan protest participants to transform how protest events were experienced, how they were witnessed, and how such witnessing then evolved into testimonies, memories, and historical records. At the same time, the highly public and spectacular nature of socially mediated protest also means that visible social media activity and content produced by participants could serve as legitimate sources of information about the protest event and its meaning.

The habit of perpetual vigilance of citizens equipped with connected digital devices was foundational to the visibility of the Euromaidan events and to the many different modes of witnessing this visibility made possible. The ubiquitous wireless connectivity, coupled with the frustration at the lack of on the ground coverage, resulted in live streams becoming a key feature of the protests' visibility. Live video reportage from the square, as well as live blogs and a constant stream of images shared on social media, contributed to making the process of witnessing one of copresence, allowing protesters in various locations (within the protest square and beyond it) to experience "being a protester" in the different modes made available to them via social media. The entanglement of material and digital elements into a single reality allowed those participating in augmented witnessing to redefine absence and presence within a protest. Being a witness was made possible on a variety of levels and included multiple temporalities, locations, and activities.

The capability to witness other people protesting, in real time or with a delay, also created a perception of affective connection to the protest events in Kyiv. The emotional component of augmented witnessing created additional opportunities for mobilization and engagement, making visible to protest participants multiple moments of inspiration, anger, despair, or hope that informed their participation. The affective component also informed the meaning-making work participants engaged in while bearing witness, with many of them conceptualizing their witnessing as commemorative and engaging in recording and capturing of events and experiences as future memories. This mindfulness of witnessing as contributing to history, memory, and meaning-making is a key feature of augmented protests.

While real-time witnessing is central to augmented dissent, socially mediated visibility also extends witnessing beyond the events, in both spatial and temporal terms. For Euromaidan, where the confrontation between protesters and government forces turned bloody and led to significant loss of life, the visibility of the protest and the many traces of witnessing became indispensable investigative materials. Activists, journalists, and witnesses combined efforts to collect, analyze, and triangulate evidence from social media, mainstream media, and other sources to recreate the events of the key days of the protest in as much detail as possible. Such projects are partially aimed at achieving justice for those who lost their lives in the protest, but they also contribute to the complex set of visuals, stories, and narratives sourced from multiple witnesses that combine to make the Euromaidan protest.

The personalized and distributed nature of witnessing with and through social media affords large-scale collective experiences of protest events, but it also enables the telling of multiple protest histories. In many ways, this augmented media witnessing casts the tripartite "participant/witness/audience" identity as both the ultimate addressee and primary producer, making the collection of engaged individuals both the subject and object of witnessing in the context of protest events, testifying to their own historical reality even as it unfolds, producing ad hoc communities of attention on both a local and a global scale (Frosh and Pinchevski 2014). We can thus understand the augmented witnessing component of protests such as Euromaidan as a "bottom-up making of the event" (Frosh and Pinchevski 2018, 137), wherein digital and material elements combine to make possible the existence of multiple protest temporalities, narratives, representations, memories, and histories. This raises further questions about the complex relationship between socially mediated visibility, witnessing and power during protest events, as control over what is made visible and through which channels becomes strategically important to both protesting citizens and the forces seeking to crush the resistance.

This in-depth examination of witnessing practices and modalities in the Euromaidan protest shows that, enabled by socially mediated visibility, they transform how a protest event is seen, recorded, and remembered. Highly visible hybrid protest activity also changes participants' experience of witnessing, giving them the ability to be part of the protest, to witness its events and to bear witness to the testimonies of others, using a combination of physical and digital means. These augmented experiences in turn impact how participants make meaning and memories of the protest events, as well as how they experience the aftermath of the protest. Understanding the intricacies of augmented witnessing in the context of protest events also underscores the core argument of the book: that protest participants see social media as contributing to a qualitatively different protest experience and as offering a variety of diverse ways of witnessing, and thus, of protesting.

Of course, without visible protest activity, both on the ground and in digital networks, there would not be much to witness. The following chapter focuses on the affordances that protesters using digital media perceived for organizing and managing protest activity and logistics. The ephemerality of mediated connections, while viewed as a limitation by some, also provided opportunities for diverse forms of engagement. Protesters also availed of the flexible temporalities intrinsic to social media use to find creative ways to participate in protest action despite the constraints of time, skills, or distance.

Chapter 6

Protest Organizing and Networked Communities

Verified: Mykhaylivska [street] needs volunteers for cleaning, garbage bags, rubber gloves and food.

Current needs of the National resistance headquarters in the Trade Unions building as of 11-12 January: Medical latex gloves (non-sterile) for volunteers; Medicines: panthenol spray, antihistamines; Toothbrushes and toothpaste; Also need top-up vouchers for any mobile providers for volunteers and coordinators. You can leave all these in the inboxes of the Trade Unions building or bring them to the Info centre on the ground floor.

Want to help Maidan but don't know how? Fill in the form at http://galas.org .ua/ (click the button in the top right corner). Describe what kind of help you can offer and leave your contact information. Our operators will contact you for more information.

These are just some of the messages that were shared in the social media communities helping to coordinate Euromaidan logistics during November–December 2013 and January–February 2014. As the Euromaidan protest grew in downtown Kyiv, it organically developed spatial and temporal rhythms of participation and organization, fusing the everyday and the extraordinary. It also encountered issues of scale. Managing thousands of people in a decentralized constellation of communities was challenging, even for the most seasoned activists. Things became even more complex once protests spread to other Ukrainian regions and gained an international presence.

This chapter focuses on protest participants' experiences of digitally augmented organizing and participation in both collective and connective action. It offers an overall context for the emergence of protest communities and networks within Euromaidan, as informed by participants' perceptions of the affordances of digital media for organizing, building social capital and trust.

Reflecting on opportunities for action for both networked communities and networked individuals within the protest, I take a deep dive into a specific case of a group of Euromaidan protest participants, a collective called Galas, that contributed to streamlining and managing the logistics of the Ukrainian protest. I find that protesters embraced the ephemeral connections afforded by social media and other online tools and used them to build networked communities of volunteers that in turn served as serendipitous connective tissue supporting the protest. The flexible temporalities of digital media also afforded networked individuals a variety of diverse, but equally meaningful modes of participation and engagement. These networked communities and individuals joined the protest action through multiple combinations of online and offline means in a range of time zones and variously augmented spaces. In this regard, Euromaidan was a highly accessible protest event even for participants who had limited resources in terms of time, funding, connectivity, or skills.

BUILDING PROTEST COMMUNITIES AND NETWORKS

Existing research on technology and society has found that networked technologies reduce barriers for creating social cohesion and organizing protest movements, and allow individuals to participate in civic and protest activity at a reduced cost and without necessarily relying on physical copresence. However, these same affordances provided by digital media also threaten traditional social movement organizations because the barriers for competitors are likewise reduced (Earl and Kimport 2011). This raises the issue of alternative forms of protest movement organization, as well as their basis and structural rigidity, and whether the latter is necessary for the protest to work or succeed.

Protest and mobilization scholars have noted that historically successful mobilization in mass protests has depended not so much on the sheer number of ties between protesters, but on the interplay between social ties created by insurgent organizations and preexisting social networks, both within protest movements and beyond their context (Gould 1991). Social media afforded Euromaidan protesters opportunities for leveraging these ties and networks in their daily organizing work and for building trust and social capital in protest communities. A number of individuals also were empowered to be significant agents of resistance and change within their personal networks, alongside more traditional protest movement organizations.

Wilson (2016) contends that the Euromaidan protests revealed that Ukrainian civil society overall was stronger and more developed in 2014 than in 2004, and that citizens and citizen groups were more proactive, modern, and technically literate than the political elites. Civil society actors, he writes, "used technology, which the political class did not" (Wilson 2016, 106) to organize and maintain communities, crowdsource human resources and funds as well as build trust within the protest movement and with external networks. While my Euromaidan interview participants provided some evidence to this effect, different groups and individuals ascribed varying degrees of importance to the internet and social media in how these afforded them opportunities to organize, build trust, and leverage networks and communities. Participants also reflected on how the presence and the use of digital media shaped the role of existing or insurgent civic organizations versus the role of individuals in the protest movement.

AUGMENTED PARTICIPATION

Much of the later literature on the Arab Spring protests reveals a more complex picture than that of a "Facebook" or "Twitter revolution": studies such as Tufekçi and Wilson's research on protest and social media in Egypt in 2012 find an enmeshed protest reality that mixes both digital and physical elements (Tufekçi and Wilson 2012). Interviews with Euromaidan participants revealed a similar set of perceptions about the nature of the Ukrainian protest. Their stories, both those of personal engagement and those of working in communities or groups, usually constituted a densely interwoven fabric of multiple online and offline spaces and connections between them, where social media, websites, email, and mobile phones were superimposed on existing social ties between friends and families, professional relationships, carpools, accidental meetings, and physical protest locations.

The recipes of this mixture of online and offline spaces, connections, activities, and opportunities differed for each participant depending on their age, technology use habits, location, and their role in the protest movement. But a common thread was that the internet and social media were more often than not combined with offline elements to tweak each particular recipe to work better in a protest context: to fix an issue, to fill in a missing link, to add an element to a process to optimize it—in other words, to augment overall protest activity or a small part of the machine by creating a *shortcut* between two "places" in the imaginary protest "mechanism" that were either not connected, were connected inefficiently, or had become disconnected due to some combination of factors, making the whole "machine" stutter and slow down. So it was not just a matter of using the internet and social media on their own, for their own sake but rather combining them with existing offline networks, resources, and opportunity structures to achieve a greater effect.

A programmer in Kharkiv who volunteered in a team that did citizen media outreach and coverage of the protests and cooperated with people in other Ukrainian cities as well, said that to achieve synergy, it was important to have a community of people whose skills and efforts complemented each other, cutting across the "physical/digital" divide:

> Someone did logistics, someone did design and printing of posters and stickers, someone did media outreach and social media, someone did internal coordination—it all worked because we each picked up the different bits we could do, online, offline, wherever—and worked on them.

There were also protest-related initiatives that started offline, then flowed online or remained floating somewhere in the enmeshed space. The data journalist interviewed in Kyiv recalled the case of IT Tent, a physical tent originally set up to offer free internet access, phone charges, and computer equipment to protesters, where people could donate used devices, USB sticks, and power cords. When "a critical mass of tech-minded individuals" accumulated around the Tent, it slowly evolved into a space where IT developers and programmers met and consulted with professional activists on a number of ICT-enabled civic projects, not only taking the collaborative coding and design online (to sites like GitHub) but also staging hackathons to work on "quick and dirty digital solutions" to various protest-related problems.

AFFORDANCES OF DIGITAL MEDIA FOR ORGANIZING

Whether the internet and social media afford certain opportunities for action is predicated on how these technologies fit into the organizational and cultural structure of protest movements. Even within Euromaidan, there were certain disparities between how strongly various groups of activists relied on digital technology to organize and communicate, depending on their previous activism experience or lack thereof. Several more experienced interview participants indicated that social media had not been a significant part of their internal organizing toolkit in previous work, and that, while they regarded it as a great public-facing tool to promote protest messages and engage with observers and the mainstream media, they largely relied on personal or direct contact to run their organizations or groups. Some also pointed out that their work during Euromaidan started with cooperating with other known activists, so there was no immediate need for digital mediation. In the words of one experienced activist,

There were quite a few people on Maidan at the start whom I knew, and there was also a lot of chaos there. Since I'm a person who has been trained to organize and manage processes, I just saw that I could help this environment, which contained so many of my friends, to become more orderly. But they were all right there [next to me].

At the same time, as the protest grew in size and drew in more participants, experienced civic organizers began to use a combination of tools to manage volunteers, delegate tasks, and plan their activity. An interviewee in Kyiv who helped coordinate housing, transport, and other logistics for the protest said ordering information and making sense of the logistics issues at scale were greatly aided by social media platforms.

At the time, I was compiling and ordering a database of volunteers and finding housing for people from out of town. This was at the point when word got out, and many people wanted to come in from the regions, at the same time many Kyivites wanted to offer their homes to them—but no one was coordinating it. So we set up a public [Facebook] page to connect these people and posted new arrivals info. That time was crazy in terms of the tempo of the work, barely two hours of sleep each night, and we spent a lot of time organizing the process, sorting the information available, but creating this public hub took some of the stress off.

For internal organizing and coordination, both experienced and novice participants reported using a mix of offline and online communications and contacts, choosing what worked best in each case and what helped them work more efficiently. Here is a description of the typical organizational communication setup in one Euromaidan community from a "new" activist in Kharkiv:

The coordinators have in-person meetings for strategy and planning, and the broader circle of volunteers and activists receives a daily briefing either via email or through personal communication with main news, what happened or was important that day, what the plans for the immediate future are, what needs to get done. We use phones as well for calls and text messages, but it is important to meet people in person as well, especially for the first time.

Another participant who had previous protest organizing experience from the 2004 Orange Revolution events and other smaller protests said the scale of Euromaidan as a protest event was "unprecedented" for anyone in Ukraine, so organizing efforts had to be scaled up as well, and the internet's "connective tissue" was helpful in establishing links between disparate protest groups and bringing some order to the enthusiastic individuals who joined the action without a clear idea of what to do.

> It's one thing to organize a sit-in or coordinate a march. But when you have all of these and more happening simultaneously, and thousands of people are join-ing, there has to be some sort of canvas that you can pin these things to, to find connections so the cumulative effect can be more productive. Just knowing that there was a way to find out about what other people were doing by looking at their pages and connecting [with them]. I've never worked with or coordinated a million people before, and having this extra layer of connections helps.

Protest participants who were engaging with the Euromaidan events over geographical distance were adamant that social media augmented their per-sonal networks in important ways to create productive relationships with protesters on the ground in Ukraine. A financial analyst whom I spoke to in Washington, DC, described the evolution of her involvement in the fundrais-ing efforts that were part of the protest activity.

> At first, the engagement to people in Kyiv was mostly through financial sup-port. I sent money to several of the people who were there but also, as this thing evolved, a couple of the activists here, in DC and New York, we formed this closed group on Facebook and connected with a couple of people in Kyiv who were helping us to buy supplies and things like that. This way we could always ask what they needed, and they could let us know if something urgent came up.

Because of the ubiquity of social media and internet access in Ukraine, for many Euromaidan participants who considered digital media part of their daily life, the mode of communication was closely connected with the mode of organization. Especially for those protest participants who were experi-encing protest organization and activity for the first time, this was the only way they knew how to communicate, coordinate, and make things work. To them, it was impractical (or often impossible) to view the digital platforms in separation from the movement they had joined.

Protesters who were used to solving management, organizational, or logis-tical problems with the help of digital technology in everyday life discussed their organizing efforts within Euromaidan through the prism of mediated communication. A programmer in Kyiv whom I interviewed in the midst of the protest in December 2013, described his initial reaction to the self-orga-nization efforts that, while "very enthusiastic," were also "totally chaotic":

> Optimization sucks, there are lots of examples of people doing the same thing twice or in parallel, and not just online or in the media—offline in Maidan itself

as well. In terms of logistics, resource centers, there are several hubs that barely interact, don't share resources effectively. Why? I think, just lack of time and attention, so of course I want to try to fix it. How can we bring order to this by automating things, optimizing things, letting people see the information at their fingertips to make better decisions?

An interviewee from Odesa who worked in management said organizing the local protest was akin to "playing an online game" in that "you had to know what [resources] you had and what you did not, and who to ask to get what you needed to win—and if you have a constantly updated dashboard showing how you're doing, that's a great motivator." In Kyiv, another interviewee explained their reliance on digital tools to coordinate local volunteers and needs as "self-evident," as they were already using these tools in their work and everyday life.

A Euromaidan activist from Kharkiv who participated in a local community that provided citizen media coverage of the protests, including online, said many of the volunteers who contributed content initially had a low level of digital media creation knowledge, which caused "lots of chaos and noneffectiveness," but noted the more experienced citizen journalists were able to work with an IT developer to "perfect the instructions and technical tools for volunteers" to make the workflow more intuitive. Such streamlining was crucial for many Euromaidan collaborative initiatives not only because they were built around online platforms but also because most of the community members were joining in to work from wherever they happened to be at the moment, so they needed ubiquitous access to documents, contact databases, and means of communications with other volunteers and coordinators, scattered around the city and the country.

DIGITAL SHORTCUTS AND HORIZONTALITY

The Euromaidan protest was to some extent reliant on digitally mediated connective action formations (Bennett and Segerberg 2012), which enabled it to scale up more quickly beyond the initial city square into a sprawling network of locations that was at times discordant in terms of political agendas, but performed well in terms of tactical diffusion and replicating protest repertoires. Using or adapting preexisting digital platforms, such as social networks, to build new kinds of activist or protest communities allowed citizens to create new pathways—digital shortcuts of a sort—between existing nodes in the network, where previously there were none, optimizing resources, time, and relationships to achieve protest organizing goals and connect existing and potential participants in new ways.

Quite a few of the protesters interviewed implied in their narratives and examples of organizing activity during the protest that they used social media to create these shortcuts in the fabric of organizing and managing protest-related work. Several referred to the necessity of training new volunteers who joined a community or an initiative. An organizer in Kyiv who I spoke to in December 2013 mentioned using Skype chats with local and regional volunteer coordinators to speed up the transfer of skills due to lack of time and human resources to do hands-on training:

> The first days in Maidan, people learned very quickly, each day was so intense it seemed like ten days. So now, a month in, we have people working on logistics who are third wave: and our regional coordinators, they were trained over chat and calls by people whom I had trained previously.

The challenge of a decentralized workflow with distributed contributors in different locations was noted by another interviewee in Kharkiv, who had spent the Euromaidan period as part of a moderator team for one of the largest protest-related Facebook communities. The moderator team for the group was scattered around Ukraine, and two of the moderators were located abroad in a different time zone, which aided in around-the-clock volunteer availability. The participant shared some of the details of the community's digitally mediated processes for making decisions and tracking the workflow.

> There wasn't really a system for making decisions: at first the several founders, they said "let's do it this way," and if these were all logical suggestions, no one opposed them, but we offered opinions. We also had a Google Doc called Memo to Moderators where we compiled how we work and tracked what we were doing, and if we saw something was going wrong, one of us, whoever saw it, suggested some means of optimization, updated the doc and made everyone aware and explained it to everyone. Other things were resolved in the group chat by the people on the shift. So somehow, we managed to get this done without a single physical general meeting or getting everyone together, everything was resolved in [the] process.

In a slightly different context from the more dispersed groups of activists who benefited from social media affording them the ability to work on a common cause without being physically copresent, a respondent in Kharkiv who worked as a volunteer psychologist offering counseling to participants in the local protest camp said she and her colleagues were rarely in the same place together simply because they all had day jobs and could only take shifts to volunteer. The psychologist said they used Facebook chat to discuss difficult cases or current events and protest news, and used a Google Docs spreadsheet to track their work:

> Time was our main common resource, so we had a timetable online with slots to take shifts and people could just add themselves there and check where and when help was needed.

Discussing the work of a decentralized team of Ukrainian Euromaidan participants based in Washington, DC, and New York who collaborated on fundraising and media outreach, one activist, a former operations manager at a software company who now co-runs the nonprofit the community has evolved into, said he and his fellow protesters relied on connections through email and social networks, as well as digital project management tools such as Basecamp to optimize their organizing efforts and to function as a coherent team:

> In terms of my profession, the main skills are getting people together to do a new thing. This is exactly what we have done here. Organizational work, communication, motivation, coming up with processes, making things work in a team, logistics—the internet played a part in each. We all did part of the hands-on work, but we needed the structure under it that these tools provided to keep in touch and work as a team.

A recurring theme in my interviews with Euromaidan participants was the self-organized or grassroots nature of the protest and the role of digital media in facilitating it. This often emerged out of participants' discussions of the organizing and group structures underlying the protest movement. More experienced activists admitted that having digital media platforms allowed for less copresence and more decentralization to make the protest activity functional, but put more emphasis on having "some organizational structure" and "clear lines of responsibilities" in order to be able to exert some authority as a cohesive movement. Newer entrants into the protest field among interviewees for the most part believed that formal organizational structures were not necessary to achieve protest-related goals, and that dividing and managing tasks and responsibilities could be achieved through as little hierarchy as possible and through having a "flat," "horizontal," and "leaderless" structure, given that the internet and social media afforded them opportunities to "coordinate," "document successes and mistakes," to keep "a public breadcrumb trail of our work" to preserve accountability, and to "let our public-facing presence speak for itself."

As early as December 2013, a little over a month into the Euromaidan protest, an interviewee in Kyiv who considered himself part of the "old guard" said:

There is very little hierarchy in all these communities that are working out
there now. All the best protest activity now happens according to the principle I
mentioned: if you want to get something done, do it yourself. The [group I work
with] and all other communities work this way.

A graduate student interviewed in Kharkiv who participated in a countrywide
legal assistance initiative during Euromaidan, said the distributed, networked
nature of their community underpinned by the digital communications
that enabled it, as well as the desire of the protest community members to
"keep everyone on an equal footing" was what made the protest tick more
generally:

What I think is unique about this movement and the many groups in it, is that
we manage to make decisions through discussion, negotiation and consensus,
not leadership. It happens organically, there is some kind of synergy, and that's
an amazing achievement.

These comments align with the ongoing cultural trend toward "horizontal,
non-institutional movements" that Tufekçi (2014) suggests predate the internet, as a precursor to new, participatory civic movements that thrive on networks and connective action and are less rigid in structure than classic social
movement organizations. Such "horizontal" protest movements are enabled
by the affordances for less formal organization provided by digital media and,
in concert with the citizens' growing distrust of institutionalized authority,
emerge as expressions of grievances and claims or statements of identity, but
rarely make sustainable structural or policy demands.

BUILDING SOCIAL CAPITAL

The affordances of social media for building relationships, trust, and expectations within the protest community, both in smaller groups and the movement
as a whole, were a recurring theme in my Euromaidan interviews. Social
movement and protest scholars collectively refer to these as *social capital*
to signify "the resources embedded in one's social networks that can be
accessed for collective action" (Lin 2008). Social capital manifests in both
structural and psychological dimensions, and is strongest in a "dense network of reciprocal social relations" that people can draw on to act upon their
interests (Putnam 2000). The psychological dimension motivates community
participation, reinforcing trust and reciprocity (Shah and Gil de Zúñiga 2008).
But accumulating social capital also depends on structural external forces that
determine the extent of opportunities individuals or groups have for creating

networks and drawing on the resources they make available (Skoric et al. 2016).

Social capital tends to foster civic participation, so researchers have studied the affordances of social media platforms for developing and maintaining bridging and bonding social capital. Bonding social capital relies on networks of strong, informal social ties that individuals maintain through frequent interactions, providing emotional and social support, access to scarce and limited resources, and promoting reciprocity (Skoric et al. 2016). Bridging social capital networks more diverse types of individuals, although these ties are relatively weak as they usually not only involve loose contact (Granovetter 1973) but also encourage those they connect to be more open-minded and view themselves as part of a broader group in a particular society.

Social media can be useful for "generating and affirming interpersonal interaction, broadening social ties, and providing information about how to become involved" (Valenzuela, Park, and Kee 2009), as well as contributing to "conditions necessary for community engagement" that, in turn, sustain social capital (Shah and Gil de Zúñiga 2008). Social media also enable users to intensify their interactions with online and offline contacts and to expand their social networks (Hampton and Wellman 2003; Sessions 2010).

In their interviews, Euromaidan participants overwhelmingly talked about relying on social media to expand their protest networks, engage in community or group efforts as part of their protest activity, with many saying social network use afforded them a greater intensity of both online and offline interactions with other protest participants and observers. An experienced activist in Kyiv who managed human resources and logistics for one of the larger Euromaidan protest communities said that, while strong ties and preexisting civic networks had enabled initial organizing, new connections on social media brought a larger circle of volunteers and new protest participants into the fold and allowed for knowledge sharing and community growth.

> I am amazed at how quickly some of the people who have never done civic activism are volunteering, connecting and learning. And we're all so different. If we met under different circumstances, we'd be unlikely to be such fast friends, because our views are very different. But in working together on this we were able to find common ground and solidarity.

A protester whom I interviewed in Washington, DC, who participated in Euromaidan action by working on financial investigations into corrupt Ukrainian officials, said that weak ties were very important in enabling the transborder work of her team, underscoring the importance of bridging social capital in loosely connected protest communities.

There's only so much of your own personal network that you have, and a lot of the times you find yourself having to seek people out and reach out to them online. For example, during one of our investigations, I had to do a check in Belgium, so I wrote in the Facebook group called "Ukrainians Abroad for EuroMaidan," and several people from Belgium replied and helped me to look for some records. The same was in Cyprus: we were looking for some companies in Cyprus, and we got people who could look through phone books locally to help us out.

Some interviewees underscored the relative importance of strong ties on social media, especially when they were used in the initial stages of the protest as a filtering mechanism to build communities from the ground up. An activist who was part of the Kyiv-based protest logistics initiative said they initially searched for moderators among close friends and acquaintances on social media by "checking their recent posts," to make sure they were recruiting among those sympathetic to the protest cause:

> We posted recruit ads for volunteers on Facebook, but made them friends-only or friends of friends, to filter it at least a little, so most people came from these networks. Since we didn't know which of our friends were sympathetic towards the protest, we didn't want to harass everyone.

In Odesa, a protest participant who helped manage a Facebook page that aggregated local protest news, information, and resources, said her small group also found it useful to connect with other willing volunteers on social media as it was fairly easy to see how people's online activity and posts reflected on their participation and willingness to help.

> The people who were around during the protest, if they didn't show up and weren't ready to work, if there wasn't this emotional connection, nothing would have happened. So it was very important to assess people and figure out what you could expect this person to do. Friendships and existing networks helped a lot, but other people simply showed up and took up work.

Some of the more popular social media platforms, such as Facebook, were used to tap into preexisting offline networks of social ties, supplemented with the site's real-name policy, which has been shown to promote reciprocity, greater trust, and commitment (Kavanaugh et al. 2005), especially when compared to more anonymous or pseudonymous platforms. A graduate student in Kharkiv said he relied heavily on the opinions and reports of his pre-Euromaidan Facebook connections, whom he had already held in high regard, in deciding to engage with the protest more fully:

For me what other people I trusted said in their [Facebook] posts was important. They weren't the ones who changed my mind, but their words resonated and pushed me to act.

One participant in Kyiv who volunteered with a group that aggregated transport and fuel supplies and used Facebook to report on the funds received and spent, said the existing networked connections who already knew each other or whose identities were easily verifiable were key to establishing trust while managing online donations in a transparent way.

Money wasn't our thing generally, mostly in-kind donations, but we did get some funds and we then did a bit of our own fundraising through friends and networks and bought easy things like a generator when we knew there was a place that needed one. We also used some of the funds to pay for firewood transport and such. Since most of our moderators are friends or people we know, the issue of trust doesn't come up.

Trust and civic engagement, according to Putnam (2000), are mutually reinforcing as people who trust their fellow citizens volunteer and participate more often in civic and political activities. Social media, in the case of Euromaidan, occasionally afforded such social trust, bolstering protesters' willingness to ascribe good intentions to other participants and creating opportunities for bridging social capital in the protest networks. Such was the case of a legal assistance initiative, which started work in Kyiv, but whose reach broadened to include other regions later in the protest timeline.

An interviewee who worked with the initiative recalled that they initially established their willingness to engage with different networks after the first cases of police brutality in Kyiv by putting up Facebook posts to solicit information and contacts from both protesters who needed legal help and volunteer lawyers who could assist in legal action. As its networks developed, the legal initiative played the role of an information hub, as it shared contacts of other protest groups, provided hotline numbers, and engaged with regional coordinators through its Facebook bridging ties. The interviewee posited that their digitally enabled openness and willingness to engage was key:

Our very public activity and always being available online, within a click of a button, our public reports on Facebook, I think it created a certain ambience, a certain environment of trust—people knew we were there for them, they relied on us, it gave them a sense of security.

Ellison, Steinfield, and Lampe (2011) find that Facebook can be particularly useful in facilitating the conversion of casual connections into weak ties that can be considered bridging social capital that could be useful in protest networks. Most interviewees said they thought internet tools, especially social networks, allowed for more effective recruitment of specific people with specific skills for Euromaidan needs, as well as a certain level of serendipity, making it easier to find professionals and verify their credentials through networked connections on sites such as Facebook and LinkedIn. Those respondents who were engaged in fundraising efforts also suggested it was easier to establish whom to trust with the money based on a combination of personal connections and social media activity of particular fundraisers or initiatives handling the funds. One respondent in Washington, DC, who helped raise funds for field medical operations in Kyiv, recalled:

> One group in Kyiv raised money for medical equipment for field hospitals, but also posted regular reports of funds spent and photos from the hospitals, so I knew where my money went.

NETWORKED PROTEST COMMUNITIES AND EPHEMERALITY

Networked social movements, replicating the underlying nature of digitally mediated communications, can be networked both offline and online, connecting both in useful ways and creating new spaces for building social capital, exchanging opinions, and engaging in protest action. In these networks, spontaneous coordination can take place, affording discontented citizens the opportunities to arrange acts of protest with minimal effort and few incentives for participation. Online social networks may also afford a greater measure of interpersonal influence that Lim (2008) suggests is key to political mobilization and engagement as the networks provide more transparency and substance in terms of the content of relationships, common interests in politics or shared political and civic identities.

In their interviews, several protesters referred to what they termed "networked communities" which they believed enabled greater levels of self-organization and were underpinned by the affordances of social media and the internet for leveraging existing networks and building new ones easily. An interviewee in Kyiv described their "networked community" of IT-savvy volunteers in the following way:

> I think it's simple, two things: we have a common network through which they [volunteers] were all found, and then the website as a platform, a technical platform that people work on together, that they use to work on something. It's not just the public interface, it's also the group chat for the team, all our social media pages, all that context and field of work.

Networked protest communities afforded by social media can be less stable and long-lasting than traditional protest movements (Kavada 2010). However, these ephemeral formations can still help mobilize resources and people and manage information more efficiently, and can act as "first responders" during the critical moments in a protest. A protester in Kharkiv who contributed to an initiative that provided online coverage of main protest events on social media and video live streams said their networked community proved to be illuminating in how productive people could be with very scarce resources when they came together and were inspired by each other:

> People pleasantly surprised me. I always knew there were tons of great people around, but that there were so many, so close and it was so easy to get things done with them—it was a revelation. The ease of people coming, joining, is one of the biggest discoveries for me.

Another protester in Kyiv, who was new to the civic action scene, said she believed that protest participants linked by networked communities created during Euromaidan would remain connected and engage in civic activity, exactly because there were no formal structures obligating them to do things "a certain way":

> I think people who simply come together and do something, with no formal structures, they will keep doing things together, they've grown friendships, got used to working together, they're staying connected on [social] networks, so I think they will want to do more together.

Though some researchers suggest that due to their mainly loose ties and flexible structure, such networked "insurgent" protest communities tend to dissolve when the crisis passes (Castells 2012), in the case of Euromaidan, the emergence of these ephemeral networked communities seems to have enabled a new kind of short-lived, but effective participatory dissent that is emerging as the next phase in the evolution of protest movements (Tufekçi 2014; Earl and Kimport 2011).

NETWORKED INDIVIDUALS AND PART-TIME REVOLUTIONARIES

The affordances of social media for connective action manifest in more than one way in the Euromaidan protest. As we've already established, it made possible organizationally enabled networks that relied on loose coordination around civic or political issues and personal action frames generated by social movement and protest organizations, but allowed individuals greater agency within digitally mediated organizational structures. But connective action also came from self-organizing ephemeral networks, bringing together "individuals with little or no organizational coordination of action" (Bennett and Segerberg 2012) whose engagement was often entirely based on personal action frames. For these individuals, engaged in personal expression and possessing a strong voice, social media played an integrative organizational role, affording them the most visible activity of the network. Such self-organized actors activated their own followers and social networks, without necessarily relying on organizations.

Dahlgren calls these highly visible individuals "online public intellectuals": digital media allows them to amplify their messages and play a significant role in alternative civic and political spaces (Dahlgren 2013). This, in turn, affords these influential users the ability to effectively activate their social networks to engage in connective action. Tufekçi (2013) conceptualizes the role these individuals play in networked protest action as "microcelebrity networked activism." She describes these microcelebrity activists as "politically motivated noninstitutional actors who use affordances of social media to engage in the presentation of their political and personal selves to garner public attention to their cause" (Tufekçi 2013, 850). In some of the movements with transborder concerns, the microcelebrities might serve as bridging agents, using different languages on social media (especially English) to draw global attention, though such dispersed messaging might in turn dilute their effect on internal protest or movement networks.

Interview participants who were protest novices or had less experience in traditional activism prior to the Euromaidan protest mentioned individual protest activity and opportunities afforded by social media more often. However, despite their general inclination to rely on movement organizations and community work, experienced activists also noted the role of prominent "opinion leaders" in the emergence of Euromaidan as a more coherent movement, citing examples such as journalist Mustafa Nayyem, whose Facebook post, though one of many calling to go on the street in November 2013, was remembered by many as a key message driving initial participation. Other examples included several anticorruption and urban activists who had a significant following online, bloggers, and journalists. An interviewee from Odesa explained the importance of these "singular voices":

> I get that not everyone might want to join an organisation or might be wary of membership. But these people, they do an important service as they raise the issues that are at the heart of the protest and allow others to engage with these issues less formally. . . . [. . .] Their posts make people think, and if you have people's attention, you can use it to ask for other kinds of help.

A journalist from an online outlet interviewed in Kyiv said that for her, having a space on social media apart from her professional work was helpful as it allowed her to engage with a diverse selection of different networks and gauge people's opinions, while also offering her own "take on things." She did note that since she already enjoyed more attention from internet users than the average citizen, she felt more responsibility for checking her facts and making sure that what she posted was "constructive [for the protest movement], rather than destructive."

Discussing their own or their protest peers' individual activity as connective action, participants said engaging with those "on the other side" and debating the merits of Euromaidan and its mission was an important, but difficult part of their networked connective practices. Only a handful of participants said they had attempted to use social media conversations to reach out to those who opposed Euromaidan, and admitted they preferred to engage with other supporters or raise awareness among those who were indifferent or agnostic, as it was "more productive."

Only one participant, a graduate student in Washington, DC, discussed at length her efforts to connect with disparate communities and individuals who were against the protest and its premises. Using Facebook and the Russian social network VKontakte (also popular in Ukraine), she engaged these individuals and tried to change their mind through providing "reasoned arguments" in favor of the Euromaidan protest.

> I'd like to say the debates were constructive, but certainly not always, and conversations would regularly dissolve into shouting matches. Sometimes it felt like people were pre-programmed to spout vitriolic anti-Ukrainian or anti-Euromaidan sentiment, and on social media this can get very ugly and personal. [. . .] Obviously, they had a different set of opinion leaders than we did, and those networks would pick up their opinions, circulate them and tout them as valid.

Technological affordances of the internet and social media often combine with users' activities and preferences to articulate each other in unexpected ways (van Dijck and Poell 2015). One of such unexpected observations made by Euromaidan participants while discussing the intricacies of what it meant to be involved and "copresent" within the context of the Euromaidan protest was how social media afforded them the capability to engage in the protests on a part-time basis, while still feeling that their activity and input was meaningful. They perceived a reduced need for collectivity and physical copresence by not only finding opportunities for action outside of the physical center of the protest but also feeling like they were present in the protest environment despite only spending a part of their day on it. Lyubashenko (in Valenzuela et al. 2014) calls such protesters "part-time revolutionaries," enabled by social networks to have "small-scale engagement on a mass level" and to join and be present in the protest environment at Euromaidan's most crucial moments, for instance, during confrontations with government forces.

Several interview participants described their involvement with Euromaidan as "part-time," explaining that they all had regular day jobs and other responsibilities that many of them could not abandon, but noting that online networks provided them with ways to have some presence within the movement. A software engineer in Kyiv who was involved in several different Euromaidan initiatives, said he was at first skeptical about whether he would be able to combine work with being a protest participant, but added that it proved to be possible, because he did not always physically have to be at the protest site and could manage his time more efficiently thanks to working online.

> I saw that you can work on several projects at once, and even though it might seem like work might put more pressure on you, you can do things in parallel when you have the right tools, [you can] manage stuff.

An interviewee in Washington, DC, who volunteered with one of the local Ukrainian protest collectives doing everything from media outreach to fundraising, said networking on social media had enabled their team to be very flexible and direct its efforts at particular causes within Euromaidan when team members had time and effort to spare.

> So, just the way this thing evolved, you see it, there is a group of about ten people who are actually very, very active, and they don't just do one thing, they come and do work or they drop out, but this very active group forms, and this is how it works.

A participant in Kharkiv who worked on one of the several teams that coordinated resources, logistics, and information for the protest, said he had mixed feelings about the part-time participation afforded by social media. She felt that more could be done, but still noted that at least this allowed more people to join in the protest and contribute to the feeling of multitudes working together and experiencing the protest as a collective phenomenon.

> It was a cocktail of this feeling of right and the satisfaction that we could, but also disappointment and sadness at lost opportunities, because there was so much to be done, still is, and we can see where we can help, but because I also combined it with work and personal life—like we all did, actually—we couldn't do everything.

A Ukrainian financial analyst living in Washington, DC, reflected on the perceptions he himself had of his part-time, long-distance involvement in the protest:

> Everyone wanted to go to Maidan [in Kyiv] to be part of the action there, because it was so exciting. . . . [. . .] But I realised that we were worth more, more useful here, with our connections and our networks of influential people. So, this is our protest experience, too, the sitting by the phone, by the laptop, the fundraising emails and Facebook auctions—that's how we protest.

Overall, participants felt that the social media-enabled networks that converged around Euromaidan allowed both groups and individuals equal access to productive collaboration and created a welcoming space, serving as evidence that a self-organized, less formal networked protest structure was not only possible, but could lead to accumulation of social capital and more sustainable transformations in how people thought about collective protest activity. In the words of one Kharkiv activist,

> To try and generalize it, I'd say it's some kind of maturity, adulthood, self-awareness, a desire and readiness to act, on their own, of some kind of internal motivation. The motives are different for everyone, [Euro]Maidan is this whole system of different groups and people with their own goals and programs, but this active position, readiness to act, self-organize, not follow someone, change the reality around you yourself—that's the main unifying thing.

CASE STUDY: GALAS

We now take an in-depth look at a specific Euromaidan initiative to illustrate the affordances of social media for flexible organizing, building social capital, ephemeral networks, and part-time participation that emerged out of the interviews discussed above. Galas was a crowdsourcing protest logistics initiative that sprang up during the protest in Kyiv at the end of 2013. Founded by a small group of enthusiasts seeking to help coordinate human, material, and other resources for Euromaidan, Galas (Ukrainian for *noise* or *ruckus*) grew into a major hub of the urban contentious effort.

Support for specific initiatives during the Euromaidan protest in Ukraine often formed spontaneously around particular needs; in some cases, just a handful of individuals were able to take projects off the ground due to the affordances of existing personal networks of relationships, as well as easily scaled free, open-source platforms that enable volunteer signup, project management, and resource mobilization. Galas appeared in response to a logistical conundrum; the management and distribution of resources (funds, transportation, lodging, and medications) at the early stages of the protest were chaotic and fragmented, despite the fact that many people in Kyiv and elsewhere expressed their desire to help the Euromaidan protesters. One of Galas' founders, who works as an IT manager at a software company, said they discussed this issue with friends (developers, programmers, and designers) and wondered if the protest movement would benefit from an organized coordination initiative that could combine material and digital efforts to manage and distribute crowdsourced resources more coherently.

Built around a loosely tied community of protesters, Galas relied on both active contact with other Euromaidan protest groups and the collection of extant, publicly available information about available resources and needs. Galas' main protest activities—the active outreach for information and the collection and curation of data that were already available—were performed through various channels, including digital online media and phone conversations, as well as face-to-face communication and distribution of visual materials in the protest camp in the city center. The initiative also worked within various spatialities and temporalities, circumscribed by the rhythms of urban life and the rhythms of the protest event.

The main protest-related activities in Galas involved the collection, curation, and dissemination of existing data and emerging information about the needs and resources within the protest movement. Spatially, this involved mapping the available information onto the network of the physical sites of resistance in the city. The map became the main symbolic representation of Galas' work. The initial core team designed both the website and the mobile apps around a real-time alert mapping platform that had already been tested during the heavy snowfalls in Kyiv the previous winter. The Galas website used the open-source Ushahidi platform for populating the interactive map with information about resources on offer and the needs of key protest hubs around the city. The main website, defunct as of June 2017, is still available to view on the Internet Archive's Wayback Machine (see figure 6.1).

The interactive map was populated with information in the following categories: (a) help needed, (b) ready to help, (c) searching for missing persons, (d) locations of help centers, (e) free Wi-Fi locations. This map was populated from messages coming in through the website's feedback form and the smartphone apps, as well as from calls, text messages, and social media exchanges, all of these curated by Galas volunteers. Additional resource-related information came in through face-to-face communication with various hubs within the central protest camp downtown, as well as through other networked protest initiatives dealing with medical needs, cooking, or transportation. One of the Galas interviewees, a volunteer coordinator, said the website was successful in raising awareness of the protest needs and connecting them to available

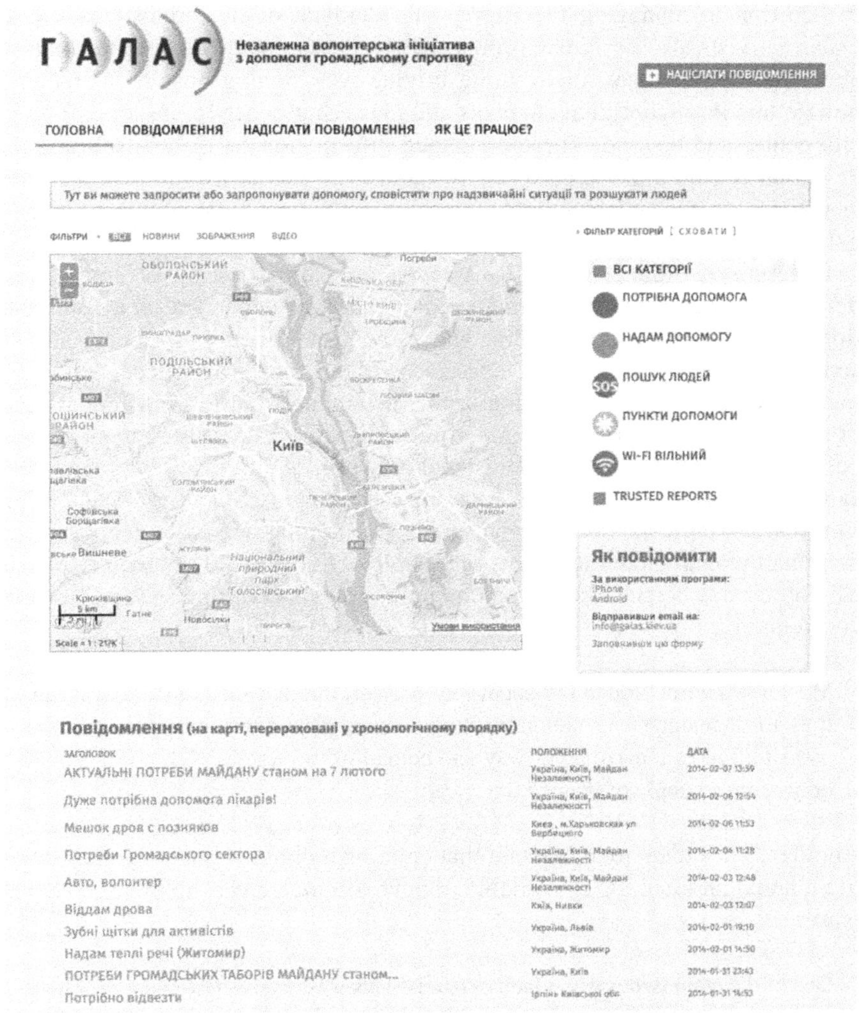

Figure 6.1   The Galas Website as Captured on February 8, 2014. Public Domain, Wayback Machine. https://web.archive.org/web/20140208062230/http://www.galas.org.ua.

resources, mainly because of regular social media updates and working on foot in the main protest locations. She also pointed out that high or low numbers of visits to the website depended on particular protest moments:

> The site was the most visited of our platforms, after November 30 [the first case of police brutality against protesters] we had a peak, December 4 we had 80K visits a day. An increase after every police clash or something big happening.

In addition to managing the supply and demand of the protest resources, Galas activists also designed, produced, and disseminated useful information about protest practices, distributing bright, eye-catching posters, maps, and newsletters through digital channels and plastering paper copies around Kyiv city center and beyond. These contained information on Galas itself and on key contact points in the protest effort and their spatial locations in the city, as well as practical advice on what to bring to the protest and where to donate extra supplies.

In terms of organization, Galas relied on a small group of activists to design and create its initial structure; the endeavor depended on a combination of volunteer work both online and in the protest locations around the city center. In spatial terms, Galas operated without a central office, relying on part-time labor from its coordinators and volunteers based in different locations around Kyiv. New part-time volunteer staff was recruited from protest participants and sympathizers on social networks and in the downtown street camp. High volunteer turnover was one of the main issues for Galas during Euromaidan protests, but the relative ease of training new volunteers and the fact that the map moderation was accessible online and did not require physical copresence helped keep the momentum going, according to the volunteer coordinator.

> Most new recruits found out about [our project] through social media, and saw it as a low-maintenance commitment that nonetheless allowed them to join the protest effort in a meaningful way and be part of the action, even if they could only spare a couple of hours a day.

Another Galas team member said that creating a digital version of their training manual and making it available to new volunteers was a key time-saving feat:

> One of the main issues was a lack of hands. This was resolved by calling for help among friends, and recruiting new friends and acquaintances and using a few new tech tools. One of our activists came up with the idea of holding webinars to train our incoming new volunteers to get them trained and acclimated faster. By that point we were so tired of teaching each new volunteer the algorithm of work. But the webinar we recorded once and then gave the link to the video to all new volunteers, and it was helpful at least in part and saved us the hassle.

Organizing a heterogeneous, ephemeral collective of protesters was challenging with regard to their varying temporalities: Most of these people worked day jobs, so they could afford to spend only a few hours each day (or sometimes night) designing and sharing content, fielding calls, inspecting donations or facilities, or adding requests for and offers of resources to the crowdsourced map and database. One Galas volunteer, a developer, said he did a lot of his protest-related work for Galas from his office, as he shared his time between work and protest-related tasks, but would "still run down to Khreshchatyk," the city's central street close to the protest camp, "after work just to add another check-in on Foursquare to the protest event there, to up the numbers." Consequently, this allowed him to feel like he was "present and involved" within the material protest space, even if he did not get to enter the physical center every day.

Galas activists maintained a regularly updated shared list of individuals, useful contacts, and daily tasks, allowing relevant actors access to necessary information from their workplaces or from smartphones if they were in the protest camp. The IT manager, a founding member of Galas, said the team relied on a number of digital tools, including social media, chat apps, and online document and storage services to get their work organized and work around the clock:

> Google docs, group chat, several documents with instructions and manuals, where we describe the basic algorithm, and where everything is stored. Several extra information resources: a history of our communications with coordinators in various places related to [Euro]Maidan, we keep a log of that, whom we called and when and what happened, and similar things for transport and such.

Though most of Galas' activity was logistically oriented and mapped onto specific locations or protest network nodes, its participants also engaged in more political and symbolic practices such as reposting and sharing protest slogans and key news about state and police reaction on their Facebook page (7,300 followers as of January 2016). But even these more symbolic communications served as evidence of Galas' embeddedness into the relational space of the protest, where the group served as an amplifier of other protest groups and communities and, in turn, expected them to amplify its own calls for help or information (many of Galas' own Facebook posts would start with the word REPOST at the top, to indicate a call for distribution beyond its initial network). The visuals designed by Galas volunteers and distributed in print and digital form throughout the protest spaces, both digital and material, served as another symbolic representation of its place and function in the protest effort—that of creating a recognizable curatorial presence, a sense of order and direction in the protest practices. Indeed, where other protest groups used art or photos in their visual communications, Galas mostly relied on infographics, text-rich posters, or maps (see figure 6.2), underscoring its mission as information collector, resource curator, and, in a sense, protest geographer.

Figure 6.2   Leaflet Produced by Galas, Mapping Key Protest Locations and Resources.
Image by teteria sonnna on Flickr, CC BY 2.0, https://www.flickr.com/photos/sonnnatete
ria/13866352295.

Throughout their organization, participation, and protest practices, Galas activists were seeking to make visible the flows of information and resources within the protest. Using both digital platforms and physical protest spaces, they collected information from heterogeneous sources, inscribed it onto a digital live map of the city, and then connected that representation back to the material locations and relational networks of the resistance movement. This hybrid nature allowed Galas to straddle the junctures between the protest square and the social web, connecting loose, informal networks and tighter, more organized protest groups to leverage information and resources. This underscores Quan-Haase and Martin's (2013) point that the material and the digital do not exist in separate spheres, but "need to be conceptualised in relation to each other" (Quan-Haase and Martin 2013, 524). Especially in the case of public or mass urban events, such as the Euromaidan protest, the augmented environment is mediated in various ways, both digital and material, that expand the definition of practices such as organization, participation, and mobilization.

Although on first approach Galas protest activity seemed to revolve predominantly around a digitally enabled platform, the case study shows that it was also firmly embedded in the material geographies, temporalities, and practices of Euromaidan, while at the same time availing itself of the increasingly common digital networks that now permeate everyday life. One of the Galas founders underscored that, while the offline protest resource management efforts benefited from an internet-based coordination tool, it was the combination of online and offline efforts that made it work:

> Without offline work, calls, trips, the map wouldn't have worked. It wouldn't work just on the internet. And the main thing that helped it happen were volunteers who worked on specific things, and connections to people on the ground, who often didn't have internet connection, and when we sent them texts, they would ask us to catch them up on what was happening in the rest of the city.

Most new recruits found out about Galas through social media, but word-of-mouth and some form of prior weak ties were crucial for securing commitment and prolonged engagement. In terms of organization, Galas' flexibility resulted not only from a reliance on digital tools (online map, shared digital spreadsheets, and contact databases) but also from the fact that urban participants often had random amounts of time they could devote to Galas work and had to balance their varying temporalities within the needs of the initiative. Some of them freelanced and had more leeway; others could only work at night or on weekends, but had unfettered internet access; yet others were self-employed or ran their own companies and could afford to take unpaid leave when needed to visit physical locations.

These temporal variations, structured by the rhythm of daily life, meant that people saw their volunteer work at Galas as a fairly low-maintenance commitment that nonetheless allowed them to "practice protest" in a meaningful way. While volunteer turnover was high, the training for volunteers required minimal effort and the decentralized nature of Galas operations meant that most practices and their evolution were extensively documented, with records made available for all community members. The flexibility of the resource management and volunteer operations structure also meant that Galas, as a project, was able to adapt quickly to the changing needs of Euromaidan, going from collecting camping gear, tea, and phone chargers at the start to crowdsourcing medical equipment and bulletproof vests when the protests turned violent.

Because Galas was responsive to the protest environment, whether digital, material/spatial, or temporal, its activists were able to recognize the space of protest as a roiling mass of hybrid human activity and interaction instead of a square in the city center filled with tents, barricades, and burning tires. They were also able to spot the opportunities for action, the "missing links" in this multispatial environment and to address these opportunities through creating spontaneous shortcuts in the ephemeral networks to gather and deliver information and resources where they were available or necessary—or, sometimes, simply to connect the right people with one another, whether face to face or via digital means. In the words of one Galas activist, "We knew where free Wi-Fi was available and we knew where you could get 100 kg of firewood. And if we didn't, we knew who to ask."

Recognizing the limitations of the various elements of this multispatial environment and attempting to overcome them by hybridizing space, technology, and human agency allowed Galas to create new connections between protest groups and to synthesize protest knowledge and practices in the process. This is reminiscent of Davies' (2012) conclusion that ephemeral social formations emerging during social and political upheaval are best seen as flexible assemblages of people, objects, spaces, and connections, able to temporarily cohere and disperse as required by the needs of the protest.

CONCLUSION

Galas was only one of the multitude of groups and communities involved in Euromaidan, but it offers a holistic example of the peculiar affordances of digital media for protest organizing and participation. Both the case study analysis and the interviews reveal the centrality of flexibility and ephemerality as key features of connective and collective action in Euromaidan.

Combining these affordances of digital media with on-the-ground efforts, Euromaidan activists were able to leverage this hybridity to create functioning protest networks, build trust and exploit social capital in the form of both strong and weak ties, and manage protest logistics. Networked technologies allowed for some degree of horizontality in protest organization and often served as impromptu shortcuts for resolving key protest tasks, be it fundraising, resource distribution, or information sharing. Although the connections in the networks were often ephemeral, they allowed for the emergence of necessary connective tissue for communication, tactical diffusion, and coordination.

Crucially, the augmented organizing and participation repertoires afforded a variety of opportunities for action for both communities and active individuals. The flexibility of digitally mediated engagement in terms of time, location, and effort allowed protesters to participate in the action in diverse, yet meaningful ways, combining elements of their digital and physical environment. The protest networks of Euromaidan, though ephemeral and pliable, extended far beyond the protest square, expanding both the reach of the protest and the access into its constellation of participating actors.

The connective tissue of augmented protest networks was put to use for managing logistics and organizing the diverse temporalities of individuals and groups joining the discontent. Protesters also made use of these connections to distribute information, both within the movement and to external audiences. As the next chapter shows, incorporating social media into the information diffusion process meant Euromaidan participants were able to frame the protest in meaningful ways and tell coherent stories about their experiences, while also having to deal with false narratives generated by rogue actors and the ephemerality and volatility of mediated attention.

Chapter 7

Information Sharing and Protest Frames

Almost two months into the protests, the public discontent became so visible and inconvenient that the authorities decided to add legislative pressure to the physical crackdowns. On January 16, 2014, the Ukrainian parliament passed a law limiting freedom of assembly and clamping down on freedom of expression. The law, billed as "protecting the security of citizens" (Bohdanova 2014), was quickly signed by then-President Yanukovych. Its provisions seemed right out of Russia's anti-protest playbook: among other things, the law criminalized libel, labeled civic organizations receiving foreign grants as "foreign agents," and introduced new, harsh penalties for any forms of protest. Importantly, it also imposed restrictions on the work of mainstream media and online activity, increasing control and surveillance of telecommunications systems and social media, under the guise of fighting extremism and violent uprisings. Reacting to the news of the law on Facebook, journalist Mustafa Nayyem marveled at the viciousness of the lawmakers, who, he said, had essentially "outlawed social media" (Nayyem 2014a).

The fact that the anti-protest law gave such prominence to the protesters' networked information activities is testament to the massive role information production, sharing, and distribution had for the protest. The grassroots organizing that made Euromaidan possible was predicated on building and maintaining networks of information exchange. The visibility of Euromaidan events, afforded in part by social media, relied on frames and narratives generated by protest participants to strategically direct attention to key events and to generate meaningful storytelling about and coverage of the protest.

Throughout, the scalability of information networks and the persistence of diverse protest frames and narratives emerged as key affordances of social media used by participants. Information sharing in the hybrid communication ecosystem of Euromaidan was scalable and persistent, yet it also relied on highly adaptive and volatile digital media mechanisms such as hashtags and network trends. Despite this ephemerality of attention-generating tools that required constant monitoring and quick reaction, Euromaidan was nonetheless successful in offering its participants a diverse range of means for participating in the exchange of information, frames, and narratives. These included publishing posts, using hashtags, translating content, reporting, sharing testimonies, following and liking, twitterstorms and similar campaigns—many of these short-lived, fickle actions that nonetheless contributed to the protest's day-to-day functioning and its continued visibility. The enmeshed nature of Euromaidan's information networks, combining offline and online elements, also created a perception of affective copresence among participants, contributing to continued participation of protesters in different locations and from different walks of life.

SOCIAL MEDIA AND INFORMATION SHARING

In a review of scholarship on social media use and participation, Boulianne (2015) finds that social networking sites emerge as "a critical mechanism for gathering information or news from family, friends, or traditional news media organisations," and afford users some potential for engaging with civic and political issues. Situating the role of digital media use in society in more political terms, Christensen points to a changing power dynamics in the political sphere, where social media have thwarted the discursive monopoly of political elites on mainstream media channels and "have made possible the presentation of alternative discourses to local and global audiences, challenging the orthodoxies of those in power" to define "what is right and wrong, what is legal and illegal, what is legitimate dissent or treason" (Christensen 2009).

Beyond the more general affordances of social media to create, distribute, and consume content and the abstract discussion of alternate discourses within a political system, social movement and protest scholars are also concerned with the kinds of interpretive work that occurs within activist and protester communities and networks. One way to consider how protesters perceive, interpret, and make meaning of their actions is by examining how the participants frame the movement and themselves within it. In social movement theory, framing is defined as "generating cognitive contexts within which data acquires meaning" (Ganz 2001). Through the prism of collective action frames, social movement and protest participants are regarded as "signifying agents actively engaged in the production and maintenance of meaning" for other participants, those they protest against, and those observing the activity (Benford and Snow 2000).

Euromaidan protesters and activists, along with the media, the state and other actors, participated in what Hall (2005) terms "the politics of signification," generating meaning in the context of the protest activity they engaged in. By using the term "framing," social movement scholars conceptualize this "signifying work or meaning construction" (Snow and Benford 1988). As an active verb, framing implies a dynamic, evolving process wherein social movement or protest movement participants exercise their agency to produce and offer contentious interpretive frames that challenge existing ones, often at the level of reality construction.

Importantly, more recent scholarly work has called for a less structural approach to understanding meaning-making in social movements, collective action, and protest activity and suggested researchers should go beyond the concept of framing and consider storytelling and narratives as central to social movement strategies and activity. Storytelling, they argue, is central to social and protest movements as it constructs agency, shapes identity, and motivates action (Ganz 2001). This was reflected in my interviews with Euromaidan participants, who discussed not only functional information sharing and distribution but also the framing of protest messages and the personal and collective narratives produced around the protest events.

NETWORKS, HASHTAGS, AND TWITTER STORMS

Research from the New York University Social Media and Political Participation lab scholars indicates that there was a clear and identifiable spike in the use of Facebook and Twitter in Ukraine during the period of the Euromaidan protests (Tucker, Metzger, and Barberá 2014), including an increase in the number of pages, new and active accounts, page views, comments, and likes. Many of my interview participants reported an increase in time spent using social media and a growing intensity of use during the events of November 2013–February 2014. Among other things, they started following new users and pages adjacent to or related to the protest movement, seeking new sources of information and new ways to share and distribute it.

Milan (2015) finds that protesters adapt the technical and design features of social media platforms to turn them into affordances for the information and communication-related needs of the protest movement or event: they use hashtags, retweets, and mentions to call people into action, raise awareness of protest causes, direct attention, and promote conversations and content exchange. In the Euromaidan context, Facebook and Twitter were particularly instrumental in affording these. Twitter, though used by a relatively small number of Ukrainians overall (hundreds of thousands as opposed to the millions using Facebook in 2014), was particularly instrumental in helping protesters connect with one another and in allowing them to inform broader networks of users (including those abroad and international observers) about developments on the ground (Tucker, Metzger, and Barberá 2014).

Protest participants used hashtags such as #євромайдан (Ukrainian), #евромайдан (Russian), and #euromaidan (English) to consolidate attention and create a visible discursive field that could be easily found by those seeking information about the protest. These hashtags became progressively more popular during the first weeks of the protests, with more than 8,000 tweets per hour published on 22 November, the second day of the protests, and as many as 4,800 per hour on 30 November, the night of the first violent crackdown by the police on student protesters (*Texty.org.ua* 2013). However, hashtags were crucial only during the first stage of organizing and mobilization, while activists positioned themselves within the protest discourse online (Lokot 2013). Once that discourse was established and the level of awareness about the protest reached saturation, users posting about Euromaidan tended to drop the hashtags, since everyone participating in the discussion already was aware of the context. A similar trend was observed by sociologist Zeynep Tufekçi during her research on the Gezi Park protests in Istanbul, Turkey, in 2013.

Hashtags, therefore, were a useful, but ephemeral tool of augmented information sharing and attention focusing in the protest. While the discussion and action online and offline remained very much alive and just as important to the outcome of the protest, they were not necessarily tagged, so those who were only relying on hashtags to follow the discussion, missed a large chunk of it. To further mark out the discursive space and establish longer-lasting, reliable information sources, within the first week of the Euromaidan action activists created "official" protest Twitter accounts—@euromaidan, @EuroMaydan, and @EuroMaydan_eng—that rapidly accumulated tens of thousands of followers and provided regular updates.

Several interview participants who said they had been generally skeptical of Twitter confessed they recognized its potential to quickly disseminate news and information and focus attention, however, one Kyiv-based respondent was still doubtful of Twitter's overall effect as a means of connecting with a mass audience.

> With Twitter, there's a very peculiar subsection of society already on it: people who are more keyed in, who follow news, so . . . [. . .] journalists, political observers, media analysts. So it's great as a tool and it's great that more people are joining, but I don't think it matters that much in the grand scheme of things.

Participants abroad had a slightly different view of Twitter's importance, noting that it gave them the ability to easily follow information streams and breaking news during the protests. Some tied it to Twitter's greater popularity in the West, and one interviewee, a graduate student, also drew attention to how well Twitter lent itself to multilingual use:

> When I looked at [Euromaidan] Twitter activity it made it seem like there was so much going on. It was probably out of proportion, the sense that every few minutes something was breaking, someone was saying or reporting something important. And I think the different language hashtags were a great idea. Plus, I saw people translating tweets on the go, to make them reach even further out to new people. At some point, I got into the translating groove as well, though it proved to be very time-consuming.

Facebook, as the more popular platform among Ukrainians, was also widely used by various Euromaidan groups and communities to establish and manage information flows and raise awareness of the protest. The most famous Facebook page, called simply "EuroMaydan," set a record in Ukraine at the time, attracting more than 76,000 followers in just eight days, and reaching more than 200,000 followers within the first ten weeks of the protests (Savanevsky 2014). Other pages and communities directed information about protest logistics, provided creative support to the movement, and engaged in aggregation of mainstream media reports about the protests and international outreach.

The predominant majority of interview participants, regardless of distance from the heart of the protest in Kyiv, said they followed the largest Euromaidan Facebook page, and many also reported joining other smaller groups. A marketing manager whom I interviewed in Washington, DC, said they were the first new addition to her Facebook Euromaidan "diet":

> Definitely, Euromaidan on Facebook. When I joined I think it was 50 thousand people, now it's over 260 or 270 thousand. So yeah, a lot of the Maidan-related ones, like Euromaidan SOS, Euromaidan . . . there's a whole bunch of them.

Other participants reported also following new individuals, usually in an organic way, because someone on their feed had reposted someone else's post with information, an opinion, or a call for help. These new sources of information included activists, reporters (both Ukrainian and international), commentators and political observers, academics and other opinion leaders. As one interviewee from Odesa remarked,

> I followed Mustafa [Nayyem] because, well, he was an online celebrity before and then everybody followed him after his post about going to protest. But over time, I also found people whose names I didn't know, but who were writing really well about the action, or who posted really good photos, so those went on my feed as well.

Generally speaking, there seems to have been a circular relationship between social media use, which initially helped to fuel protest mobilization and action, and the protest events themselves, which, in turn, increased user demand for digitally mediated information. Most respondents said the combination of personal connections and extended social networks online, such as Facebook and Twitter, was one of the most useful tactics that afforded them opportunities for engaging in protest-related information exchange and discussions. This mixture not only allowed them to exploit their existing strong ties in online networks but also afforded wide reach to the weak ties in the broader networks to share information, event announcements, and reports. Those respondents who used social media to catch the attention of other observers of Euromaidan said they thought internet tools, especially social networks, significantly amplified their efforts and messages in cases of raising awareness. A human resources specialist in Kyiv who worked on coordinating protest efforts from the first days of the civic occupation of the city center said in a December 2013 interview that, a little over a month into the protest, their Facebook page gained thousands of followers almost immediately and was far more popular than their standalone website.

> We have a Facebook page. We also have a separate website, but it's kind of lame, not enough people to keep it up. Facebook functions well, it's updated daily with dozens of posts, 80% is our own news produced by us. We're at about 6-7K followers right now, after 10 days of existing.

An IT manager in Kyiv who helped run a crowdsourced logistics initiative for the protest said their website became a well-known source of information about the protest needs in large part due to the information sharing work they were able to do on social media. Traffic, he said, very much depended on the volume of their posts to social media, as well as Facebook reposts and retweets.

Another activist in Kyiv said their group combined working with traditional media and citizen networks to amplify their voice and bring more attention to the work they were doing within the context of Euromaidan.

> And collaborating with other public pages and traditional media like radio, we worked with civic media. The Euromaidan public (the most popular page) was super-helpful for us in terms of driving attention. Without them and their reposts we would probably be able to do a lot less.

Respondents in regional protest hubs, such as Kharkiv and Odesa, not only reported similar dynamics of building presences on Facebook and (to a lesser extent) Twitter, and working with local independent media but also said they connected with Kyiv-based groups and sources online. Regional protest groups relied on them for up to date information about events at the center of the action, which they often reshared and reposted to their own pages, but also worked to push out their own local protest news, related statements, manifestos, and claims to a broader audience focused mainly on Kyiv and the events and discourse emerging from there. An activist in Kharkiv who worked with a group that reported on Euromaidan-related rallies and events in the city said their photos and videos were often picked up by more prominent communities on social media, giving them a boost in views and sometimes creating a cascading attention effect typical of the hybrid media and attention systems Chadwick (2017) describes:

> A retweet from Euromaidan Press would get us massive traffic, and if the tweet they retweeted had a link to our Facebook page, that went up as well. And if a major Kyiv community retweeted you, it was more likely the media and the foreign reporters would notice, too.

In terms of international outreach, activists used a variety of approaches to attract the attention of foreign media and to secure support and a loyal audience from users abroad. Protesters undertook long-term crowdsourcing translation efforts to share the latest news about Euromaidan (Bohdanova 2013), creating Facebook communities such as Euromaidan As It Is and Maidan Needs Translators. The translation initiatives also provided content for English-language protest update Facebook pages such as Euromaidan in English, Euromaidan Updates in English and Euromaidan News and Analysis. The process of selecting and translating content was quite decentralized and relied on volunteer labor, so the groups were also constantly seeking new volunteers, including native speakers able to proofread the updates in several languages.

Some of the interviewees also said they engaged in individual content translation efforts on Twitter and Facebook. This was especially popular as an activity with respondents abroad, one of whom said that translating important posts and news was a way of "being useful" while situated very far from the protest action on the ground, as translations helped spread awareness of protest events beyond the Russian- and Ukrainian-speaking online and offline networks and provided an alternative dimension to the international mainstream media coverage of Euromaidan. A Washington, DC, resident described it thusly:

> It helped alleviate the guilt of not being there a little [. . .] a small thing, sharing the news widely, retweeting the images, the livestreams, translating what I retweeted into English, to make sure the important stuff gets seen. Some other

Ukrainians here were doing this as well, so it was just our personal contribution, but it also gave us something to do besides simply taking in the news.

Other international awareness-raising efforts online included circulating viral video appeals to international viewers and organizing mass "Twitter storms" to bring Ukraine-related hashtags to the top of worldwide Twitter trending topics (Minchenko 2014). Ukrainians living abroad and representatives of the Ukrainian diaspora were at the heart of these social media activities and helped increase Euromaidan's visibility and promote its message abroad. For instance, on January 27, 2014, a Ukrainian #DigitalMaidan hashtag briefly held the number one position in Twitter's worldwide trending topics, due to a concerted campaign by Euromaidan activists from around the world (Lokot 2014b). The Facebook event page for the January 27 #DigitalMaidan Twitter storm effort provided access to a number of precomposed messages for sharing and offered a detailed explanation of how a Twitter storm was supposed to work:

> Have you been a part of a Twitter storm before? If not, here's how they work: A Twitter storm is when people, at a specific time, bombard Twitter with the same hashtag. Just before the Twitter storm starts, a page of around 80 pre-made tweets will be shared here on this event page. The pre-made tweets target TV stations, newspapers, officials, celebrities. [. . .] By all of us tweeting the same 80 messages with the same hashtag at various media and VIPs, we can get our message trending. ("EuroMaidan: #DigitalMaidan Twitter Storm" 2014)

During that particular hour in January 2014, over 60,000 tweets with the #digitalmaidan hashtag were published on Twitter, leading to the appearance of the hashtag in the trending topics. These efforts were deliberately ephemeral (nothing ever stays trending for very long), as they exploited the mechanics of attention on social media to drive short-term, but concentrated levels of attention to the events in Ukraine. They were also strategically constructed, providing social media users with premade content that was aimed at key accounts and easy to share on the hashtag, offering a different mode of engagement through information sharing and frame diffusion for those who could not participate in the events on the ground. As one Twitter user participating in the storm put it, "When we don't lay siege to administration, we lay siege to Twitter" (@Lil_Tolstoy, January 27, 2014).

MANAGING THE FLOOD

As the number of protesters ballooned and the attention grew, so did the amount of content generated around Euromaidan. At times, it almost seemed like too much. In their interviews, respondents shared the various ways in which social media platforms were useful for them as means of managing the overwhelming flow of information as the Euromaidan events gained in size, volume, and speed. The affordances of social networks to curate, aggregate, and prioritize information (Boulianne 2015; Valenzuela 2013) proved to be useful for both internal communications inside Euromaidan groups and for external uses of those participants and supporters who consumed, produced, and shared information online.

One of the more experienced organizers within the Kyiv interview pool said both mobile communication and social media were useful in directing the multiple flows of information that coordinators inside the protest needed to convey, which was often difficult to do in a densely people-packed protest camp where, in her own words, "despite the huge stage and [. . .] broadcasting of stuff from there, there were tons of people who had no idea what was happening and would come up to tents or booths and ask 'What's happening? What's going on?'" Social media were also useful in coordinating and sorting through information that went out to different groups of people scattered around Kyiv, and, later, to the regions of Ukraine as well. The organizer in Kyiv, interviewed in December 2013, reflected:

> [During] the first days in Maidan, people learned very quickly, each day was so intense it seemed like ten days. The flow of information is humongous, I wake up in the morning after two-three hours of sleep and I have 26 missed calls, so we have to spread the work around, and Facebook proved to be a good way to make stuff available to many people at once, but also to have a controlled way of sharing information and contacts with a select group.

Another Kyiv-based respondent who helped manage a community that coordinated the needs of protest participants and the resources available to them said that, while they had a dedicated website with an interactive crowd map through which information could be submitted, social networks were still the major source of information for project administrators and moderators, and also served as an amplifying mechanism for the most urgent requests for help.

> Where do we get info from? The website is only the top of the iceberg, we might get hundreds of messages only through the web interface. The rest— the majority—comes through email or social media. Everything that ends up on the website (the map) is then reposted on Facebook (on our page) and then it is reposted by other people there—we ask our friends to repost, and at some point, we also hooked up with the aggregator pages, like [the] main Euromaidan one.

He also added that the wide reach of some of their need-based Facebook posts and the actual reaction of people who participated in the protest or were sympathetic toward the movement served as evidence of the network and its serendipitous connections being effective at affording access to a broader pool of users who might not have otherwise seen their messages.

> As a channel, as a media, Facebook worked great, and we have confirmation that the ads and calls for help we posted on Facebook, they were shared, they didn't just stay up there, they were read and people bought stuff and brought it where it was needed. You can't measure it, since we didn't track the history. . . . But there was definitely an effect.

A protester interviewed in Odesa said he had seen a fair amount of criticism from those who felt online efforts to direct information and resources were largely useless, but contended that for him "the internet and social media played a huge role for me and meant a lot" in terms of how informed and engaged he felt during the protests.

> I don't watch TV, all news I found out from Facebook mostly all of this time, so I don't know [. . .] it's obvious that it had a great impact, maybe from my place I'm blowing its importance out of proportion. For me this all unfolded through the prism of the internet and social networks. Even in places I felt a sense of guilt: oh, here I am clicking on buttons instead of making sandwiches somewhere there, on the ground.

In an autoethnographic participant observation report of his own engagement with Euromaidan and its information and communication context during the protests, Ukrainian media and politics scholar Volodymyr Kulyk writes that because of the overwhelming amount of news and a lack of time to look through everything, he found himself paying attention "only to those texts from foreign media that were reposted on Facebook by my friends or friends of friends whose recommendations promised quality or at least relevance" (Kulyk 2014, 181) and notes that he consumed local media and news in much the same way.

Among my interview participants, many reported that they used their Facebook and Twitter feeds in a similar fashion, unsatisfied with the overall quality of media coverage and trusting that their existing network and the new people and groups they were adding to it would supply them with a selection of news and information that would be at once reflective of the situation on the ground, relevant in terms of proffered opinions, and reliable. At the same time, many of those who consumed news this way said they still felt overwhelmed by the constant barrage of information, saying the "information field" influenced them "quite heavily emotionally" and created a "feeling of constant hyperawareness." One respondent in Kharkiv described it as a somewhat difficult experience, referring especially to the instances of brutality against protesters and the clashes that took place in Kyiv and other cities, which caused a sense of vicarious trauma:

> It's almost like PTSD in a way. We see awful stuff, both online and on the street, people attacked, firebombs, Molotovs . . . and then we see it all echoing around the [social] networks, and we can't stop watching. It becomes this nervous habit, almost, checking for new messages and refreshing feeds, to see if anything else has happened. And after a few months, it seems like you're desensitized, but seeing an image, a video or reading about someone hurt is still horrible.

As interview participants discussed the affordances of social networks to manage and aggregate information and connections for organizing and informing protest participants, as well as to curate their own news consumption patterns, there were also instances of using social media to create "shortcuts" between the private and public communications of protest participants. This intentional context collapse, echoing boyd's (2010) observation about the blurring of public and private in networked publics, occurred serendipitously when the circumstances required it, and protesters tended to bridge different forms of digital media when creating these previously nonexistent connections. Examples of such "shortcuts" afforded by social media included copying and posting information from text messages and message apps into public Facebook posts and tweets to make the private public. Occasions for such cross-context dissemination included seeking help or offering available resources, looking for missing persons, and issuing urgent warnings of riot police action. An example of the latter, offered by one interview participant, is an anonymized public Facebook post from February 18, 2014, that was shared by one of her Facebook friends. The post is essentially a word-for-word reproduction of someone else's text messages, copied and pasted by the Facebook user into a public posting. It is translated into English and reproduced below:

> [17:37:51] Dasha: BERKUT [riot police] IS LOADING INTO THE METRO AT DARNITSA!!!!!!!!
> [17:39:33] Dasha: Info from subway staff: Berkut is being brought to the depot en masse and then loaded onto trains to be taken to central stations to crack down on the people.

During the months of Euromaidan Facebook was used for a variety of purposes by activists: groups were created for specific events, such as Sunday rallies, or ongoing activities, providing information support and publishing previews for things like the Maidan University (a series of public lectures on various social and political topics). Special pages curated information from the protest camp and reported on the current needs of protesters (Kulyk 2014).

Another important subsection of activist social media, including individual pages and topical groups on Facebook, collected, archived, and shared various Euromaidan-related documents, evidence, programmatic statements and artworks, both verbal and audiovisual. These collections were perceived by protesters to be important markers of a political, civic, and cultural milestone that was Euromaidan, but reflecting on the archival work later, interview participants said they realized that this digitally generated and stored content not only had historical or cultural value but also came to serve as key evidence in investigations of the violence, crimes, and human rights violations that occurred during the protests.

Live, unedited video streams, discussed at length in chapter 5, proved to be one of the more compelling kinds of content made and shared in the Euromaidan protest, which led to them becoming significantly more mainstream in the eyes of Ukrainian internet users. Because of their multiple viewpoints, extreme mobility, and interaction with viewers via social networks, live casting journalists and citizen reporters were instrumental in providing timely updates and performing prompt fact-checking to debunk rumors and misinformation. Though interview participants on the ground confessed they were often too busy to watch the live streams when they actually went live, some noted that archived videos were still useful to rewatch later, to spot provocateurs in the crowd and discuss tactics for protecting the protest camp. Interviewees who were further away from the protest camp in Kyiv said they watched the live streams religiously, and protesters in other regions of Ukraine said they soon adopted the practice for broadcasting and documenting their own protest gatherings and police brutality. Later on in the protest, some activists even used drones with affixed video cameras to capture the size of the protest camp and show the scale of the human presence in the capital, which by that time was playing host to thousands of protesters who had traveled from other towns. Videos of the drone-enabled footage were recalled by several interviewees as an example of technological innovation and became another popular symbol of the protest, while also assisting in capturing accurate information about its size.

MISINFORMATION, BOTS, AND HACKING

The acceleration of information flows and networked nature of social media mean that news and useful information are not the only thing that travels fast. Especially in a crisis situation, such as a mass protest where people are already experiencing intense information-related stress, rumors and fakes spread just as easily. Respondents who were in Kyiv during the protest were especially dismissive of social media's ability to spread unverified and false information, with one Kyiv-based interviewee recalling the story of a volunteer medic who was shot by government forces during one of the more dangerous days of the protest (Sevilla 2014).

> Do you remember this story? It went viral, I think. This medic girl got shot in the throat and tweeted that she was dying before losing consciousness. Then someone posted a photo of her with a bloody neck, and the social media went wild. What's worse, mainstream media took the story and ran with it. And then it turned out she survived, so they had to publish retractions.

Interestingly, when asked why she tweeted as her "last word" instead of calling someone or sending a text, the volunteer medic reportedly said that she thought a public post would get out and reach her family faster, in case they were not looking at their phones (Sevilla 2014).

This story exemplifies the numerous instances of publishing unverified information or misstating the facts discussed by participants, who complained this sometimes resulted in wasted resources or time. Even worse, according to some interviewees, were some of the international media outlets who often borrowed "sensational" photos published by Euromaidan protesters and used them in their coverage, but "misunderstood the context" and often used social media posts and content without bothering to confirm the provenance of the images or information.

There were also instances of intentional manipulation and disinformation by rogue actors who were not part of the protest. As early as late November 2013, internet users reported concerted attempts by social media accounts to spread rumors and false information about the protest. Twitter accounts (with both male- and female-presenting profile images) tweeted that they were invited to Euromaidan and offered 100 hryvnias (about $12 at the time), but that they were instead choosing to "take my wife to the theatre" (Savanevsky 2013). Other Twitter accounts expressed skepticism about the protest, asking how much the protesters were being paid or claiming the protest was disbanded because of bad weather. These messages were replicated by dozens of different accounts posting to the #euromaidan hashtag—a clear sign of mass manipulation by bots or cyborg accounts.

On Facebook, manipulators chose a different tactic—skeptical opinions or posts containing disinformation would be seeded in the comments on popular posts by opinion leaders, aiming to capitalize on the attention already accumulated there (Savanevsky 2013). While overall the efficacy of such manipulation attempts was likely negligible, activists still suggested report-ing or blocking these accounts to stop the spread of false information. Other protest participants used technology and media skills to monitor information manipulation on social media, tracking the most popular tweets for every hour and attempting to divine whether these were published by protest sup-porters or by "trolls," "opponents of Euromaidan," or spammers (*Texty.org .ua* 2013).

Although bothersome overall, this propensity of social media to spread both facts and fakes led some participants to think more critically about their digital media literacy skills and to attempt to engage in verification and debunking practices on the very platforms which were spreading unveri-fied or blatantly fake information. These activities involved fact-checking suspicious information in the comments to Facebook posts or replies and mentions on Twitter; asking multiple individuals to confirm something someone had reported online as happening; asking for images or video from a reported location or event to support a claim; and networking with other social media users to find related or similar posts reporting the same incident. One Kharkiv-based activist joked that "people became very suspicious very quickly and learned to be cautious of everything," but said that despite an increase in digital media literacy practices, "false alarms and rumors" were still quite persistent on social media, and were often hard to lay to rest "once they got picked up by mainstream media."

A limited number of hacking attacks was also used by both the protest supporters and anti-protest actors during Euromaidan to influence the infor-mation ecosystem. On December 1, 2013, right after the brutal dispersal of protesters in the city center, a number of government websites, including the official website of the President of Ukraine and the website of the Interior Ministry, were taken down by anonymous DDoS[1] attacks and were unavail-able (*Radio Svoboda* 2013). Immediately after, some of the most popular independent media websites in Ukraine, such as Ukrainska Pravda, Dzerkalo Tyzhnya, and Livyy Bereh, were also targeted by DDoS attacks inhibiting their availability, and a few others were hacked and taken down (*Ukrainska Pravda* 2013). These attacks further limited the already diminished capacity of official or mainstream sources of information, and highlighted the role of distributed networks of information sharing, verification, and curation under-pinned by social media affordances.

CONTESTING MAINSTREAM MEDIA FRAMING

The popularity of social media in Ukraine grew during Euromaidan, trig-gered by the turbulent protest activity and led to a shift in information consumption patterns. During the period between the autumn of 2013 and the spring of 2014, the number of click-throughs from social media to Ukrainian news websites (many of them partisan or independent) rose to almost 2.5 million per day (Valenzuela et al. 2014). This signaled the decreasing ability of the authorities and government-friendly media owners to control the flow of information or impose their dominant narrative through traditional media.

However, a significant number of interview participants reported consuming some mainstream media content related to the Euromaidan protests and commented on the use of social media by protesters to contest and shape the Euromaidan news frames appearing on traditional media channels.

Generally, participants reported getting their news from a collection of sources, which included some traditional media, some citizen media outlets that emerged during Euromaidan, and social media communities created by activists to curate, aggregate, and disseminate Euromaidan-related content. Here is an example of a typical media consumption pattern from an activist in Kharkiv:

> Mostly it's online TV, like Hromadske, Spilne. There are actually a couple of websites that allow you to watch six [channels] at the time, so I've been watching that. Also, reading newspapers, [Ukrainska] Pravda, ZiK, and several other publications. I also follow, read Dozhd and Echo Moskvy, just to get the other perspective. And obviously Facebook and VKontakte. But you need to have like, nerves of steel, to read a lot of the stuff there.

Interview participants said they were concerned about not only mainstream Ukrainian media outlets but also international media, as a source of information about what was happening in Ukraine and in relation to the Euromaidan protests. They were also worried about how media owners and editors wanted their outlets to represent these events, that is, how ready they were to present an "independent, unbiased, inclusive" depiction of protest events, or even to "support the protesters rather than Yanukovych's government" through their news framing.

In view of this, several protesters said they tried to use social media to influence the mainstream media frames, including communicating directly with journalists of various media outlets on their social media accounts, reaching out to media outlets with opportunities for interviews about protest activity and the work their initiatives were doing within Euromaidan, producing press releases and making visual content such as photos and images available to the press online; staging and participating in social media flash mobs and "storms" to raise the profile of the protest in general and of specific protest claims, to gain media visibility.

Of those activists who used social media to engage with traditional media outlets, a few of the less experienced protesters remarked on the scale of effort and skill necessary to successfully relay the ideas behind the protest and to influence the frames the media imposed on Euromaidan events, often indulging in what interviewees scoffed at as "sensationalist coverage." One participant interviewed in Kyiv during the protest, who was a founding member of a Euromaidan-related logistics crowdsourcing initiative, confessed he had never had to deal with journalists directly before, but found it necessary to raise the profile of their project:

> One of the challenges was this public nature of the activism and being open to dealing with the outside, with other people working in other places, press, interviews, this was completely new and uncomfortable. I recently gave an interview to a German TV [channel] and made a complete fool of myself.

Euromaidan participants abroad also came together to crowdsource a community of semi-professional and professional English-speaking pundits to represent Ukrainians and the Euromaidan cause and offer succinct comments to U.S.-based and other foreign media. A protest participant interviewed in Washington, DC, said their larger protest network included a media relations wing:

> I was not part of that group, but there's a big media and public relations part of it, people were giving interviews to local media, going on places like Voice of America, CNN, things like that, spreading the message.

As evident from the participant responses, social media platforms were used widely in the protest networks to compensate for lack of accurate media coverage, as well as to establish rapport and connections with reporters in a bid to influence their framing of the protest events. Protesters also exploited the power of mediated copresence, engaging in their own framing of the events via testimonies and visual records of the protest action.

VISUAL FRAMING OF PROTESTS

Discussing the kinds of content and information that was the most popular on social media and was shared widely by Euromaidan protesters, interview participants in all locations were united in suggesting that visual content, including images, photos, art, video, and animated materials were the most powerful, both in terms of reach and in terms of the potential emotional effect. Scholars have noted the power of images to "place" those viewing them in specific viewing positions and convince them to view events or subjects in a certain way (Lister and Wells 2001) and suggested the potential of certain "persistent images" to contest or even reframe the dominant media narratives (Andén-Papadopoulos 2008).

Though art and images were, of course, very much present in the protest camp in Kyiv's Independence Square and other locations, it was on social media that activists were able to express their creativity, solicit ideas for the protest's visual language, and create memorable visuals, many of which came to be associated with the protest itself. Several of the activists who had worked in or near the protest square in Kyiv remembered that a good share of the printed art and images hung around the camp came from various social media communities—and just as many were created at the physical protest site and then went to become viral on social networks, creating a kind of never-ending online-offline circuit of information dissemination.

Several communities were created by activists on Facebook to create and curate evocative protest-themed art and slogans: СтрайкПлакат (StrikePoster) brought together graphic artists who created and shared free Euromaidan posters aimed at keeping protesters motivated, with one respondent recalling that he and his fellow protesters regularly printed out posters from the community to put up in the city "as a kind of paper graffiti."

Another online initiative, which brought together participants of all kinds, including designers, advertising managers, and other creative professionals, was called "I Am a Drop in the Ocean" (Я—крапля в Океані), inspired by the idea that everyone's small contribution ("a drop") counted toward the achievement of a common goal. The group created its own visual language, using the image of a water drop and the title of the community and made available poster templates where anyone could add their own personal expressions and meanings of what it felt like to be "part of a huge community of like-minded people." The group also designed complete posters, videos, and put together a visually evocative website with stories about Euromaidan and its participants.

Some interviewees said images were an easy way to express your identification with a cause. One interviewee in Washington, DC, recalled that during the many days of mourning the increasing number of those who died during the government-sanctioned violence toward the end of Euromaidan, countless Facebook and Twitter users changed their avatars on social networks—a practice common for online awareness campaigns (as seen in Vie 2014)—to black squares crossed with a ribbon in Ukrainian flag colors, yellow and blue:

> Suddenly everyone's profile pic looked the same and, overall, it made quite a powerful impression—that of a country, a people in mourning.

In an account of the interactions between traditional media and new media during the first months of the Syrian uprising, Trombetta found that activists used social media as "the press-office for the protests, providing daily bulletins of the regime's victims and violations" (Trombetta 2012, 7) and using images and videos to great effect. Graphics, visual explainers, and summaries were a similarly popular format for sharing information among Euromaidan communities and making it easily identifiable and memorable, according to one interviewee who worked on an initiative coordinating logistics and resources for the protest in Kyiv.

> We came up with good formats—graphic formats like digests which are images with lists of needs, they are shared quite well and attract attention. Then we do offline work, so we print these graphics out and stick them up in key places of the protest [camp], so people can find us online or call us and ask, and bring their needs, information, or resources to us in this way as well.

Reflecting on the power of amateur photography, Sjøvaag suggests that images possess "affective and evidentiary force" (Sjøvaag 2011, 84) as carriers of information and can become focal points for political debate and public reaction, including public outrage. A participant in Washington, DC, who was involved in fundraising activity said evocative images were helpful in attracting attention to their cause (collecting funds for medical supplies for one of the protest's volunteer medical facilities) and creating the right emotional message for potential donors:

> Images and pictures work wonders for increasing sharing and driving traffic on social media. And there were so many amazing photos coming out of Euromaidan. We used them a lot.

Euromaidan protesters in my interviews were clearly cognizant of the affordances of social media such as scalability, persistence, and visibility and their role in offering alternatives to mainstream media frames. Protesters used these affordances to fill in the gaps in traditional media coverage of the protest, availing of the opportunities for live coverage of events, using powerful imagery, and sharing opinions that contributed to creating an accessible space for political and civic debate.

SHAPING PROTEST FRAMES AND NARRATIVES

Considering the potential for social media to disrupt the media agenda and framing monopoly of political elites (Christensen 2009), recent Euromaidan research using large-scale analysis of social network data and Ukrainian and Russian mainstream media content during the protest found some cross-directional information flows of frames, narratives, and viral memes between the media coverage of protest events and their discussion on Twitter (Karamshuk et al. 2016). Some of the persistent politically charged "buzzwords" emerged within mainstream media discourse and were later picked up by Twitter users, pointing to circumstantial evidence of propaganda and information manipulation. However, in other cases, social media denizens were able to create their own frames and viral terms tied to key moments in the protest and push them out to the mainstream media agenda.

Though Facebook, Twitter, and other networks allow protesters to organize and contest event and news frames, Milan (2015) argues that the downside of social media in the context of protest action is their tendency to listen to and echo the voices of like-minded people, discouraging critical engagement or healthy debate. While several respondents mentioned talking with people they knew in their social network circles who did not support the protests and trying to convince them and give them the facts, only one respondent said she regularly discussed these issues with people on social networks and made systematic efforts to raise these people's awareness of the political, social, and human rights contexts in Ukraine and to try to provide a convincing narrative about "the reasons for the protests and the facts about the situation in Ukraine."

From my interviews with protest participants, three main protest-related frames emerged, often supplemented by personal stories or community narratives: that of the *self-organized or grassroots* nature of the protest, that of the shift from a *single-issue protest* to a *multiple-issue* one with a broad spectrum of claims, and that of the *protest that the internet made possible*. Some of these frames that participants said they observed on social media, though dominant in a number of discussions, were also contested by some of the interviewees, who recognized their existence but argued they were not entirely reflective of their perception and experience as Euromaidan participants. Most of the differences in framing lay along the lines of disparity between experienced and "newbie" protesters, and between people who had been physically located at the site of the protest in Kyiv and those who had participated from elsewhere.

When interview participants talked about the *self-organized or grassroots protest* frame of social media protest activity, they usually referred to social media discussions and posts containing terms such as "citizen," "decentralized," "from the ground up," "self-organized," "public," "open-source," "nonpolitical," and "do-it-yourself." In terms of discourses, the absence of "political party leadership," no affiliation "with any specific political party," "horizontal organizing structures," and "ad-hoc" strategic and tactical decisions made by "loose communities of protesters" emerged as the main discursive markers of the self-organized protest frame. These discursive markers triangulate with Karamshuk et al.'s finding in their social media data analysis of Euromaidan framed as a "leaderless protest" (2016). With regard to the specific affordances of social media platforms which helped perpetuate this frame, participants talked about the "public nature of social media," the "networked" nature of relationships on Facebook and Twitter, the power to "bypass mainstream media and mainstream politics," the "ubiquitous nature" of digital devices and the preexisting "habit of using the internet to organize our own lives."

The *self-organized/grassroots protest* frame was the least contested one throughout the interviews: multiple participants, including seasoned and "new" activists, offered their own stories of self-organization or observations of such self-organization occurring both online and offline. The more experienced protest participants leaned toward a greater role of preexisting civil society networks and protest experience in affording Euromaidan its grassroots nature, while the novices mostly believed that overall enthusiasm, a desire to "join the action," coupled with the viral potential of social media and personal strong-ties and weak-ties connections on social networks were key for the genuinely grassroots mobilization, organizing, planning, and action within Euromaidan.

When interview participants talked about the framing of Euromaidan as shifting from a *single-issue protest* to a *multiple-issue* one they discussed social media protest activity using terms such as "revolution of dignity," "fed up," "disillusionment," fighting against "corrupt authorities," "not just pro-European," "human rights," "justice," and "reforms." Discourses mentioned within this frame were suggestive of a broad spectrum of claims and included, along with the initial "EU-directed movement," discussions of human rights and dignity as "lacking" in the country, the need to reform the law enforcement and judiciary "co-opted by the authorities," "economic reforms," as well as broader comments on the "equality" of claims brought by various participants to the protest, and the overall role of civil society in making decisions about the country's "future development and reforms." Social media were said to provide opportunities for these "multiple maidans," per Wilson (2016), within one protest movement. This was possible, interviewees said, through allowing for "a plurality of voices," affording "anyone a platform to speak their mind," "connecting people across political divides," and creating "multiple self-contained, but connected communities" whose protest claims and goals could overlap productively to achieve "greater synergy."

Interviewees from all groups mainly supported the frame of a *single-issue protest* shifting to a *multiple-issue* one, but offered varying and sometimes competing narratives of how and when the shift had occurred. While some cited the first cases of violence in the protest square and their amplification by social media as the turning point in the programmatic development of the protest, others said the shift came later, as the protest gained a more solid foundation through the crystallization of key protest communities and physical, digital, and communicative infrastructure. Still others credited the lack of a coherent agenda, clear leadership, and defined political aims after Euromaidan "outgrew" its initial grievance with the EU Association Agreement failure with enabling the "multifaceted," all-encompassing nature of the protest movement and affording it the opportunity to be "about many things at once."

When framing Euromaidan as the *protest that the internet made possible*, participants discussed the prominent role of digital technology in general and social media in particular using terms such as "real-time information," "borderless communication," "instant access," "going viral," "hashtag activism," "Facebook mobilization," "live-tweeted protest," "live-streamed protest," "digital citizen" journalism, and "constantly connected." The discourses revolving around internet affording expressions of dissent around Euromaidan included mentions of "higher internet penetration" in Ukraine, the "ubiquitousness" and "user-generated" nature of social media, the pre-existing "transborder" and "transcultural" connections between Ukrainians in the country and abroad that afforded "a broader reach" to protest claims, and the availability of free and open digital tools for "mobilization, building civic structures, disseminating messages" and "creating alternative spaces for debate." Participants who advocated this frame drew on differences with earlier protests in Ukraine and argued that it was digital technology and social media that made Euromaidan "grow so quickly and find such overwhelming support" among Ukrainians and even beyond Ukraine, diminishing the costs of joining the protest activity and providing "constant and convincing evidence that the protesters were in the right."

Less experienced protesters and those interviewees who engaged with Euromaidan protest activity from a distance were most enthusiastic about the *protest that the internet made possible* frame, citing many of the factors described above in their reasoning. At the same time, more experienced activists and participants who spent more time in the protest square held a more skeptical view of this frame for their protest experience. They said that, among other things, "existing civil society networks" and the general level of "citizens' disillusionment with the political elites" were equally mobilizing factors. They were adamant that in terms of organization and building protest communities and structures, personal connections and face-to-face communication had also served a purpose. Some of the criticism was directed at activities on Facebook that "did not necessarily help those on the ground" (Kulyk in his 2014 participant observation account notes that "all too often," the Facebook activity "served as an ersatz" of the action in the protest camp). Seasoned protesters also found fault with those who, instead of doing anything useful for the protest cause, whether online or offline, criticized various protest activities or decisions, disseminated sensational "facts" and gloomy predictions, and otherwise contributed to general anxiety. These "armchair analysts" and their behavior were said to be one of the less helpful elements in the discourse about the *protest that the internet made possible* frame.

CONCLUSION

Lyubashenko (in Valenzuela et al. 2014) posits that while social media was not in itself the cause of Euromaidan, it afforded the protest the potential to achieve scale and intensity. Despite the critiques of the latter of the three protest frames that emerged in the interviews, there was a general consensus that the internet and social media did contribute to a sense of what Gerbaudo (2016) calls "digital enthusiasm": a significant enough number of activists who did use social media to organize, coordinate, and otherwise mediate protest action produced a "hopeful narrative" that less experienced participants and protest observers were receptive to, which generated a process of "emotional contagion" (Gerbaudo 2016) or, in this case, framing and narrative contagion that enabled mass protest participation. While such moments of enthusiasm are rare and ephemeral, they are nonetheless important in the overall momentum of political and social change that the affordances of social media help make possible.

The scalability and persistence afforded by social media were instrumental for sharing protest-related news and information, but were also exploited by those seeking to manipulate public opinion about Euromaidan and inject disinformation and confusion into the hybrid information ecosystem. Protesters using social networks to share and follow protest updates found themselves also engaging in policing the information field to weed out manipulative content and ill-intentioned actors. Moreover, protest participants availed of the volatile and ephemeral, but highly scalable toolkit of social media vernacular, such as hashtags, live-tweeting, trending topics, and profile photos, to contest mainstream media framing of Euromaidan and formulate their own protest frames. Especially through the use of powerful visuals and witness reports, participants constructed a sense of augmented copresence afforded by online platforms to draw attention to the events of Euromaidan and to create stronger affective connections within the protest community.

Though the importance attributed to social media in the context of sharing information and shaping protest frames differed among protesters with varying levels of experience and proximity to the protest square, these different accounts also serve as evidence of the diversity of modes of participation afforded by social media. One of the protest frames formulated by the interviewees themselves was that of "a protest that the internet made possible." The deterministic nature of this frame is certainly questionable: would the protest have been possible without social media? Of course. But would it have happened in the same way? Probably not. These nuances of the overall dynamics of mediated event framing, narrative construction and information diffusion are illustrative of the overall argument of the book: that the affordances of social media introduced subtle, but distinct augmentations into the Euromaidan protest, making engagement and participation possible in a broader variety of ways and opening the protest up to a diverse selection of actors with all kinds of experience, all manner of political persuasions, and in all sorts of locations relative to the protest square.

Chapter 8

Russia

Protest in the Age of Networked Authoritarianism

The detailed examination of Ukraine's Euromaidan protests in the previous chapters underscores the complexity of augmented dissent. Affordances of digital media for protest are highly context-dependent, so the nature of governance in a given state, based on either democratic deliberation or authoritarian rule, is one of the factors shaping possibilities and limits of digitally mediated action. The actors—in this case, citizens and civil society activists—further shape these possibilities and limits due to their shared histories of dissent, social movement experience, and digital media skills. Finally, the technologies themselves shape the forms and structures of participation, guiding the opportunities and restrictions arising from the environment and the actors along the grooves of platform vernaculars, temporalities, and features.

In Ukraine, a weak and corrupt state operating under the guise of a declarative democracy was mostly concerned with co-opting the mainstream political and economic structures and gaining control over strategic traditional media assets. This left the digital media sphere free and opened up space for all sorts of experimental protest-related activity. Ukrainian citizens, though coming to the protest with various levels of relevant experience (or none at all), also brought different social media and internet use habits, stemming from their everyday life. In a protest environment, these habits took on new significance and transformed their relationships and connections, their information sharing routines and meaning-making practices, and their perceptions of what and how social media make visible. Specifically, the ephemeral connections and flexible temporalities of social media afforded protesters a multitude of ways to organize and manage the protest events, opening up protest participation to people with different skills and resources. The scalable and persistent nature of digitally mediated information not only provided a variety of ways to capture public attention but also meant activists had to deal with highly adaptable misinformation attempts and volatile social media trends. Socially mediated visibility, while exposing protesters to potential hostile actors, also afforded Euromaidan participants diverse ways of witnessing the protest, resulting in a sense of augmented eventfulness and affording the creation of multiple visual and textual records of Euromaidan, and thus, a plurality of protest histories.

The developing Russian scenario for augmented dissent is interesting because, while the actors and the technologies seem broadly similar to the Ukrainian case, the context for expressions of discontent and online expression more generally in the country has been increasingly different. In this chapter, I examine how these conditions have shaped the affordances of digital media for dissent in Russia. The state, spooked by a wave of discontent from the Arab Spring and the "color revolutions" in a number of post-Soviet states, became even more concerned with controlling the digital public sphere after its importance was highlighted in the Russian 2011–2012 protest rallies and the Euromaidan protest in Ukraine in 2013–2014. This meant that by 2016, Russian activists found themselves operating within an increasingly restricted environment both online and offline. While this pressure imposed certain limitations on their digital media use, it also pushed them to be more creative in adapting the affordances of the internet and social media in such a way as to make resistance to state pressure and dissent possible. I argue that, though the Russian context is much more restrictive due to government surveillance, tighter regulations, and creeping co-optation of internet infrastructure, Russian activists were still able to augment their repertoires of contention through the use of digital media, which afford them a variety of alternative ways to make their work visible, engage the public, organize protest actions, manage their own and their supporters' security, and negotiate state pressure and sanctions.

RUSSIA'S EVOLVING INFORMATION CONTROLS

In the decade since 2011, it has become evident that the Russian state is perturbed with the potential of the free internet and seeks to cement control over the national online sphere and its users. It has made legislative, regulatory, and economic efforts to wrest control of the digital space away from dispersed private actors and to centralize internet governance, content regulation, and network infrastructure. Regulatory bodies such as Roskomnadzor, tasked by the state with oversight of the internet, media, and telecommunications, have taken on a more prominent role. Laws such as the data localization bill, the anti-extremist legislation package policing online speech, encrypted communications and user privacy, and the more recent internet sovereignty law (aimed at co-opting telecommunications infrastructure along with increased filtering of citizen communications) exemplify this push for control on the part of the state.

In the past several years, Russian authorities have routinely outlawed what had previously been ordinary online activity. A number of recent legislative acts contribute to the normalization of state censorship and surveillance in digital spaces, both for organizations such as media outlets and NGOs and for private citizens. These include the infamous bloggers' law that required popular bloggers with over 3,000 daily views to register with the state and disclose their personal information; the law creating a state-run list of "organizers of information distribution" and requiring social network websites, portals and similar sites to register and share certain data with the state; measures limiting anonymous use of public Wi-Fi networks and banning sales of prepaid SIM-cards to customers without state IDs.

Some of the most damaging surveillance-oriented legislation has been passed just in the past several years and includes the data localization law that came into force in 2016 and requires internet companies to store Russian users' data on servers located within Russia. Though some companies (e.g., Viber, Booking.com) have complied with the demands, others (such as Facebook and Twitter) have yet to move to do so, and face potential fines or blocking: the professional social network LinkedIn has already been blocked in Russia for failing to move Russian users' data to Russia (Lunden 2016). Another major recent surveillance tool—the so-called Yarovaya Law passed in the summer of 2016 and taking effect in 2018 (Luganskaya 2017)—is an "anti-extremism" package of amendments that includes anti-dissent measures such as increased sentences for the use of "extremist" language online, a push for internet companies to share encryption keys with the state and to decrypt user communications, and requirements to store user data (content) for six months and metadata for up to three years. Most recently, in July 2017, Russian lawmakers voted to ban anonymous use of messenger apps and services (*Meduza* 2017), further broadening the surveillance powers of Russian security services and law enforcement. The use of anonymizing VPN/proxy servers is also being treated as potentially illegal (Idrisova 2017), all in an attempt to gain greater control over online communications and critical expression and cement state power over every byte and pixel that passes through the Russian internet.

At the same time, the Kremlin has also displayed a growing preoccupation with mass protest. Article 31 of the Russian Constitution guarantees its citizens the "right to assemble peacefully," but the reality is quite different. A whole new wing of internal military forces, called Rosgvardia (The Russian National Guard), was created by a Presidential decree in April 2016 to police protest activity in public spaces (*TASS* 2016), and is subordinated directly to the Russian president. A string of recent legal amendments has almost completely outlawed impromptu expressions of public discontent. Protest rallies involving more than one person can only happen with an official blessing from local authorities, and organizers have to apply for permits in advance (Kohen 2019). Participation in unsanctioned rallies carries increasingly severe penalties: organizers and participants can face arrest, administrative, or criminal charges. Fines for unsanctioned protesting were raised in 2012, and criminal sanctions, including jail sentences, were introduced in 2014 (*The Moscow Times* 2019). Even single-person pickets, while technically allowed to take place without prior planning, are regulated by strict rules: for example, picketers are not allowed to stand closer than 50 meters apart (Smirnova 2019). No protest activity, group or individual, is allowed near presidential buildings, courts, prisons, and other key infrastructure facilities—and Russian lawmakers are considering further amendments to restrict the list of locations where protests can and cannot be held (*The Moscow Times* 2019). Despite these harsh penalties and limits, the number of citizens charged with participating in unsanctioned rallies has skyrocketed in 2017–2019 (Kartsev 2019).

Catching up with the activists, the state has exhibited awareness of the affordances of digital media for protest organizing and information sharing. Internet users sharing information about protest events or even retweeting someone else's post about an unsanctioned rally, have been charged with calls or incitement to "mass riots" and have faced fines, community labor or arrests (Shedov, Smirnova, and Glushkova 2019). At the same time, researchers from OVD-Info and HRC Memorial point out that disseminating information about "mass riots" and "unauthorized public events" online is essentially equated with event organization, leading to yet higher fines for those charged, or, in the case of multiple violations, up to five years in prison (Shedov, Smirnova, and Glushkova 2019). Increasingly, the authorities in Russia draw no distinction between online and offline activity related to protest or political activism: they see them as an equally real threat to national security (and their regime stability) and happily dish out punishments for both.

AUGMENTED DISSENT IN MODERN RUSSIA

In this atmosphere of pervasive pressure and curtailing of the freedom to protest in both digital and physical realms, the opportunities for augmented dissent for Russian activists have been shaped as much by state-imposed restrictions as by their own ingenuity and the capabilities of the platforms and technologies they use. Though they faced different challenges than the Euromaidan participants, they nonetheless exploited some of the same affordances of digital media to organize, share information, and build affective connections with the broader public.

In particular, the affordances of socially mediated visibility and scalability were used strategically by protest organizers and participants to circumvent government censorship and provide real-time updates on protest activity and to retain a visible and transparent presence for the public. While it made key protest actors vulnerable to state repressions, the visibility underpinned by social media also allowed activists to promote their security and digital literacy practices in a conspicuous manner, normalizing these in response to the highly securitized state approach to policing online spaces and protest in Russia. At the same time, the ephemerality afforded by encrypted social media communications allowed protest networks to have flexible organizational structures, to evade state surveillance and to preserve the invisibility of key parts of the *connective tissue* of the protest fabric. Finally, digital media use afforded Russian protesters additional agency as they could exercise sousveillance during protest rallies and outside of them by using social media and networked technologies to counter-monitor state officials, law enforcement, and other actors seeking to crush augmented dissent.

CASE STUDY: 2017 ANTI-CORRUPTION PROTESTS

The ethnographic data for this chapter was collected around the anti-corruption protests in Russia on March 26 and June 12, 2017, and focuses on publicly available content from key protest organizers. The 2017 protests, as well as the Voters' Boycott marches of January 2018 and the most recent protests for free access to municipal elections in Moscow, exemplify the newest wave of protest activity in Russia. These protests emerge not only in response to controversial actions on the part of the state, such as unfair elections but also due to mediated activism aimed at exposing government corruption or injustice. Yet public engagement in these protests was comparatively large, and online activity around them equally significant. The first anti-corruption protest on March 26, 2017, saw reports of between 36,000 and 88,000 people taking to the streets in ninety-seven different cities (*OVD-Info* 2017), with many of these rallies unsanctioned.

One of the driving factors behind the protest in March 2017 (and a second one in June 2017) was a short investigative documentary "Don't Call Him Dimon"[1] ("Он вам не Димон" in Russian). Released on YouTube in early March by opposition politician Alexey Navalny and the Anti-Corruption Foundation, the fifty-minute video detailed Russian Prime Minister Dmitry Medvedev's ties to secret luxury properties and caused a wave discontent that resulted in mass protests.

The Anti-Corruption Foundation or FBK (an acronym of its Russian-language title, Фонд Борьбы с Коррупцией) is an interesting case study in augmented dissent. My decision to study the digital-mediated practices of this particular group was informed by the central role that FBK and Navalny's supporters play in the Russian opposition and protest movement (Laruelle 2014; Gel'man 2015) as they bridge political and civic concerns (White 2015). I was especially interested in seeing how a non-technology-centric and a non-internet-freedom-centric activist community (such as FBK) engages with issues of digital surveillance, privacy, and security in the context of protest activity in Russia, and what their experience can tell us about the broader affordances of digital media for protest and activism as perceived by the Russian civil society and political activists.

Virtual ethnographic observation for this case study involved content posted around the 2017 protests on public opposition websites https://navalny .com/, the main website of opposition leader Alexey Navalny, and https:// fbk.info/, the website of the Anti-Corruption Foundation; public Twitter feeds and Telegram channels of FBK staff, activists, and consultants; and FBK- and Navalny-created online video programming on the public Navalny LIVE YouTube channel. Unstructured ethnographic observation was also conducted on a number of public social media accounts of the members of FBK, based on the list of FBK staff on their website.[2] The netnography sample also included the accounts of several other activists close to the organization and working with FBK on digital security matters.[3] Where possible and necessary, quotes and observations from particular accounts have been anonymized.

The extant data collected from these publicly available sources between August 2016 and August 2017 made visible both the perceptions of digital media by the activists and the protest-related practices afforded by networked technologies. The mediated protest practices adopted by the FBK community and their networks in the state-conditioned environment of surveillance and censorship demonstrate that Russian activists approached the affordances of digital media strategically, and deployed them selectively to mitigate security threats, limits on information diffusion and visibility issues.

STRATEGIC VISIBILITY AND SCALABILITY

The primary mission of the Anti-Corruption Foundation (FBK) is to investigate, expose, and fight "corruption among high-ranking Russian government officials" ("About Us" 2017). In addition to the NGO's core staff of about thirty people, founder and opposition leader Alexey Navalny, who is himself a lawyer, also operates an election campaign headquarters network, with a central Moscow office and regional outposts. This network stems out of his initial bid to run for Moscow mayor in 2013 (Oliphant 2013) but has grown as he fought to gain access to the presidential electoral race in 2018 and later establish his own political party, Future Russia. Throughout their investigative activity, campaigns, and protest efforts, FBK, the regional HQ network and the community that emerged around them have made extensive use of digital tools and social media, and have proven themselves to be savvy in harnessing the power of internet-enabled communications. Unlike digital rights activists such as RosKomSvoboda or the Pirate Party in Russia, FBK and its allies have never explicitly made it their mission to fight internet censorship or to raise awareness of the Kremlin's crackdown on free expression online and mass discontent. And yet, since 2017, the activities on FBK-affiliated online platforms have increasingly focused on protest-related activity, dealing with physical and digital surveillance, online censorship and its circumvention, and attacks on activists and protesters, both digital and physical.

Why were opposition activists suddenly publicly preoccupied with digital surveillance and security? And how did they deal with these concerns in the context of a growing protest agenda? I find that FBK activists came to accept state surveillance and crackdowns on dissent as routine and inevitable, but they also devised strategies to counter them. The affordances of socially mediated visibility and scalability allowed for heightened but more controlled presence that, coupled with their security practices, emerged as a mitigating mechanism in the face of pervasive state pressure and restrictions.

During key protest events, FBK activists and their allies made strategic choices about their public visibility in online spaces, while also working to make the protest action on the ground visible to the broader protest networks. This focus on *strategic* visibility here is intentional, as the tensions between private and public lives and spaces of Russian dissidents and citizens go back in history. Siegelbaum notes that in totalitarian regimes (of which the Soviet Union is an example), the state exerts "an all-embracing despotic interference in all manifestations of life" and that the Soviet period was characterized by "a balanced system of total surveillance" (Siegelbaum 2006, 2). To some extent, the advent of the internet has granted ordinary citizens, and Russian dissidents in particular, a greater measure of control over their private sphere and their public image, but the state has been quick to move in on the free territory. As the activists find their private spheres under threat of constant surveillance as much as their public work, they choose to exercise the control they do have online over what to reveal and to what effect. Such strategic visibility work often seeks to forestall state-sanctioned leaks or accusations of unscrupulous activity aimed at discrediting the dissenters. In this way, by taking back some control and being visible on their own terms, the activists' visibility practices served as a mechanism of resisting state pressure during protest events. The observation and analysis of public online activities of the FBK community and their allies before, during and after the 2017 protests revealed several kinds of visibility-related practices that took advantage of socially mediated visibility in different ways.

As a combined measure against both state censorship and state surveillance, FBK and other opposition activists actively used all available informal channels to remain visible and accessible during the protest, and to promote protest-related frames and claims. As they were basically barred from state-run federal media and exercised little control over state media narratives, they resorted to alternative channels such as the Telegram messenger, Facebook, VKontakte, and YouTube. They frequently posted and shared promos of their own investigative and protest-related content, often produced in-house and then broadcast on YouTube or teased on Twitter. They also actively used memes and viral content, exploiting the networked logic of spreadable media (Jenkins, Ford, and Green 2013). With Russian mainstream media, especially television channels, under complete state control, protest organizers felt it necessary to create their own platforms and channels, attempting to remain visible in the public eye and to operate outside mainstream media logics and agendas. It is worth noting that the authorities have attempted to shutter these alternative visibility channels: after the Medvedev documentary became a viral sensation, Russian billionaire Alisher Usmanov, who featured in the investigation, sued Alexey Navalny for libel and demanded that the YouTube video be removed from the internet (Borzenko and Dmitriev 2017). Despite the threat of fines and possible further court proceedings for noncompliance, FBK refused to take down the investigation, YouTube has not taken down the video either, and it is still available on the website today.

As with Ukraine's Euromaidan protests, online video live streams and real-time content distribution were crucial during the 2017 protests in Russia. Unedited live footage of multiple rallies was supplemented with live casting of interviews or daily news briefs, YouTube-powered online real-time shows, and updates on court hearings provided as live text blogs. By making street protests in Moscow and multiple Russian cities visible, and supplying unedited content delivered to the viewers or readers in real-time mode increased public trust, allowing citizens to see the levels of participation and the instances of police brutality with their own eyes. Again, using social media live streams allowed protesters to not only bypass the deafening lack of protest coverage in state-controlled mainstream media but also gave them the opportunity to control the narrative. For instance, the large-scale anti-corruption protests on March 26, 2017, had FBK delivering syndicated live streams from protesters on the ground at rallies around Russia, showing both the scale and the breadth of the rallies, as well as documenting detentions, beatings, and arrests. The main protest live stream, run by FBK, was active for over ten hours on March 26, 2017, and attracted over 170,000 simultaneous views, with almost four million people viewing the recorded stream after it was over. These numbers are significant even when compared to Russian mainstream media and support the argument that grassroots, social media-based channels that aggregate protest video streams and narratives from numerous locations and can scale viewership and attention quickly through easy sharing can be a viable countermeasure to censorship, become a source of protest visibility and help consolidate the feeling of togetherness and unity.

Social media and live streaming augmented protest visibility in constructive ways, while also shaping participants' understanding of what it means to be copresent and to bear witness together. First, they made visible the huge efforts undertaken to mobilize, organize, and coordinate the protest, as well as to mitigate the damage from the state crackdown. In Russia, the various protest locations joined the live stream set up by the organizers, tuning in one by one from the country's multiple time zones. Once protesters were arrested, coordinators followed up with an offer of distributed legal help—also through social media. Post-protest, smaller pickets in support of those detained and court hearings featuring protest participants were often live streamed as well, to raise the profile of each individual participant, and to document and make public possible abuses of justice.

When crackdowns do happen (and in autocracies, they happen sooner rather than later), broadcasting visceral images of police violence and detentions live serves a two-pronged cause: the live visuals show an uncensored picture of how much the government and law enforcement care for the right to free expression their citizens claim, but they also serve as a record of these abuses for future human rights investigations and courts. The socially mediated records made by Russian protesters in 2017 and in other protests, featured both police brutality and police van selfies by relatively unharmed protesters, including foreign reporters. The latter might seem frivolous, but were important for documenting who was detained and where, so human rights activists could follow up on detentions the next day. Over 1,300 protesters were detained in Moscow on March 26, 2017, with dozens apprehended elsewhere in Russia, and making each one of them visible was of utmost importance. This visibility and transparency of backstage activity is important in environments where trust is thin on the ground, and where showing your work matters.

The live streams and photos shared on social media also amplified the numbers of bodies occupying city squares and main streets and made them visible across distances and time zones, creating a sense of community that does not rely on physical copresence alone. This is especially important for countries such as Russia, with vast land mass and citizens scattered across thousands of kilometers. Letting protesters in different cities and locations see each other made every person both a participant and a witness, affecting morale and giving citizens a more comprehensive understanding of the scale of the discontent.

Another way Russian activists used socially mediated visibility to build trust was by engaging in radical transparency with regards to their funding and operations. A significant proportion of their funds comes from donations and crowdfunding, so transparency is a necessary measure to remain accountable to their funders. As financial and operational surveillance of FBK work is widespread, the organization and its community also see being public and transparent about their funding, budgets, and other activity as a self-defense mechanism. They regularly publish financial reports on their expenses, explanations on how their campaigns were run, offering behind the scenes content, instructions on how to build and run campaigns or investigations, as well as photos and video reports from on-the-ground activity. Such radical transparency seeks not only to raise the level of trust among the community's supporters but also to neutralize ongoing and potential surveillance efforts by the state and security services aimed at extracting information that could be used to discredit the activists and their activity. Especially since a favored narrative of the Russian state with regard to any activism, campaigns or protests they perceive as antigovernment is to blame "foreign agents" and thus, suspicious funding and external support, it is especially important for FBK to make their operations visible and fully transparent.

CONSPICUOUS SECURITY PRACTICES

While socially mediated visibility afforded Russian activists access to alternative attention channels during protest events, as well as platforms for affective engagement and copresence and radical transparency, it was also instrumental in making visible the security and safety concerns involved in practicing activism and dissent. Increasingly, protesters and activists in Russia recognize pervasive state surveillance as a normal part of protest participation. A persistent theme in the online practices of FBK activists and their allies in 2016–2017 was making visible the growing number of surveillance-related threats and attacks on their community. The activists documented these attacks and threats meticulously in public social media posts, offering details and speculating about the reasons for the surveillance, the possible perpetrators, and their connections to the state. Examples of surveillance included physical monitoring such as individuals following Navalny campaign activists and even premeditated physical attacks. Navalny's website documented such an attack on the partner of FBK lawyer Lyubov Sobol, who was ambushed by an unknown assailant near their home and drugged in November 2016 (Navalny 2016). Documented examples of combined physical and digital surveillance included plain-clothes law enforcement officers filming participants of protest rallies in March, June, July, and August 2017 with digital cameras and later detaining them based on video evidence, as well as confiscating computers, live streaming and data-storing equipment from FBK and campaign headquarters in Moscow and around Russia.

Activists also documented multiple examples of networked surveillance, based around digital platforms and employing digital tools. These range from innocuous keyword-triggered Twitter bots (replying to tweets critiquing certain officials or mentioning the protest) to more serious instances such as the monitoring and closure of e-payment accounts that FBK and Navalny used to solicit donations and crowdfund investigations and the hacking of private email inboxes. Other examples included an attempt to hijack the Telegram accounts of several high-profile activists in April 2016, including Georgiy Alburov, head of investigations at FBK, and civic activist Oleg Kozlovsky. Subsequently, Kozlovsky reported that the social network and email accounts of multiple Russian journalists, activists, and human rights advocates had also been hacked, or an attempt to hack them had been uncovered (Shedov, Smirnova, and Glushkova 2019). This particular case was investigated by the victims and their allies in great detail and their public digging led them to conclude that the mobile provider MTS cooperated with Russian security services and attempted to remotely hack their accounts by tampering with Telegram's SMS login feature (Bonch-Osmolovskaya et al. 2018). The activists believed intruders wanted to gain access to their personal communications, including contact lists and other sensitive data. Such extensive documentation of instances of state surveillance and attacks provided the activists with an opportunity to reflect on how secure their communications and information are and to raise awareness of security issues among their supporters and protest participants more generally.

The cases above are stark examples of the environment of normalized surveillance practices exercised by the Russian state against those it sees as threats to its hegemony. However, the FBK team and allied opposition activists did not simply document and make visible the instances of being watched, recorded, or hacked. While they admitted state-perpetrated spying and pressure were broad and multipronged, they also adopted a more proactive position in addressing the attacks and threats by engaging in conspicuous security practices on their public online platforms. These practices were conspicuous because they emerged on platforms where previously discussion had centered only around issues of politics and state corruption, and become part of routine activist and protester discourse. They were also conspicuous because activists explicitly and overtly acknowledged the fact of the surveillance and attempted to mitigate or minimize security risks posed by state spying, while also demonstrating in detail how this could be achieved.

First, they used each suitable surveillance case to stage a public deconstruction of what happened and how one could avoid the same happening to them (as in the case with the attempted Telegram hacks). They also promoted digital literacy and security literacy in other ways, offering advice, guides, and explanations about key security tools such as the Tor browser, end-to-end encryption, and two-factor authentication. Leonid Volkov, Navalny's longtime ally and head of his election campaign, began hosting a regular online video segment on the Navalny LIVE YouTube channel called "The Cloud," where he specifically focused on issues of online privacy, anonymity, and security, often bringing on expert guests such as security experts and digital rights advocates. In Volkov's show segments, as well as on their Telegram channels, FBK staff and allies often offered advice on using specific anti-surveillance tools, such as VPNs and proxy services.

Other examples of conspicuous security practices employed by opposition activists included moving away from Russia-based online services and moving their content and activity to servers and platforms outside of Russia. After Navalny's official website was briefly blacklisted in Russia in 2015, and especially with the advent of the Russian data localization law, opposition activists focused on moving all possible resources to hosting providers outside of Russia, as well as making use of social media platforms that have not conceded to storing Russian users' data inside the country. Activists have taken the time to explain their decisions and discussed the use of platforms such as YouTube, Twitter, Facebook, and Telegram in the context of Russia's environment of political repressions and the tightening space for online free expression.

Finally, FBK and other opposition activists practiced conspicuous security by directly involving themselves in the development and creation of digital security and anti-surveillance tools and by supporting others who wished to lend their hand to improve the community's digital arsenal. This is in line with Lysenko and Desouza's observations about the co-evolutionary nature of state surveillance and counter-protest measures and activist digitally enabled tactics to overcome counterrevolutionary and restrictive measures in the former Soviet Union states (Lysenko and Desouza 2014). Such projects included the Red Button, an app developed by a team led by Alex Litreev, an IT expert and FBK consultant, in April 2017 (Litreev 2017). The app allowed protest and rally participants to react quickly in cases of police pressure and to let their friends and family know they have been detained. Another project was a Telegram-based VPN bot developed by Vladislav Zdolnikov, a longtime FBK contributor and IT-entrepreneur (TgVPN 2017). The bot, launched in May 2017, allowed for quick delivery of VPN services via Telegram messenger and offered an easy way to begin using the anti-surveillance technology that also allowed access to websites banned in Russia.

Broader protest networks have embraced the conspicuous security approach and have adapted security and literacy efforts to suit the needs of the protest movement. After the March 2017 anti-corruption protest, that saw scores of protesters arrested, FBK coordinators followed up with an offer of distributed legal help on Twitter: "Our lawyers are providing support to all illegally detained at the March 26 rally" (@fbkinfo, March 27, 2017). OVD-Info has been tracking detentions and arrests during protest rallies in Russia, offering regular online updates on the numbers and legal advice for detainees. To track new and ongoing cases of protest participants prosecuted for offline and online activity, activists have set up a Telegram messenger channel called "You will go to prison for a like" ("Ты Сядешь За Лайк [You Will Go to Prison for a Like]" 2017). Another Telegram channel, run by Apologia of Protest project, set up by lawyers from human rights organization Agora in 2018 ("Апология Протеста [Apologia of Protest]" 2018), also provides regular updates on court proceedings and sentences received by protest participants, with Agora lawyers offering their services to protesters pro-bono.

As an additional visibility-driven security measure, protesters have also engaged in counter-surveillance of law enforcement officers during protest rallies by posting regular updates to social media and providing photographic and video evidence of police presence, police surveillance efforts, and any altercations or arrests. Human rights activists have also educated citizens about their rights with regard to documenting police presence at protest events.

Such public management of state repression against dissent through explicit acknowledgment, visible analysis, and mitigation of protest-connected risks at scale makes these security practices conspicuous and underscores the key role of socially mediated visibility and scalability in shaping protest affordances.

EPHEMERALITY VERSUS VISIBILITY

In their strategic approach to socially mediated visibility in protest-related activity, Russian protesters and activists were also strategic about what remained invisible and hidden. This interpretation of the ephemerality afforded by social media as the other side of the coin was crucial, as it also afforded protest organizers and participants greater agency in the shrinking space of public discontent. FBK and other protest organizers used encrypted messengers such as Telegram to build and maintain coordinating networks, especially with regional headquarters that organized activist campaigns and local protest rallies. Telegram in particular allowed for strategic applications of visibility and ephemerality, as it allows for both one-to-one and many-to-many private communications (and self-destructing chats), and public groups and channels. Even in publicly accessible groups, local coordinators and administrators were often pseudonymous and therefore under less risk of pressure from the state and law enforcement. Combining the affordances of social media for visibility and ephemerality in this way gave protest organizers the ability to have both visible and ephemeral protest leadership, and to use both strategically for drawing attention to protest claims and for coordinating action online and offline.

In a sense, even the live streaming operation, while producing highly visible protest visuals, was ephemeral in nature. The syndicated live streams from the March and June 2017 protests relied on local video streams from regional protests. After the FBK head office was visited by law enforcement officers on March 26 under the pretense of a reported bomb threat, but in reality, seeking to shut down the live broadcast from the protest, FBK and its allies started to operate their own live streaming from more than one location, which proved to be helpful as police visits to FBK offices became a regular occurrence during later protests.

CONCLUSION

As evident from the Russian case study, the affordances of digital media for protest manifest in different ways when protesters face a hostile regime that is equally interested in exploiting these affordances or limiting the opportunities for civic and political action. As in the Ukrainian case, the socially mediated visibility and scalability of protest networks and messages afforded Russian activists possibilities of alternative channels for garnering public attention and communicating their claims. But beyond circumventing government censorship and making possible real-time mediated engagement and affective copresence, Russian protest organizers also found they were more vulnerable because of their visibility. They therefore relied on socially mediated visibility to make their operations more transparent to avoid accusations of malpractice and build civic trust. They also used their visible presence to engage in conspicuous security practices, at once letting the state know they were aware of being watched, and at the same time educating other protesters and supporters about basic security practices, both digital and physical, necessary for engaging in anti-government activism and dissent. They also publicly documented state surveillance and attacks, provided analysis of them and built or recommended tools that activists and protesters could use to protect themselves from state spying, all in an effort to mitigate increasing state pressure on those who contest its status quo.

Along with their visible work, protest organizers in Russia also found themselves relying heavily on the ephemerality afforded by social media for coordinating the loose networks that underpin their activist and protest organizing across the many Russian regions. The anonymity and pseudonymity of encrypted messaging platforms, as well as the portability of digital technologies used for live streams, website hosting and other protest work, became important to protesters in Russia for opening up spaces for the hidden work of dissent that necessarily occurs alongside the more visible elements of protest.

The challenge for activists organizing and joining protests in Russia today is that they are facing a state that feels actively threatened both by political opposition and the affordances of digital media that enable dissenting voices. Though to some extent those protesting in Russia are able to benefit from the more varied opportunities for dissent and more diverse modes of protest engagement, they also have to exploit the same affordances to confront state surveillance, hostile attacks, and growing restrictions on public assembly and free expression in the hybrid media space. This context shapes their perception of the potential for augmented protest, where the material and networked elements work in concert to create space for dissenting voices and opportunities for change. Increasingly, such a confrontational environment also leads to the gradual convergence of the spheres of citizens' digital rights and their rights to protest. Both the state and the activists now see the two as intrinsically linked, and this is reflected in the state's efforts to regulate and control both civic freedoms and digital infrastructure, and in the protesters' changing ideas about visibility, security, and individual agency.

Chapter 9

Conclusion

Beyond the Protest Square

How can we understand the affordances of digital media for protest through the prism of a hybrid conceptualization of society, media, and technology, where the online and offline aspects of protest activity augment each other in complex ways?

While far from being the only factor enabling dissent and empowering protest participants in modern societies, information and communication technologies matter as they have the potential to augment the opportunities for action and to allow citizens to engage in protest activity in a number of different ways, shaping the repertoires of contention. Increasingly integrated into our personal, social, and political lives, the internet and social media contribute to shifts in how citizens approach protest organizing and mobilization, how they participate, talk about and remember protests, as well as how they conceive of their personal and collective protest identities.

The research that powers this book had two main aims. The first aim was to examine the affordances of digital media for protest in Ukraine and to offer a detailed analysis of how the affordances framework may work in different ways, depending on the context, actors and technology use. The second, more ambitious aim was to use this analysis to develop the concept of augmented dissent as a useful way to explain how protest happens in the hybrid spaces where material and digital elements enmesh. Understanding how digital media augment modern protest activity, whether by affording new opportunities for participation or limiting action possibilities, is valuable as it informs how networked technologies can be designed, regulated, and critiqued when we think of them in the context of political contestation. Another valuable insight this book offers is that the same affordances of digital media can empower and restrict protesters in very different ways, as evident from applying the findings of Ukraine's Euromaidan analysis to more recent protests in

Russia. These differences depend on how aware the governing regime is of these affordances and how actively it attempts to police the networked space as part of a greater effort to restrict free expression and political pluralism.

The book's core argument is that protesters perceive digital media as affording them a qualitatively different experience of protest. When protest activity is augmented by the joining together of offline and online structures and mechanisms, it offers individuals a variety of modes of participation and makes the action accessible to a diverse range of actors. This variety and diversity, however, are modulated by the context in which protest participants choose to make use of the opportunities for action they perceive. Factors such as the absence or presence of strong democratic institutions or a mature civil society and experienced social movement organizations influence the possibility and scale of protest in general. Increasingly, we are also seeing a connection between these factors and the levels of internet freedom and everyday media use, as well as levels of state control, censorship, and surveillance in the digital realm. Combined, these factors result in a particular environment that influences how activists perceive the internet and social media, and how they are able to use them for protest. As we've seen in this book, the contexts in Ukraine and Russia differed significantly in this regard, so the opportunities and limitations of digital technologies and networks augmented protest activity and strategy in each country in a very different manner.

This book contributes to existing scholarly work proposing that the internet and social media sites offer multimodal communicative affordances that can supplement traditional methods of protest engagement and offer new spaces and strategies for information gathering, political debate, and participation (Vitak et al. 2011). My research also underscores the need to study both the mundane and the revolutionary uses and affordances of digital media for citizen engagement to better understand how particular technology features and participant identities merge with the political, cultural, and social environment of the protest in question to translate into affordances for protest participation.

The key protest-related affordances of social media—visibility, scalability and persistence, ephemerality and flexibility—were perceived by Ukrainian and Russian protesters and activists as allowing for different kinds of action, to reach distinct protest goals. Importantly, in Ukraine the state reacted to protest activity in mostly material terms, and attempts to quash discontent mainly boiled down to brute force and some mainstream media silencing. Because the internet and the digital media sphere remained mostly free, Ukrainian protesters were able to incorporate these into their protest activity as a natural element and to explore the opportunities offered by networked technologies in creative and expansive ways. In Russia, the authorities likewise cracked down on the "protest square" in material terms, through police pressure on rallies and mainstream media censorship. But beyond that, the Kremlin became aware of the affordances of digital media for protest and has been co-opting them or imposing limitations on the networked public sphere, modifying the possibilities for augmented dissent. Russian activists, in response, have had to adapt to these hybrid pressures, availing of the same affordances not only to pursue their protest goals but also to negotiate their security, promote digital literacy, and carve out a space for resistance despite the vulnerability of their visible efforts.

In both Ukraine and Russia, the structures of political and social opportunities become inextricably linked with how the state and the citizens conceive of and use networked media platforms. These hybrid imaginaries come to shape a structure of protest opportunities that is made up of both atoms and bits, interpenetrating, but always differently configured. These different possibilities of what a protest could look like hint that augmented dissent is a complex construct exactly because the protest square could be variously augmented, depending on who and how gets to access the networked technologies and to shape the capabilities for action they contain.

AUGMENTED DISSENT IN UKRAINE: EXPLORING THE POSSIBILITIES

The nature of augmented dissent in the Euromaidan protest in Ukraine in 2013–2014 was *exploratory*, *bridging*, and *expansive*. Digital media were largely perceived by protest participants as offering a range of possibilities for action and few limitations. Despite the fact that the Ukrainian authorities at the time wielded some mainstream media control and instigated repressive physical attacks against the protest on the ground, they were blithely ignorant of the affordances of digital media for protest. Their attempts to limit digital media use by protesters (as described in chapter 7) can best be summed up as "too little, too late." As a result, protesters' perceptions of action opportunities afforded by the internet and social media were shaped mostly by other contextual factors: the size and scale of the protest; the participants' own activism and protest experience; their digital media habits; and their location and distance from events in the protest square in Kyiv. Dealing with threats to bodies gathered in the square, but not to the technologies connecting them and other bodies located elsewhere, Euromaidan participants were able to negotiate a number of communicative and organizational challenges through the use of connected devices and social media.

First, Ukrainian protesters had the space to explore the various possibilities for protest participation that emerged at the nexus of actors and technologies coming together around Euromaidan. As they dealt with increasing physical pressure, the availability of a free internet and unfettered access to social media provided them with space to be creative, to experiment, and to discover a number of ways for using protest-related affordances. In another sense, Ukrainian protesters relied on the internet and social media to help them bridge physical, temporal, experiential, and existential distance both between each other and between themselves and the protest as a phenomenon in which they wanted to engage. The exploratory and bridging nature of augmented protest also led to it becoming expansive, growing to encompass a broader set of agendas and claims, and stretching beyond the protest square, past the city limits, and past the country borders.

Key affordances of digital media such as visibility, scalability, persistence, ephemerality, and flexibility allowed the protesters to augment their participation in Euromaidan, resulting in a number of distinct modes of augmented participation. These included participation as witnessing, participation as organizing and building networked communities, and participation as information sharing and frame management.

Participation in the form of augmented witnessing was underpinned by socially mediated visibility as a root affordance of digital media. The capability of social media to make events in the protest square highly visible and to create a sense of affective copresence transformed participants' experience of witnessing, whereby they were able to be part of the protest, to witness its events and to bear witness to others' testimonies, using a combination of physical and digital means. The experience of the event and its story/narrative enmeshed and became one, complicating the process of witnessing historic events by mixing offline and online components and extending them into each other. In this case, the personalized and distributed nature of the internet and social media, coupled with their real-time reporting capabilities, afforded participants both large-scale collective experiences of protest events, and the telling of "multiple protest histories" based on individual experiences. The more complex, hybrid process of witnessing also impacted how participants made meaning of the protest events, how they constructed post-protest memories, and how they dealt with the massive amount of visual and other records in the aftermath of the protest.

Digital media augmented mediated copresence in different ways for Euromaidan participants, depending on their proximity to the epicenter of the protest and their civic activity experience. However, across the board respondents noted that using digital media gave them a new understanding of "being present" and "being together" within the protest movement. To participants at the protest's physical core, social media afforded an expanded protest experience in which physical presence (and copresence) was augmented by mediated awareness of other people who were engaging with the protest elsewhere. To participants who were engaging remotely, social media afforded an experience mediated by live video streams, Facebook posts and tweets, enabling a sense of togetherness beyond physical copresence. For participants of all kinds, the internet and social media also provided a common visual and symbolic protest language of posters, photos, slogans, and hashtags, demonstrating how the concept of copresence can be rearticulated given that it might not necessarily be tied to physical proximity or geographical colocation.

Examining augmented protest participation in the form of organizing and network-building revealed flexibility and ephemerality as the central affordances for connective and collective action in Euromaidan. Euromaidan activists were able to leverage the hybridity of digital and material connections to create functioning protest networks, build trust and exploit social capital in the form of both strong and weak ties, and manage protest logistics.

Networked technologies allowed for some degree of grassroots horizontality in protest organization and often served as impromptu shortcuts for resolving key protest tasks, be it fundraising, resource distribution, or information sharing. Although the connections in the networks were often ephemeral, they allowed for the emergence of necessary connective tissue for communication, coordination, and tactical diffusion. Given the mix of experienced and novice participants connected by overlapping networks, Euromaidan became a fertile ground for experimentation and spontaneous communities of people taking on various tasks based not only on their activism experience but also their skills, knowledge, and availability more generally.

The augmented organizing efforts and networks of participation afforded a variety of possibilities for action for both communities and active individuals. Among other things, social media enabled Euromaidan participants to be "part-time revolutionaries," allowing for meaningful engagement within limited time or with limited resources and creating a broader network of participants who were feeling involved and useful despite having made only a partial commitment to the protest cause. What this book suggests is that partial was enough—that asynchronous protest activities that took place primarily in the online sphere were not only effective but incredibly powerful for individuals and communities alike. Especially for those engaging with the Euromaidan protest at a distance, digital media helped reduce the need for physical copresence and allowed citizens to be emotionally, organizationally, and meaningfully involved in the protest activity. Thus, the augmented protest networks of Euromaidan extended far beyond the protest square, expanding both the reach of the protest movement and the access to the engaged space of protest.

Participation in the form of curating and aggregating information about Euromaidan and managing protest frames hinged on the scalability and persistence afforded by social media. Protesters took advantage of these to share news and information about the protest within its networks and with external audiences. The propensity of social media for scalable and persistent discourse was also available to counter-protest actors (both within and outside Ukraine), and protesters had to thwart attempts to spread false and manipulative information, mitigate rumors and perform information verification in the quickly developing context of protest events to weed out fakes and hostile actors.

Milan (2015) suggests that while the life cycles of social media-enabled protests are typically very short and tend to disappear as quickly as they emerge, the visibility of such protest movements can gain traction through frequent repetition of messages and claims, both online and offline, often aided by additional exposure via mainstream media. As Tufekçi (2017) finds, social media can amplify protest movements as well as undermine their longevity, as they make some elements of protest building (e.g., quick mobilization) easier than others (e.g., sustainability and entrance into mainstream discourse). Gerbaudo (2016) argues that social media enable "moments of digital enthusiasm" through making public hopeful and inspiring narratives on community pages and platforms that in turn get promoted across the networks by less experienced protest participants and observers. Aware of the volatility and ephemerality of social media attention cycles, Ukrainian protesters relied on social media genres and forms such as hashtags, live-tweeting, trending topics, and branded profile photos to contest mainstream media framing of Euromaidan and formulate their own protest frames. They were able to build on a sense of affective copresence afforded by online platforms and used evocative images and striking witness reports to draw attention to the events of Euromaidan and to create stronger emotional connections within the protest community.

Protesters attributed different significance to social media in the context of sharing information and shaping protest frames depending on their prior experience and proximity to the protest square, but these differences of opinion underscore the diversity of modes of participation afforded by social media. One of the protest frames formulated by the interviewees themselves was that of "a protest that the internet made possible," but it existed alongside other protest frames, for example, the self-organized or grassroots protest frame, and the evolving multiple-issue protest frame, propagated through the protest's hybrid media system.

Thus, the affordances of social media introduced subtle, but distinct augmentations into the practices of mediated event framing, narrative construction and information diffusion, enabling different modalities of participation, and opening the protest up to a diverse selection of actors with a spectrum of experience, all manner of political persuasions, and variously removed from the protest square.

AUGMENTED DISSENT IN RUSSIA: CONFRONTING THE STATE

For the Russian anti-corruption protesters in 2017, using networked technologies gained a different meaning. Less a matter of creativity and free exploration, they perceived augmented dissent as *strategic, contested,* and *survival-oriented.* By then, the Russian authorities had cottoned on to the action opportunities the internet offered to citizens in an otherwise co-opted information environment, and were seeking to limit them. The affordances of digital media for protest themselves became a space of contestation, where protest action potentialities clashed with draconian regulations and overt abuse of power. Coupled with physical crackdowns on street rallies and activist organizing structures, the hybrid pressure from the state was a key factor that shaped protesters' perceptions of possibilities for action that the internet and social media held and of how these were limited in the context of networked authoritarianism in Russia. Other factors, such as the geographical scale of the protest network, the protesters' digital and protest literacy, also played a role. But it was the double threat to bodies in the protest square and to the technologies connecting bodies across time, space, and circumstance that resulted in the peculiar way Russian opposition activists negotiated and interpreted the affordances of digital media for protest.

Having seen the gradual restriction of free expression and dissent in online spaces following earlier waves of protest within and outside Russia, activist and protest groups in 2017 understood that digital media were a contested environment that, while offering comparatively more freedom for protest activity, required clever strategies on the part of opposition activists, digital rights advocates and protest participants to carve out a space for discontent. Efforts to preserve digital freedom and digital rights, therefore, became a small but significant part of the protest agenda. In this contested space, activists also found they had to be strategic in their choices with regards to digital media affordances if they wanted to avoid state surveillance and compete with state-controlled mainstream media. Beyond circumventing state limitations, strategic thinking about how to best use the limited action opportunities to reach more people, build trust and generate public debate about contentious issues was a necessity. Finally, the affordances of digital media were also seen as tools of survival, as protesters explored their opportunities for self-defense, operational security, and privacy of communications.

In these challenging circumstances, the same affordances of digital media that were central to Ukrainian protest activity—visibility, scalability, persistence, ephemerality, and flexibility—augmented protest participation in Russia in vastly different ways. Locked in a constant battle against restrictions and obstacles to discontent online and offline, Russian activists found ways to use the alternative capabilities of networked technologies to make their activity visible and credible, engage the public, organize protest events, manage their security needs, and negotiate increasing state repressions and abuse.

Socially mediated visibility and scalability afforded protest organizers opportunities to circumvent government censorship and provide real-time updates from protest events. Activists also made strategic decisions about creating and maintaining a visible and transparent profile for the protest movement, instrumental for building public credibility. While it meant that visible protest leaders were vulnerable to state attacks, the visibility under-pinned by social media also allowed activists to raise awareness of security and digital literacy issues as crucial to the survival of the protest. Digital threats and security incidents were dissected in public and security was practiced in a conspicuous manner, as a reaction to the highly securitized government approach to policing both protests and digital media. Along with digital literacy, activists in Russia also organized to provide legal assistance and advice to participants of hybrid protests, educating citizens about relevant regulations and basic security measures, both digital and physical, necessary for engaging in anti-government activism and dissent.

The visibility afforded by social media also meant protesters were not the only visible actors in the game. In the face of pervasive government surveil-lance, digital media afforded Russian protesters additional agency by allow-ing them opportunities for counter-surveillance during protest events and outside of them. Activists regularly used social media and networked tech-nologies to monitor the actions of state officials, police, military personnel, and other actors seeking to curtail their augmented protest efforts.

Along with highly visible and conspicuous activity, the ephemerality afforded by encrypted messaging platforms and other secure communica-tion tools allowed for the flexibility and invisibility of protest networks. Relying on this hidden connective tissue underpinned by the anonymity and pseudonymity of encrypted messaging, protesters were able to evade state surveillance to some extent. Ephemerality in the form of portability of digital technologies used for live streams, website hosting, and other protest logistics, was also important to protesters in Russia for opening up spaces for the hidden work of dissent that necessarily occurs alongside the more visible elements of protest.

Organizers and participants of the Russian 2017 protests found their oppor-tunities for resistance heavily modified by the growing state pressure on both the space for protest and the digital public sphere. Along with a variety of opportunities for dissent and more diverse modes of protest engagement for citizens, digital media also afforded the authorities opportunities for surveil-lance, misinformation, and persecution. This meant protesters had to resort to the same affordances of digital media they used for protest to confront state spying, as well as threats to bodies coming together and to the free use of communication technologies. As in the Ukrainian case, the environment in which augmented protest happened influenced how it was augmented and how atoms and bits could coalesce to create or defend space for the possibility of discontent, resistance, and change.

THEORISING AUGMENTED DISSENT

How do we understand augmented dissent? What are the factors that shape how bodies and technologies can be configured in the space of protest? What emerges from the research in this book is that the affordances of a free networked public sphere can shape a very different kind of augmented protest compared to the affordances of an internet that is under siege.

In both Ukraine and Russia, digital media provided citizens with opportunities to renegotiate what it meant to be a protest participant when one was afforded new, meaningful ways to be copresent, to bear witness, and to connect with others within the protest movement. In Ukraine, this meant building digital shortcuts in serendipitous ways, exploiting the effervescence of social media streams to promote protest claims, and making multiple, but legitimate protest histories. In Russia, it meant using visibility strategically to promote protest claims, build public trust, and educate protesters about digital self-defense, but also relying on ephemerality and invisibility to protect protest networks from state surveillance and crackdowns. In both cases, these affordances emerged from the melding of the online and offline realities into one, augmented reality of dissent.

While digital technology and social media do not by themselves cause political or even revolutionary change, they do provide new opportunities (Howard 2010) and impose new constraints on actors in society (Deibert 2012), as they afford individuals and communities the power to renegotiate local or national contexts in both political and social activity. Because of this importance of context, our understanding of the role of digital media benefits from close analysis of how technology is entangled in protest events in specific countries, like the ones examined in this book.

Using the internet and social media for mobilization and political protest, citizens connect their daily self-representation online with an understanding of their roles as individuals in more complex political systems, and of how those roles are mediated by networked spaces. How citizens perceive the affordances and limitations of digital media, therefore, is a useful measure of political and social "change for the individual" (Oates 2013), and augmented dissent can be seen as an emerging form of democratic engagement in a not only more independent but also more contested space of interaction between individuals, places, and networked technologies.

Scholarly research on the role of digital media in activism and protest has reached a stage where studying digital technologies as an autonomous sphere is no longer possible. The challenge of studying the affordances of the internet and social media for dissent, then, is to scrutinize how cultural values, user practices, political and civic contexts, and technological infrastructures are "constantly and intricately entangled" (van Dijck and Poell 2015), transforming civic action, political engagement, and protest practices. The dialogic nature of the internet and the technologies it underpins, its changing notions of time and place, its affordances for erasing or replicating modes of inequalities or for creating the spaces for oppositional discourse must be examined in the context of how the digital extends into, augments and is augmented by the physical or material, and not regarded as a separate, "virtual" plane of operation. Such a comprehensive approach allows to better understand what new types of participation and discourse are possible once the internet is in play, and how citizens and communities living in this augmented reality can engage in dissent.

As we move toward a world in which the internet and digital technologies increasingly permeate every layer of existence, be it political, social, or cultural, we must shift away from a duality of the "virtual" and the "real," or the artificial divide between online and offline activism and protest action, since most active citizens, and, increasingly, political regimes are always-already both. The internet as a new layer or flavor of reality redefines relations between humans and reconfigures relations of technology to culture and politics, necessarily demanding a new discourse about the effects of technology on political change and social transformations.

Although we may be tempted to consider digital media as enabling new, digital, noncorporeal forms and means of political and civic engagement, this book demonstrates that human bodies remain present in these interactions and continue to influence the discourse and the potential for political and civic transformations, as they are augmented and limited by digital platforms and connections. In Ukraine's Euromaidan protest, physical distance and protest experience were mitigated by digitally enabled shortcuts and new means of witnessing and engagement, resulting in augmented organizing, augmented information flows, augmented copresence, and augmented protest frames, never only digital or physical, but always, to different degrees, both. In the Russian anti-corruption protests, state restrictions and pressure on both bodies on the streets and digital networks were mitigated by strategic uses of visibility and ephemerality, and the emergence of conspicuous security practices and digital literacy efforts as a necessary part of augmented protest activity.

Theorizing about the role of digital media in political change, social movements, and dissent gains more depth if we choose to understand these technologies as embedded in the fabric of society and everyday life, and their use and perception as a part of our personal and collective identities. This book argues for a comprehensive theory of *augmented dissent* that considers how the digital and the physical aspects augment each other and work in concert; how the augmentation is shaped by the affordances of social media and by the environment in which they emerge; and how citizens (and states) perceive this augmentation. Understanding modern protest as *augmented* is a useful approach to understanding the impact of emerging media technologies on the rapidly shifting scene of political and social transformations. The social movements and protests in modern societies increasingly exist both online and offline, negotiating the entanglement of the physical and the digital, the ties between atoms and bits, and they should be studied as such.

FROM AUGMENTED DISSENT TO AUGMENTED CITIZENSHIP

While this book was being written, the environments shaping the possibilities for augmented dissent in Ukraine and Russia have inevitably shifted and changed. The countries now find themselves embroiled in a conflict, and this has meant that spaces for dissent and online freedoms in both societies are under threat. In Ukraine, concerns about cyberwarfare and disinformation have resulted in tighter regulation of the internet, the blocking of popular Russian social networks and websites, and a general sense of pessimism about the power of social media to spread information and capture attention. At the same time, the post-Euromaidan civic regeneration, bolstered by the needs of the conflict in Eastern Ukraine and occupied Crimea, has preserved a sense of hope about the possibilities for action that digital media offer to volunteer organizations, activist networks, and protest movements. In Russia, the state has further consolidated control over the digital sphere, introducing more draconian legislation curtailing free expression online and public assembly and, more recently, making moves to take over digital communications infrastructure in the country justified by an "internet sovereignty" doctrine. For activists, this has meant that many of the action possibilities afforded to them by digital media, even beyond explicit protest activity, are being delegitimized, making the tension between the visibility of their work and the ephemerality of their networks even greater.

These confrontations and tensions between how states seek to police and regulate expression and civic action in hybrid spaces and how citizens seek to practice their rights to free speech and discontent in the same environments mean that we are going beyond the protest square in more than one sense. The interlinked digital and physical realities of protest are extending into the broader reality of citizenship and human rights, which we can also conceptualize as augmented. Both the state and the citizens increasingly understand the spheres of citizens' digital rights and their right to protest and participate in politics as convergent and linked. This is reflected in the states' efforts to regulate and control both civic freedoms and digital infrastructure, often within the same legislative acts, and in the protesters' changing ideas about free expression, security, privacy, and individual agency.

In Russia, for instance, both internet freedom and the right to protest are now advocated as human rights: the civic groups that monitor internet censorship, offer legal advice to protesters, and support those charged with internet-related crimes are often the same people. Almost every piece of legislation adopted in the country in recent years that deals with regulating speech, public assembly or political activity also contains provisions for regulating their digital equivalents. Ukrainian lawmakers are definitely taking notes, judging by the growing number of internet-related legislative initiatives passing through Parliament, as free speech advocates and civic activists push back on these attempts, while sharing concerns about cybersecurity and misinformation.

There is an intrinsic connection between the freedom of the internet and freedom to protest and express alternative opinions. In fact, they are becoming one and the same. We are seeing a gradual transformation of digital rights and civil rights into a right to augmented dissent, and from that, to augmented citizenship. It is not simply a matter of how the augmented reality affords or limits our right to protest—it is now a matter of how we understand our identities, rights, and obligations as augmented citizens and how the states confront our interpretations with their own ideas about individual privacy, personal data, and political agency.

Beyond insights about affordances of the internet and social media for augmented dissent, the research in this book contributes to the development of the concept of digital citizenship, articulated by Isin and Ruppert (2015) as the ability of individuals to participate in society online and to "make rights claims about how their digital lives are configured, regulated and organised" (Isin and Ruppert 2015, 5). As Wahl-Jorgensen, Bennett, and Taylor assert (2017, 742), digital citizenship is essentially an expression of the power relations between states, citizens, and the networked platforms mediating these relations. Experiences of augmented dissent analyzed in this book serve as evidence that affordances of digital media for protest and the activity they circumscribe are clearly linked not only to democratic action but also to human rights issues such as freedom of expression and freedom of assembly. The centrality of these affordances for performing dissent also makes them central to the performance of augmented citizenship and to the shaping of power relations between states and their citizens writ large.

The implications of this shift are not just relevant for faltering democratic states such as Ukraine or authoritarian regimes such as Russia. As the world's democracies feel increasingly threatened by state and non-state actors with hostile intentions, be it terrorist groups, trigger-happy dictators or anonymous hackers and trolls, we see more and more attempts to justify granting states (or private corporations) greater control over digital networks, private communications, and personal data. When these decisions are made, the repercussions extend into the interplay of power between individuals and states in societies. Digital rights are human rights, so choices about how to regulate freedoms and expression online inevitably impact the opportunities and limits for augmented dissent. More than that, they impact how citizen agency and individual liberty are encouraged—or constrained—in a world where atoms and bits are intricately entangled.

Notes

CHAPTER 2

1. After the Bolotnaya square, the key protest location in Moscow in 2011–2012.

2. The blacklist of banned websites, or the "Unified Register of Domain Names, Internet Website Page Locators, and Network Addresses that Allow to Identify Internet Websites Containing Information Prohibited for Distribution in the Russian Federation," is run by Roskomnadzor, Russia's state internet watchdog. The blacklist database is accessible via a search form on https://eais.rkn.gov.ru/, and Russian internet rights organization RosKomSvoboda maintains a mirror database at https://reestr.rublacklist.net/.

3. Disclaimer: The author was a contributor to Freedom House's *Freedom on the Net* report in 2012–2016.

CHAPTER 3

1. The Russian spelling would usually transliterate as "Kharkov," which is still the more common English spelling. Here it is transliterated from the Ukrainian. The same applies to Odesa (the Ukrainian spelling used in this book) versus Odessa (the more common Russian spelling often used in English).

CHAPTER 4

1. The Holodomor was a manmade famine orchestrated by the Soviet authorities in the Ukrainian Soviet Socialist Republic in 1932 and 1933 that killed an estimated 2.5–7.5 million Ukrainians.

2. *Maidan*, the Ukrainian word for "square," became the generic designated term for "protest" in Ukraine after the 2004 Orange Revolution, which centered on Maidan Nezalezhnosti (Independence Square) in Kyiv.

CHAPTER 5

1. Instytutska Street is a central street in Kyiv, near the Independence Square, that houses key government buildings, and was an important site of the Euromaidan protest. Part of the street has been renamed as the Alley of the Heavenly Hundred to commemorate the protesters who were killed in the last days of Euromaidan.

CHAPTER 7

1. A DDoS, or "distributed denial of service," attack occurs when multiple systems flood the bandwidth or resources of a targeted website with requests, resulting in overloading the web server and shutting down access to the website.

CHAPTER 8

1. The documentary is available on YouTube at the link: https://www.youtube.com/watch?v=qrwlk7_GF9g.

2. FBK's official website at https://fbk.info/about/.

3. The complete list of accounts is not being made public to protect the identities of the activists, many of whom are at risk of state pressure or repressions for their work.

References

"About Us." 2017. *Anti-Corruption Foundation*. https://fbk.info/english/about/.

Adachi, Yuko. 2006. "The Ambiguous Effects of Russian Corporate Governance Abuses of the 1990s." *Post-Soviet Affairs* 22 (1): 65–89. doi:10.2747/1060-586X.22.1.65.

"Aftermath VR: Euromaidan." 2017. *Kickstarter*. https://www.kickstarter.com/projects/1275823698/aftermath-vr-euromaidan.

Andén-Papadopoulos, Kari. 2008. "The Abu Ghraib Torture Photographs: News Frames, Visual Culture, and the Power of Images." *Journalism: Theory, Practice & Criticism* 9 (1): 5–30. doi:10.1177/1464884907084337.

———. 2013. "Media Witnessing and the 'Crowd-Sourced Video Revolution.'" *Visual Communication* 12 (3): 341–57. doi:10.1177/1470357213483055.

"Апология Протеста [Apologia of Protest]." 2018. Telegram Channel. *Апология Протеста [Apologia of Protest]*. https://t.me/s/apologia.

Barassi, Veronica. 2013. "Ethnographic Cartographies: Social Movements, Alternative Media and the Spaces of Networks." *Social Movement Studies* 12 (1): 48–62. doi:10.1080/14742837.2012.650951.

Bennett, W. Lance, and Alexandra Segerberg. 2012. "The Logic of Connective Action: Digital Media and the Personalization of Contentious Politics." *Information, Communication & Society* 15 (5): 739–68. doi:10.1080/1369118X.2012.670661.

Bohdanova, Tetyana. 2011. "Ukraine: Netizens Criticize Chaotic Construction in the Nation's Capital." *Global Voices*, February 11. https://globalvoices.org/2011/02/11/ukraine-netizens-criticize-chaotic-construction-in-the-nation's-capital/.

———. 2013. "Ukraine: Translators Organize on Facebook to Provide Live #Euromaidan Updates." *Global Voices*, December 9. https://globalvoices.org/2013/12/09/ukraine-translators-organize-on-facebook-to-provide-live-euromaidan-updates/.

———. 2014. "Ukraine Stifles Freedom of Speech, Peaceful Protest with New Law." *Global Voices*, January 17. https://globalvoices.org/2014/01/17/ukraine-stifles-freedom-of-speech-peaceful-protest-with-new-law/.

Bonch-Osmolovskaya, Tatiana, Aurélia Dondo, Laurens Hueting, and Sergey Parkhomenko. 2018. "Russia's Strident Stifling of Free Speech 2012–2018." *PEN International*. https://pen-international.org/news/new-report-pen-international-highlights-russias-relentless-crackdown-on-free-expression.

Borzenko, Aleksandr, and Denis Dmitriev. 2017. "Навальный Отказался Удалять Фильм «Он Вам Не Димон». Что Теперь Будет с Роликом? [Navalny Has Refused to Delete the 'Don't Call Him Dimon' Film. What Will Happen to the Video Now?]." *Meduza*, May 31. https://meduza.io/cards/navalnyy-otkazalsya-udalyat-film-on-vam-ne-dimon-chto-teper-budet-s-rolikom.

Boulianne, Shelley. 2015. "Social Media Use and Participation: A Meta-Analysis of Current Research." *Information, Communication & Society* 18 (5): 524–38. doi:10.1080/1369118X.2015.1008542.

———. 2016. "Online News, Civic Awareness, and Engagement in Civic and Political Life." *New Media & Society* 18 (9): 1840–56. doi:10.1177/1461444815616222.

boyd, danah. 2011. "Social Network Sites as Networked Publics: Affordances, Dynamics and Implications." In *A Networked Self: Identity, Community and Culture on Social Network Sites*, edited by Zizi Papacharissi, 39–58. New York, NY: Routledge.

Brighenti, Andrea M. 2010. *Visibility in Social Theory and Social Research*. Basingstoke, Hampshire, England and New York, NY: Palgrave Macmillan.

Bruns, Axel, Gunn Enli, Eli Skogerbø, Anders Olof Larsson, and Christian Christensen. 2016. *The Routledge Companion to Social Media and Politics*. http://site.ebrary.com/id/11136821

Castells, Manuel. 2009. *Communication Power*. Oxford and New York, NY: Oxford University Press.

———. 2010. *The Rise of the Network Society*, 2nd ed., with A new pref. The Information Age: Economy, Society, and Culture, vol. 1. Chichester, West Sussex and Malden, MA: Wiley-Blackwell.

———. 2012. *Networks of Outrage and Hope: Social Movements in the Internet Age*. Cambridge, UK and Malden, MA: Polity Press.

Chadwick, Andrew. 2017. *The Hybrid Media System: Politics and Power*, 2nd ed. Oxford Studies in Digital Politics. New York, NY: Oxford University Press.

Chadwick, Andrew, James Dennis, and Amy P. Smith. 2016. "Politics in the Age of Hybrid Media: Power, Systems, and Media Logics." In *The Routledge Companion to Social Media and Politics*, 7–22. New York, NY: Routledge.

Christensen, Christian. 2009. "Iran: Networked Dissent?" *Le Monde Diplomatique*, July 2. http://www.mondediplo.com/blogs/iran-networked-dissent.

"Citizen Lab Summer Institute." 2015. *Citizen Lab*, June 19. https://citizenlab.ca/summerinstitute/2015.html.

Couldry, Nick, Sonia Livingston, and Tim Markham. 2007. "Connection or Disconnection?: Tracking the Mediated Public Sphere in Everyday Life." In *Media and Public Spheres*, 28–42. Basingstoke: Palgrave Macmillan.

Dahlgren, Peter. 2003. "Reconfiguring Civic Culture in the New Media Milieu." In *Media and the Restyling of Politics: Consumerism, Celebrity and Cynicism*, edited by John Corner and Dick Pels, 151–70. London and Thousand Oaks, CA: SAGE.

———. 2013. *The Political Web: Media, Participation and Alternative Democracy.* Houndmills, Basingstoke, Hampshire and New York, NY: Palgrave Macmillan.

Davies, Andrew D. 2012. "Assemblage and Social Movements: Tibet Support Groups and the Spatialities of Political Organisation: Assemblage and Social Movements." *Transactions of the Institute of British Geographers* 37 (2): 273–86. doi:10.1111/j.1475-5661.2011.00462.x.

Deibert, Ronald, John Palfrey, Rafal Rohozinski, Jonathan Zittrain, and OpenNet Initiative, eds. 2010. *Access Controlled: The Shaping of Power, Rights, and Rule in Cyberspace.* Information Revolution and Global Politics. Cambridge, MA: MIT Press.

Della Porta, Donatella, and Sidney G. Tarrow, eds. 2005. *Transnational Protest and Global Activism.* People, Passions, and Power. Lanham, MD: Rowman & Littlefield.

Dijck, José van, and Thomas Poell. 2015. "Social Media and the Transformation of Public Space." *Social Media + Society* 1 (2): 1–5. doi:10.1177/2056305115622482.

Dyczok, Marta, and O. V. Gaman-Golutvina, eds. 2009. *Media, Democracy and Freedom: The Post-Communist Experience.* Interdisciplinary Studies on Central and Eastern Europe, vol. 6. Bern and New York, NY: Peter Lang.

Earl, Jennifer, and Katrina Kimport. 2011. *Digitally Enabled Social Change: Activism in the Internet Age.* Acting with Technology. Cambridge, MA: MIT Press.

Edenborg, Emil. 2017. *Politics of Visibility and Belonging: From Russia's "Homosexual Propaganda" Laws to the Ukraine War.* Interventions. London and New York, NY: Routledge, Taylor & Francis Group.

Ellis, John. 2009. "Mundane Witness." In *Media Witnessing: Testimony in the Age of Mass Communication*, 73–88. London: Palgrave Macmillan.

Ellison, Nicole B., Charles Steinfield, and Cliff Lampe. 2011. "Connection Strategies: Social Capital Implications of Facebook-Enabled Communication Practices." *New Media & Society* 13 (6): 873–92. doi:10.1177/1461444810385389.

"EuroMaidan: #DigitalMaidan Twitter Storm." 2014. *Facebook*, January. https://www.facebook.com/events/341170319354082/.

EuroMaydan. 2014. "'Шановний Абоненте, Ви Зареєстровані Як Учасник Масових Заворушень' ['Dear Subscriber, You Have Been Registered as a Participant of Mass Protest']." *Facebook*, January 20. https://www.facebook.com/EuroMaydan/posts/553098384786503.

Fayard, Anne-Laure. 2012. "Space Matters, But How? Physical Space, Virtual Space, and Place." In *Materiality and Organizing: Social Interaction in a Technological World*, edited by Paul M. Leonardi, Bonnie A. Nardi, and Jannis Kallinikos, 1st ed., 177–95. Oxford: Oxford University Press.

Flyverbom, Mikkel, Paul Leonardi, Cynthia Stohl, and Michael Stohl. 2016. "The Management of Visibilities in the Digital Age: Introduction." *International Journal of Communication* 10: 12.

Fossato, Floriana, John Lloyd, and Alexander Verkhovsky. 2008. *The Web That Failed: How Opposition Politics and Independent Initiatives Are Failing on the Internet in Russia.* Oxford: Reuters Institute for the Study of Journalism. https://reutersinstitute.politics.ox.ac.uk/our-research/web-failed.

"Freedom of the Press 2013: Russia." 2013. *Freedom House*. https://freedomhouse
.org/report/freedom-press/2013/russia.

"Freedom on the Net 2013: Ukraine." 2013. *Freedom House*. https://freedomhouse
.org/report/freedom-net/2013/ukraine.

"Freedom on the Net 2014: Ukraine." 2014. *Freedom House*. https://freedomhouse
.org/report/freedom-net/2014/ukraine.

"Freedom on the Net 2015: Russia." 2015. *Freedom House*. https://freedomhouse
.org/report/freedom-net/2015/russia.

Frosh, Paul, and Amit Pinchevski. 2009. "Introduction: Why Media Witnessing? Why Now?" In *Media Witnessing: Testimony in the Age of Mass Communication*, 1–19. London: Palgrave Macmillan.

———. 2014. "Media Witnessing and the Ripeness of Time." *Cultural Studies* 28 (4): 594–610. doi:10.1080/09502386.2014.891304.

———. 2018. "Media and Events after *Media Events*." *Media, Culture & Society* 40 (1): 135–38. doi:10.1177/0163443717726007.

Gainutdinov, Damir, and Pavel Chikov. 2018. "Internet Freedom 2017: Creeping Criminalisation." *Agora International*. http://en.agora.legal/articles/Report-of-Agora-International-"Internet-Freedom-2017-Creeping-Criminalisation"/8.

Ganz, Marshall Louis. 2001. "The Power of Story in Social Movements." *Annual Meeting of the American Sociological Association*, Anaheim, CA. https://dash.ha rvard.edu/bitstream/handle/1/27306251/Power_of_Story-in-Social-Movements.pd f.

Gel'man, Vladimir. 2008. "Party Politics in Russia: From Competition to Hierarchy." *Europe-Asia Studies* 60 (6): 913–30. doi:10.1080/09668130802161165.

———. 2015. "Political Opposition in Russia: A Troubled Transformation." *Europe-Asia Studies* 67 (2): 177–91. doi:10.1080/09668136.2014.1001577.

Gerbaudo, Paolo. 2016. "Rousing the Facebook Crowd: Digital Enthusiasm and Emotional Contagion in the 2011 Protests in Egypt and Spain." *International Journal of Communication* 10: 254–73.

Gibson, James J. 1979. *The Ecological Approach to Visual Perception*. Boston, MA: Houghton Mifflin.

Goldstein, Joshua. 2007. "The Role of Digital Networked Technologies in the Ukrainian Orange Revolution." *SSRN Electronic Journal*. doi:10.2139/ssrn.1077686.

Gould, Roger V. 1991. "Multiple Networks and Mobilization in the Paris Commune, 1871." *American Sociological Review* 56 (6): 716. doi:10.2307/2096251.

Granovetter, Mark S. 1973. "The Strength of Weak Ties." *American Journal of Sociology* 78 (6): 1360–80. doi:10.1086/225469.

Greene, Samuel A. 2012a. "How Much Can Russia Really Change? The Durability of Networked Authoritarianism." *Policy Memo. PONARS Eurasia*. http://www. ponarseurasia.org/memo/how-much-can-russia-really-change-durability-networked-authoritarianism.

———. 2012b. *The End of Virtuality*. Moscow: Center for the Study of New Media & Society. https://web.archive.org/web/20140916030515/http://www.new mediacenter.ru/2012/01/18/the-end-of-virtuality/.

———. 2014. *Moscow in Movement: Power and Opposition in Putin's Russia*. Stanford, CA: Stanford University Press.

Gunitsky, Seva. 2015. "Corrupting the Cyber-Commons: Social Media as a Tool of Autocratic Stability." *Perspectives on Politics* 13 (1): 42–54. doi:10.1017/ S1537592714003120.

Hall, Stuart. 2005. "The Rediscovery of 'Ideology': Return of the Repressed in Media Studies." In *Culture, Society and the Media*, edited by Tony Bennett, James Curran, Michael Gurevitch, and Janet Wollacott. Hoboken, NJ: Taylor and Francis. http://qut.eblib.com.au/patron/FullRecord.aspx?p=242285.

Hampton, Keith, and Barry Wellman. 2003. "Neighboring in Netville: How the Internet Supports Community and Social Capital in a Wired Suburb." *City and Community* 2 (4): 277–311. doi:10.1046/j.1535-6841.2003.00057.x.

Hanson, Elizabeth C. 2008. *The Information Revolution and World Politics*. New Millennium Books in International Studies. Lanham, MD: Rowman & Littlefield.

Hoskins, Andrew, and Ben O'Loughlin. 2010. *War and Media: The Emergence of Diffused War*. Cambridge: Polity.

Howard, Philip N. 2010. *The Digital Origins of Dictatorship and Democracy: Information Technology and Political Islam*. Oxford Studies in Digital Politics. Oxford and New York, NY: Oxford University Press.

Idrisova, Ksenia. 2017. "Explainer: What Is Russia's New VPN Law All About?" *BBC News*, November 1. https://www.bbc.com/news/technology-41829726.

Ilko Kucheriv Democratic Initiatives Foundation. 2014. "Річниця Майдану— Опитування Громадської Та Експертної Думки [Maidan Anniversary—A Public and Expert Opinion Poll]." *Ilko Kucheriv Democratic Initiatives Foundation*. https ://dif.org.ua/en/article/richnitsya-maydanu-opituvannya-gromadskoi-ta-ekspertnoi -dumki.

Interfax-Ukraine. 2011. "Poll: Ukrainian Government Losing Citizens' Trust." *Kyiv Post*, March 9. https://www.kyivpost.com/article/content/ukraine-politics/poll-ukrainian-government-losing-citizens-trust-99343.html.

International Business Publications. 2008. "Internet in Ukraine." In *Ukraine Telecom Laws and Regulations Handbook*. Richmond, TX: International Business Publications USA.

Isin, Engin, and Evelyn Ruppert. 2015. *Being Digital Citizens*. London, UK: Rowman & Littlefield.

Jenkins, Henry, Sam Ford, and Joshua Green. 2013. *Spreadable Media: Creating Value and Meaning in a Networked Culture*. Postmillennial Pop. New York, NY and London: New York University Press.

Karamshuk, Dmytro, Tetyana Lokot, Oleksandr Pryymak, and Nishanth Sastry. 2016. "Identifying Partisan Slant in News Articles and Twitter During Political Crises." In *Social Informatics*, edited by Emma Spiro and Yong-Yeol Ahn, 10046:257–72. Cham: Springer International Publishing. doi:10.1007/978-3-319-47880-7_16.

Kartsev, Dmitry. 2019. "Russia's New Resistance 'Meduza' Analyzes the Rise of a New Wave of Protest Movements." *Meduza*, August 7. https://meduza.io/en/feat ure/2019/08/07/russia-s-new-resistance.

Kavada, Anastasia. 2010. "Activism Transforms Digital: The Social Movement Perspective." In *Digital Activism Decoded: The New Mechanics of Change*, edited by Mary Joyce, 101–18. New York, NY: International Debate Education Association.

Kavanaugh, Andrea, John M. Carroll, Mary Beth Rosson, Than Than Zin, and Debbie Denise Reese. 2005. "Community Networks: Where Offline Communities Meet Online." *Journal of Computer-Mediated Communication* 10 (4). doi:10.1111/j.1083-6101.2005.tb00266.x.

Kendall, Lori. 1999. "Recontextualizing 'Cyberspace': Methodological Considerations for Online Research." In *Doing Internet Research: Critical Issues and Methods for Examining the Net*, 57–74. Thousand Oaks, CA: Sage Publications.

Kiryukhin, Denys. 2016. "Roots and Features of Modern Ukrainian National Identity and Nationalism." In *Ukraine and Russia: People, Politics, Propaganda and Perspectives*, 59–68. Bristol, UK: E-International Relations Publishing. http://www.e-ir.info/wp-content/uploads/2016/06/Ukraine-and-Russia-E-IR-2016.pdf.

Kohen, Hilah. 2019. "'The Art of Rejection' A New Report Reveals the Hidden Mechanisms Authorities Use to Restrict Protests in Russia." *Meduza*, January 10. https://meduza.io/en/feature/2019/01/10/the-art-of-rejection.

Koliska, Michael, and Jessica Roberts. 2015. "Selfies: Witnessing and Participatory Journalism with a Point of View." *International Journal of Communication* 9: 1672–85.

Kubicek, Paul. 2009. "Problems of Post-Post-Communism: Ukraine after the Orange Revolution." *Democratization* 16 (2): 323–43. doi:10.1080/13510340902732524.

Kulyk, Volodymyr. 2014. "The Media at the Time of Unrest: A Report of a Maidan Participant." *Russian Journal of Communication* 6 (2): 181–85. doi:10.1080/1940 9419.2014.908695.

Kyj, Myroslaw J. 2006. "Internet Use in Ukraine's Orange Revolution." *Business Horizons* 49 (1): 71–80. doi:10.1016/j.bushor.2005.06.003.

Laruelle, Marlene. 2014. "Alexei Navalny and Challenges in Reconciling 'Nationalism' and 'Liberalism.'" *Post-Soviet Affairs* 30 (4): 276–97. doi:10.1080/1060586X.2013.872453.

Lim, C. 2008. "Social Networks and Political Participation: How Do Networks Matter?" *Social Forces* 87 (2): 961–82. doi:10.1353/sof.0.0143.

Lin, Nan. 2008. "A Network Theory of Social Capital." In *The Handbook of Social Capital*, edited by Dario Castiglione, Jan W. van Deth, and Guglielmo Wolleb, 50–69. Oxford and New York, NY: Oxford University Press.

Lipman, Masha, and Michael McFaul. 2001. "'Managed Democracy' in Russia: Putin and the Press." *Harvard International Journal of Press/Politics* 6 (3): 116–27. doi:10.1177/108118001129172260.

Lister, Martin, and Liz Wells. 2001. "Seeing beyond Belief: Cultural Studies as an Approach to Analysing the Visual." In *Handbook of Visual Analysis*, edited by Theo Van Leeuwen and Carey Jewitt, 61–91. London and Thousand Oaks, CA: SAGE.

Litreev, Alexander V. 2017. "Мы Запускаем Красную Кнопку [We Are Launching the Red Button]." *Telegraph Post*, April 22. http://telegra.ph/My-zapuskaem-Kras nuyu-Knopku-04-22.

Lokot, Tetyana. 2013. "As Ukraine's Protests Escalate, #Euromaidan Hashtag Lost in a Sea of Information." *Global Voices*, December 6. https://globalvoices.org/2013/12 /06/as-ukraines-protests-escalate-euromaidan-hashtag-lost-in-sea-of-information/.

———. 2014a. "Ukrainian #DigitalMaidan Activism Takes Twitter's Trending Topics by Storm." *Global Voices*, January 27. https://globalvoices.org/2014/01/27 /ukrainian-digitalmaidan-protests-twitter-trending-topics-storm/.

———. 2014b. "New Book Tells the Story of Ukraine's Euromaidan Protests in Facebook Posts." *Global Voices*, November 12. https://globalvoices.org/2014/11 /12/ukraine-book-euromaidan-protests-facebook/.

———. 2015a. "Ukrainian MP Pushes for Carbon Copy of Russian Blogger Law, Meets Resistance." *Global Voices*, February 16. https://globalvoices.org/2015/02 /16/ukraine-russia-blogger-law/.

———. 2015b. "Mapping the 2012 Election: Use of Crowdmapping in Ukraine." *The Civic Media Project*, March 10. http://civicmediaproject.org/.

Luganskaya, Dariya. 2017. "OpenEconomy: Как Российские Власти Будут Контролировать Интернет. Три Основных Способа [OpenEconomy: How the Russian Authorities Will Control the Internet. Three Main Ways]." *OpenRussia*, April 23. https://openrussia.org/notes/708721/.

Lunden, Ingrid. 2016. "LinkedIn Is Now Officially Blocked in Russia." *TechCrunch*, November 17. https://techcrunch.com/2016/11/17/linkedin-is-now-officially-blocked-in-russia/.

Lysenko, Volodymyr V., and Kevin C. Desouza. 2014. "Charting the Coevolution of Cyberprotest and Counteraction: The Case of Former Soviet Union States from 1997 to 2011." *Convergence: The International Journal of Research into New Media Technologies* 20 (2): 176–200. doi:10.1177/1354856512459716.

MacKinnon, Rebecca. 2012. *Consent of the Networked: The World-Wide Struggle for Internet Freedom*. New York, NY: Basic Books.

Majchrzak, Ann, Samer Faraj, Gerald C. Kane, and Bijan Azad. 2013. "The Contradictory Influence of Social Media Affordances on Online Communal Knowledge Sharing." *Journal of Computer-Mediated Communication* 19 (1): 38–55. doi:10.1111/jcc4.12030.

Makarenko, Olena. 2018. "Two Photographers Recreate Bloodiest Days of Euromaidan with Virtual Reality." *Euromaidan Press*, February 20. http:// euromaidanpress.com/2018/02/20/two-photographers-ukraine-recreate-euromai dan-massacre-with-virtual-reality/.

Maréchal, Nathalie. 2017. "Networked Authoritarianism and the Geopolitics of Information: Understanding Russian Internet Policy." *Media and Communication* 5 (1): 29. doi:10.17645/mac.v5i1.808.

Mattoni, Alice, and Emiliano Treré. 2014. "Media Practices, Mediation Processes, and Mediatization in the Study of Social Movements: Media Practices, Mediation Processes, and Mediatization." *Communication Theory* 24 (3): 252–71. doi:10.1111/ comt.12038.

Meduza. 2017. "Russia's Senate Adopts New Legislation Cracking Down on Internet Anonymity. All That's Left Now Is Putin's Signature." July 25. https://meduza. io/en/news/2017/07/25/russia-s-senate-adopts-new-legislation-cracking-down-on-internet-anonymity-all-that-s-left-now-is-putin-s-signature.

Milan, Stefania. 2015. "From Social Movements to Cloud Protesting: The Evolution of Collective Identity." *Information, Communication & Society* 18 (8): 887–900. doi:10.1080/1369118X.2015.1043135.

Minchenko, Olga. 2014. "I Am a Ukrainian: Відео Про Події в Україні Перегляну ли 8 Млн Користувачів На YouTube [I Am a Ukrainian: A Video about Events in Ukraine Has Been Viewed by Eight Million YouTube Users]." *Watcher*, March 14. http://watcher.com.ua/2014/03/14/i-am-a-ukrainian-video-pro-podiyi-v-ukrayi ni-perehlyanuly-8-mln-korystuvachiv-na-youtube/.

Morozov, Evgeny. 2011. "Tunisia, Social Media and the Politics of Attention." *Foreign Policy*, January 14. http://neteffect.foreignpolicy.com/posts/2011/01/14/ tunisia_social_media_and_the_politics_of_attention.

Morton, Elise. 2017. "Ukraine to Block Russian Social Media Sites VKontakte and Odnoklassniki." *The Calvert Journal*, May 16. https://www.calvertjournal.com /articles/show/8293/ukraine-to-block-russian-social-media-sites-vkontakte-and-odnoklassniki.

Nagy, Peter, and Gina Neff. 2015. "Imagined Affordance: Reconstructing a Keyword for Communication Theory." *Social Media + Society* 1 (2). doi:10.1177/2056305115603385.

"Nations in Transit 2013: Russia." 2013. *Freedom House*. https://freedomhouse.org/ report/nations-transit/2013/russia.

Navalny, Alexey. 2016. "Нападение На Мужа Юриста ФБК Любови Соболь [Attack on the Husband of FBK Lawyer Lyubov Sobol]." *Navalny*, November 28. https://navalny.com/p/5142/.

Nayyem, Mustafa. 2014a. "Социальные Сети Объявлены Вне Закона [Social Networks Have Been Outlawed]." *Facebook*, January 16. https://www.facebook .com/Mustafanayyem/posts/10201517585407567.

———. 2014b. "Uprising in Ukraine: How It All Began." *Open Society Foundations*, April 4. https://www.opensocietyfoundations.org/voices/uprising-ukraine-how-it-all-began.

"Nebesna Sotnya." 2014. *Ukrainska Pravda*. http://nebesna.pravda.com.ua/.

Norris, Pippa. 1999. *Critical Citizens: Global Support for Democratic Government*. Oxford and New York, NY: Oxford Univ. Press. http://public.eblib.com/choice/ publicfullrecord.aspx?p=3053220.

Oates, Sarah. 2013. *Revolution Stalled: The Political Limits of the Internet in the Post-Soviet Sphere*. Oxford Studies in Digital Politics. Oxford and New York, NY: Oxford University Press.

Oates, Sarah, and Tetyana Lokot. 2013. "Twilight of the Gods?: How the Internet Challenged Russian Television News Frames in the Winter Protests of 2011–12." *SSRN Electronic Journal*. doi:10.2139/ssrn.2286727.

Oliphant, Roland. 2013. "Alexei Navalny Rattles Kremlin in Moscow Mayoral Race." *The Telegraph*, September 7. http://www.telegraph.co.uk/news/worldnew

s/europe/russia/10293384/Alexei-Navalny-rattles-Kremlin-in-Moscow-mayoral-r
ace.html.

Onuch, Olga. 2014. "Social Networks and Social Media in Ukrainian 'Euromaidan'
Protests." *The Washington Post*, January 2. http://www.washingtonpost.com/blogs
/monkey-cage/wp/2014/01/02/social-networks-and-social-media-in-ukrainian-
euromaidan-protests-2/.

———. 2015. "'Facebook Helped Me Do It': Understanding the EuroMaidan
Protester 'Tool-Kit.'" *Studies in Ethnicity and Nationalism* 15 (1): 170–84.
doi:10.1111/sena.12129.

OVD-Info. 2017. "Сколько Людей Вышло На Акции 26 Марта и Чем Все Закон
чилось: Карта ОВД-Инфо и «Медузы» [How Many People Came out for March
26 Rallies and How It All Ended: A Map by OVD-Info and Meduza]." June 7.
https://ovdinfo.org/articles/2017/06/07/skolko-lyudey-vyshlo-na-akcii-26-marta-i
-chem-vse-zakonchilos-karta-ovd-info-i.

Pearce, Katy E., Jessica Vitak, and Kristen Barta. 2018. "Socially Mediated Visibility:
Friendship and Dissent in Authoritarian Azerbaijan." *International Journal of
Communication* 12: 1310–31.

"Percentage of Individuals Using the Internet." 2013. *International Telecommunication
Union*. http://www.itu.int/en/ITU-D/Statistics/Pages/stat/default.aspx.

Peters, John Durham. 2009. "Witnessing." In *Media Witnessing: Testimony in the
Age of Mass Communication*, 23–48. London: Palgrave Macmillan.

Pishchikova, Kateryna, and Olesia Ogryzko. 2014. *Civic Awakening: The Impact
of Euromaidan on Ukraine's Politics and Society*. Madrid: Fundación para las
Relaciones Internacionales y el Diálogo Exterior.

Putnam, Robert D. 2000. *Bowling Alone: The Collapse and Revival of American
Community*. New York, NY: Simon & Schuster.

Quan-Haase, Anabel, and Kim Martin. 2013. "Digital Curation and the Networked
Audience of Urban Events: Expanding La Fiesta de Santo Tomás from the Physical
to the Virtual Environment." *International Communication Gazette* 75 (5–6):
521–37. doi:10.1177/1748048513491910.

Radio Svoboda. 2013. "Хакери Атакують: «лежать» Сайти Януковича Та МВС
[Hackers Attack: The Websites of Yanukovych and Interior Ministry Are Down]."
December 1. https://www.radiosvoboda.org/a/25185814.html.

Reporters Without Borders. 2014. "Ukrainian Parliament Approves Very Dangerous
Draft Law on First Reading." *Reporters Without Borders*, August 12. https://rsf.org
/en/news/ukrainian-parliament-approves-very-dangerous-draft-law-first-reading.

Rothrock, Kevin. 2012. "Russia: A Great Firewall to Censor the RuNet?" *Global
Voices*, July 10. https://globalvoices.org/2012/07/10/russia-a-great-firewall-to-ce
nsor-the-runet/.

Runet Echo. 2018. "Russian Anti-Corruption Activists Are Jailed for 'Inciting Riots'
Based on Their Tweets and Retweets.' *Global Voices*, May 25. https://global
voices.org/2018/05/25/russian-anti-corruption-activists-are-jailed-for-inciting-r
iots-based-on-their-tweets-and-retweets/.

Ryabinska, Natalya. 2011. "The Media Market and Media Ownership in Post-Communist Ukraine: Impact on Media Independence and Pluralism." *Problems of Post-Communism* 58 (6): 3–20. doi:10.2753/PPC1075-8216580601.

Saunders, Clare, Maria Grasso, Cristiana Olcese, Emily Rainsford, and Christopher Rootes. 2012. "Explaining Differential Protest Participation: Novices, Returners, Repeaters, and Stalwarts." *Mobilization: An International Quarterly* 17 (3): 263–80. doi:10.17813/maiq.17.3.bqm553573058t478.

Savanevsky, Maksym. 2013. "Боти Намагаються Засмічувати Інформаційне Поле #євромайдан—Як з Цим Боротись [Bots Are Trying to Muddy the #euromaidan Information Field—How to Deal with It]." *Watcher*, November 25. http://watcher.com.ua/2013/11/25/boty-namahayutsya-zasmichuvaty-informatsiyne-pole-yevromaydan-yak-z-tsym-borotys/.

———. 2014. "10 Цифр Про Український Facebook, Яких Ви Могли Не Знати [10 Figures about Ukrainian Facebook That You May Not Have Known]." *Watcher*, February 4. http://watcher.com.ua/2014/02/04/10-tsyfr-pro-ukrayinskyy-facebook-yakyh-vy-mohly-ne-znaty/.

Semetko, Holli A., and Natalya Krasnoboka. 2003. "The Political Role of the Internet in Societies in Transition: Russia and Ukraine Compared." *Party Politics* 9 (1): 77–104. doi:10.1177/135406880391005.

Sessions, Lauren F. 2010. "How Offline Gatherings Affect Online Communities: When Virtual Community Members 'Meetup.'" *Information, Communication & Society* 13 (3): 375–95. doi:10.1080/13691180903468954.

Sevilla, Cate. 2014. "The Ukrainian Medic Who Tweeted She Was Dying Is Actually Alive." *BuzzFeed*, February 21. https://www.buzzfeednews.com/article/catesevilla/the-ukrainian-medic-that-tweeted-she-was-dying-is-actually-a.

Shah, Dhavan V., and Homero Gil de Zúñiga. 2008. "Social Capital." In *Encyclopedia of Survey Research Methods*, edited by Paul J. Lavrakas, 824–25. Thousand Oaks, CA: SAGE Publications.

Shedov, Denis, Natalia Smirnova, and Tatyana Glushkova. 2019. "Limitations on and Restrictions to the Right to the Freedom of Peaceful Assembly in the Digital Age." *OVD-Info*. https://ovdinfo.org/reports/freedom-of-assembly-in-the-digital-age-en.

Shklovski, Irina, and Bjarki Valtysson. 2012. "Secretly Political: Civic Engagement in Online Publics in Kazakhstan." *Journal of Broadcasting & Electronic Media* 56 (3): 417–33. doi:10.1080/08838151.2012.705196.

Siegelbaum, Lewis H., ed. 2006. *Borders of Socialism: Private Spheres of Soviet Russia*, 1st ed. New York, NY: Palgrave Macmillan.

Sjøvaag, Helle. 2011. "Amateur Images and Journalistic Authority." In *Amateur Images and Global News*, edited by Kari Andén-Papadopoulos, 79–95. Bristol: Intellect.

Skoric, Marko M., Qinfeng Zhu, Debbie Goh, and Natalie Pang. 2016. "Social Media and Citizen Engagement: A Meta-Analytic Review." *New Media & Society* 18 (9): 1817–39. doi:10.1177/1461444815616221.

Smirnova, Natalia. 2019. "Одиночные Пикеты. Ограничения в Теории и На Практике [Single-Person Pickets. Limitations in Theory and in Practice]." *OVD-Info*. https://ovdinfo.org/reports/odinochnye-pikety.

Snow, David A., and Robert D. Benford. 1988. "Ideology, Frame Resonance, and Participant Mobilization." *International Social Movement Research* 1 (1): 197–217.

Snyder, Timothy. 2018. *The Road to Unfreedom: Russia, Europe, America*, 1st ed. New York, NY: Tim Duggan Books.

Soldatov, Andreĭ, and I. Borogan. 2015. *The Red Web: The Struggle between Russia's Digital Dictators and the New Online Revolutionaries*, 1st ed. New York, NY: Public Affairs.

Szostek, Joanna. 2017. "The Power and Limits of Russia's Strategic Narrative in Ukraine: The Role of Linkage." *Perspectives on Politics* 15 (2): 379–95. doi:10.1017/S153759271700007X.

TASS. 2016. "Kremlin: National Guard Likely to Be Involved in Suppression of Unauthorized Mass Actions." April 5. https://tass.com/politics/867506.

Texty.org.ua. 2013. "#Євромайдан: Що Відбувається у Твітері. Спецпроект, Частина №1 [#Euromaidan: What Is Happening on Twitter. Special Project, Part 1]." November 29. http://texty.org.ua/pg/news/editorial/read/50061/Jevromajdan _shho_vidbuvajetsa_u_Tviteri_Specprojekt_chastyna.

TgVPN. 2017. "VPN в Telegram [VPN in Telegram]." Medium blog. *TgVPN*, May 31. https://medium.com/@TgVPN/vpn-%D1%81%D0%B5%D1%80%D0%B2% D0%B8%D1%81-%D0%B2-telegram-b63f1d02a6b0.

The Moscow Times. 2018a. "Man Gets 2-Year Suspended Sentence for Criticizing Putin on Social Media." June 6. https://www.themoscowtimes.com/2018/06/06/man -gets-2-year-suspended-sentence-for-criticizing-putin-on-social-media-a61693.

———. 2018b. "Vkontakte Announces Privacy Reforms After Spate of Extremism Prosecutions." August 13. https://www.themoscowtimes.com/2018/08/13/vko ntakte-announces-privacy-reforms-after-spate-of-extremism-prosecutions-a62512.

———. 2019. "Russia Moves to Tighten Protest Laws Amid Moscow's Opposition Uprising." April 9. https://www.themoscowtimes.com/2019/08/09/russia-moves-to -tighten-protest-laws-amid-moscows-opposition-uprising-a66783.

Thompson, John B. 2005. "The New Visibility." *Theory, Culture & Society* 22 (6): 31–51. doi:10.1177/0263276405059413.

"Three Days in February." 2017. *Texty.org.ua.* http://texty.org.ua/d/maidan_maps _eng/.

Toor, Amar. 2014. "How Putin's Cronies Seized Control of Russia's Facebook." *The Verge*, January 31. https://www.theverge.com/2014/1/31/5363990/how-putins-c ronies-seized-control-over-russias-facebook-pavel-durov-vk.

Trombetta, Lorenzo. 2012. "Altering Courses in Unknown Waters: Interaction between Traditional and New Media during the First Months of the Syrian Uprising." *Global Media Journal-German Edition* 2 (1): 1–13.

Tucker, Joshua A., Megan Metzger, and Pablo Barberá. 2014. *Tweeting the Revolution: Social Media Use and the #Euromaidan Protests*. New York, NY: Social Media and Political Participation Lab, New York University. https://sm appnyu.org/wp-content/uploads/2018/11/Ukraine_Data_Report.pdf.

Tufekçi, Zeynep. 2013. "'Not This One': Social Movements, the Attention Economy, and Microcelebrity Networked Activism." *American Behavioral Scientist* 57 (7): 848–70. doi:10.1177/0002764213479369.

———. 2014. "After the Protests." *The New York Times*, March 19. http://www.nytimes.com/2014/03/20/opinion/after-the-protests.html?_r=5.

———. 2017. *Twitter and Tear Gas: The Power and Fragility of Networked Protest.* New Haven, CT and London: Yale University Press.

Tufekçi, Zeynep, and Christopher Wilson. 2012. "Social Media and the Decision to Participate in Political Protest: Observations from Tahrir Square." *Journal of Communication* 62 (2): 363–79. doi:10.1111/j.1460-2466.2012.01629.x.

"Ты Сядешь За Лайк [You Will Go to Prison for a Like]." 2017. Telegram Channel. *Ты Сядешь За Лайк [You Will Go to Prison for a Like]*. https://t.me/s/zalayk.

Ukrainska Pravda. 2011. "Генсек 'Репортерів Без Кордонів' Стурбований Наміром Депутатів Обмежити ЗМІ [Reporters Without Borders General Secretary Concerned with MP's Intention to Limit Mass Media]." October 28. http://www.pravda.com.ua/news/2011/10/28/6711923/.

———. 2012. "Більше Половини Українців Не Користуються Інтернетом [Over Half of Ukrainians Don't Use the Internet]." March 15. http://www.pravda.com.ua/news/2012/03/15/6960641/.

———. 2013. "Українські Інтернет-ЗМІ Піддаються Масовим Атакам Хакерів [Ukrainian Internet Media Suffering Mass Hacking Attacks]." December 2. https://www.pravda.com.ua/news/2013/12/2/7004463/.

Uldam, Julie. 2018. "Social Media Visibility: Challenges to Activism." *Media, Culture & Society* 40 (1): 41–58. doi:10.1177/0163443717704997.

Valenzuela, Sebastián. 2013. "Unpacking the Use of Social Media for Protest Behavior: The Roles of Information, Opinion Expression, and Activism." *American Behavioral Scientist* 57 (7): 920–42. doi:10.1177/0002764213479375.

Valenzuela, Sebastián, Namsu Park, and Kerk F. Kee. 2009. "Is There Social Capital in a Social Network Site?: Facebook Use and College Students' Life Satisfaction, Trust, and Participation." *Journal of Computer-Mediated Communication* 14 (4): 875–901. doi:10.1111/j.1083-6101.2009.01474.x.

Valenzuela, Sebastián, Valgeir Valdimarsson, Nwachukwu Egbunike, Matthew Fraser, Araba Sey, Tohir Pallaev, Pavin Chachavalpongpun, Erkan Saka, and Igor Lyubashenko. 2014. "The Big Question: Have Social Media and/or Smartphones Disrupted Life in Your Part of the World?" *World Policy Journal* 31 (3): 3–8. doi:10.1177/0740277514552964.

Varnelis, Kazys, and Anne Friedberg. 2008. "Place: The Networking of Public Space." In *Networked Publics*, 15–42. Cambridge, MA: MIT Press.

Vie, Stephanie. 2014. "In Defense of 'Slacktivism': The Human Rights Campaign Facebook Logo as Digital Activism." *First Monday* 19 (4). doi:10.5210/fm.v19i4.4961.

Vitak, Jessica, Paul Zube, Andrew Smock, Caleb T. Carr, Nicole Ellison, and Cliff Lampe. 2011. "It's Complicated: Facebook Users' Political Participation in the 2008 Election." *Cyberpsychology, Behavior, and Social Networking* 14 (3): 107–14. doi:10.1089/cyber.2009.0226.

Wahl-Jorgensen, Karin, Lucy Bennett, and Gregory Taylor. 2017. "The Normalization of Surveillance and the Invisibility of Digital Citizenship: Media Debates after the Snowden Revelations." *International Journal of Communication* 11 (2017): 740–62.

Walgrave, Stefaan, Ruud Wouters, Jerome Van Laer, Joris Verhulst, and Pauline Ketelaars. 2012. "Transnational Collective Identification: May Day and Climate Change Protesters' Identification with Similar Protest Events in Other Countries." *Mobilization: An International Quarterly* 17 (3): 301–17.

Wanenchak, Sarah. 2013. "Toward an Augmented Eventfulness." *Cyborgology*, May 2. http://thesocietypages.org/cyborgology/2013/05/02/toward-an-augmented-event fulness/.

White, David. 2015. "Political Opposition in Russia: The Challenges of Mobilisation and the Political–Civil Society Nexus." *East European Politics* 31 (3): 314–25. doi :10.1080/21599165.2014.990628.

Wilson, Andrew. 2016. "Ukrainian Politics since Independence." In *Ukraine and Russia: People, Politics, Propaganda and Perspectives*, 101–8. Bristol, UK: E-International Relations Publishing. http://www.e-ir.info/wp-content/uploads/2016/06/Ukraine-and-Russia-E-IR-2016.pdf.

Zelinska, Olga. 2015. "Who Were the Protestors and What Did They Want?: Contentious Politics of Local Maidans across Ukraine, 2013–2014." *Demokratizatsiya: The Journal of Post-Soviet Democratization* 23 (4): 379–400.

Index

Page numbers in italics reference to figures and tables.

affordances, 3; concept of, 4; of digital technology, 21; of ICTs, 119; imagined affordances, 4–5; of the internet, 5, 28, 43; of networked media, 4, 11, 57; of online media, 39; of technology, 3, 4, 72, 105

affordances of digital media, 1–2, 4, 10, 28, 48, 90; for activism, 8; citizens' perception of, 165; for dissent in Russia, 7, 8, 12, 142, 157–58, 163–64; in Euromaidan protests, 5, 9, 11, 157–58, 159–60; factors affecting, 158; horizontal protest movements, 98; for information sharing, 144; for organizing, 92–95; for protest, 48, 144, 154, 157–59, 168–69

affordances of social media, 5, 43, 81, 98, 99; for connective action, 103–4; ephemerality, 154, 158; ephemeral networks, 107; flexibility, 158; flexible organizing, 107; online public intellectuals and, 104; part-time participation, 107; persistence, 134, 158; protesters use of, 134; protest participation and, 162; scalability, 134, 158; social capital,

building, 107; visibility, 134, 154, 158

"Aftermath VR: Euromaidan" project, 84–85

agency, 2, 13, 15, 16, 104, 119; digital media and, 39; digital rights and, 169; Euromaidan protesters and, 67; in post-Soviet states, 24; Russian protesters, 145, 153, 155, 164, 168; social media and, 42, 70

Agora, 153

Alburov, Georgiy, 151

algorithms, 3, 12, 16, 110, 111

Amazon Smile, 64

Anti-Corruption Foundation (FBK), 145–46; anti-surveillance tools, 152; conspicuous security, 151–52, 153, 166; digital literacy and security, 152; digital media use, 148; financial transparency, 150; legal help offer, 153; networked surveillance, 151; police visits to offices, 154; primary mission of, 146–47; public deconstruction of surveillance, 152; state surveillance of, 146, 150–52; strategic visibility and ephemerality,

153–54; strategic visibility and scalability, 146–50; surveillance-related threats/attacks, 150; video live streams, 148–49, 154

anti-corruption protests, 166; counter-surveillance by protesters, 145, 153; detentions, 149, 153; encrypted messaging platforms, 155; online video live streams, 148–50; police violence, 149; in Russia, 4, 5–6, 7, 8, 26, 145–46, 163; state surveillance/attacks, documentation of, 154

anti-government protests, in Russia, 11–12

anti-surveillance technology, 152

anti-Trump movement, 3

Apologia of Protest project, 153

Arab Spring protests, 3, 91, 142

Armenia, 3

augmented citizenship, 167–69

augmented dissent, 12–13, 28, 165–67; Anti-Corruption Foundation, 145–46; augmented citizenship and, 167–69; concept of, 2, 5, 157; Euromaidan protest, 159; national and political contexts, 5–6; real-time witnessing and, 86; in Russia, 5, 142, 144–45, 163–65; theorising, 165–67. *See also* augmented protest

augmented eventfulness, 73, 142

augmented media witnessing, 86

augmented participation, 91–92, 160

augmented protest, 2, 12, 161; live streaming, 149; networks, 115; in Russia, 155, 158; social media and, 10, 72–73; as visible spectacle, 72–73; witnessing, 86

augmented witnessing, 74–75, 83–87, 160

authoritarianism, 13, 15, 16, 22, 25, 39, 141, 163, 169

AutoMaidan drivers, 48

avatars on social media, 42, 66, 133

Baraboshko, Oleksandr (Krus Krus), 76

Basecamp (project management tool), 97

Belarus, mass protest events, 3

blogs/bloggers, 19, 21, 39, 43; Krus Krus (Ukrainian student), 76; in Russia, 25, 143; in Ukraine, 18, 20–21, 70, 76, 85, 104

Bolotnaya rallies (2011–2012), 3, 12, 171; regime reactions to the, 24

bots, 128–30, 151, 152

Boulianne, Shelley, 118

boyd, danah, 127

Buzzfeed, 33

Castells, Manuel, 53

censorship, in Russia, 22, 143, 147, 148, 159

Chadwick, Andrew, 5, 123

Chicago, 65

China, 51

Christensen, Christian, 118

citizen journalism, 18, 48, 76, 95, 137

civic activism, 34, 35, 36, 37; affordances of digital media, 49–50; examples of, 42; internet use, 42–43; in Kyiv, 42; perception of, 41–42

civic engagement, 29, 34, 41, 63, 101, 166

collective action, 98, 114, 118, 119, 161

colocation, 161

Columbia University, School of International and Public Affairs, 49

commemorative witnessing, 80–82

connective action, 11, 89, 95, 98, 103–5

copresence, 10, 72, 75, 77, 97; affective, 118, 150, 154, 160, 162; augmented, 138, 166; common protest language, 72; concept of, 161; mediated, 132, 160; physical, 57, 90, 105, 110, 149, 160, 161; process of witnessing, 85

Couldry, Nick, et al., 38

Crimea, 58, 167

crowdsourced investigations, 82–83; citizen video footage of shootings, 82–83; election monitoring in Ukraine, 21

crowdsourcing, 132
cybersecurity, 25, 27, 46, 168
cyberutopianism, 16
cyberwarfare, 167
cyborg accounts, 129
Cyrillic web, 7

Dahlgren, Peter, 38, 104
Davies, Andrew D., 114
DDoS. *See* distributed denial-of-service
  (DDoS)
Deibert, Ronald, et al., 23
democracy, 15–17, 19, 21, 25, 27, 39, 141
digital citizenship, 137, 168
digital media: affordances of, 4, 5,
  10, 11, 12, 157–58; affordances
  for organizing, 92–95; augmented
  dissent and, 2; augmented protest
  and, 10; change in mode of use, 47;
  contested environment in Russia,
  163; cybersecurity, 46; development
  in Russia, 10; development
  in Ukraine, 10; Euromaidan
  participants' perception of, 38;
  Euromaidan protest (2013–2014),
  6–7, 43–48, 67; everyday rights,
  management of, 38–40; everyday
  use of, 38–40; factors affecting
  affordances, 158; habits, remaking
  of, 46; literacy skills/practices, 130,
  152; protesters' perception of, 9–10,
  158; protest organization, 11, 16;
  public debates, 3; role in activism
  and protest, 166; role in human
  lives, 3; in Russia, 158; Russian
  protesters and, 2; security tools, 152;
  in Ukraine, 158; Ukrainian protesters
  and, 2; verification, 130. *See also*
  affordances of digital media
digital networks, social movements'
  reliance on, 50
digital rights, as human rights, 168, 169
digital shortcuts, 95–98, 165, 166
disinformation on social media, 129–30,
  138, 167

distributed denial-of-service (DDoS),
  20, 130, 172
Dnipropetrovsk, Ukraine, 58
Donetsk, Ukraine, 58, 59
"Don't Call Him Dimon"
  (documentary), 145, 148
Dzerkalo Tyzhnya, 130

Earl, Jennifer, and Katrina Kimport, 57
Electric Yerevan rallies (2015), 3
Ellis, John, 71–72
Ellison, Nicole B., et al., 101–2
encrypted messaging platforms, 145,
  153, 155, 164
ephemerality, 5; digital technologies
  and, 164; encrypted social media
  communications and, 145;
  Euromaidan and, 161; of Galas, 107,
  110, 114; of mediated connections,
  87; networked protest communities
  and, 102–3, 104; protest organizers
  in Russia, 155, 164; versus visibility,
  153–54
Espreso TV, 76
EU Association Agreement, 6, 44;
  Euromaidan Protest and, 50, 58, 137;
  Yanukovych's refusal to sign, 1, 6,
  43, 52, 58, 61
#euromaidan, 45, 74, 120, 129
Euromaidan Donetsk, 59
Euromaidan Kharkiv, 59
Euromaidan movement: emergence of,
  7; pre-Euromaidan routines, 40–43
Euromaidan posters, 133
Euromaidan Press, 84, 123
Euromaidan protesters, 29–48; age
  range, 31; deaths, 81, 82–83, 133;
  device use/internet access, *34;*
  diversity of, 48; education, level of,
  31; employment, 31; internet use,
  36, 38, 40; interviewees, summary
  of information about, *30;* interview
  locations, 51–52; media coverage,
  dissatisfaction with, 126; media
  habits/internet use, 31, 32–34, 43–

48; new protesters (novices), 34, 35,
36, 37, 48; old protesters (returners),
34–35, 37, 48; online digest of news/
events, 37; pre-Euromaidan routines,
40–43; professional skills, use of,
36–37; self-organization, 36, 97;
social media and, 90; synergy, 92;
visual memorials to, 81
Euromaidan Protests (2013–2014), 1, 3,
4, 5, 25, 26; accounts made public
during protest, 47; affordances of
digital media, 5, 9, 11, 157–58,
159–60; affordances of networked
platforms, 11; affordances of
social media, 5, 158; affordances
of the internet, 5, 11; ambushes/
kidnappings, 46; anti-protest
legislation, 117; awareness of,
55–56; commemorative witnessing,
80–82; communications, common
strategy and, 61; digital media,
change in mode of use, 47; digital
media use during, 43–48, 160–61;
digital shortcuts, 95–98, 165,
166; dual local/global nature of,
50–51; ephemerality, 5; Facebook
communities, 123; Facebook use, 6,
34, 40, 43–44, 61, 119, 122, 127–28,
161; flexibility, 5; framing of, 132,
134–38, 162; geographical distance,
effects of, 65–66, 94; grassroots
movement, 6, 97; Group Skype
calls, 57; hacking attacks, 130;
information flows in protest camp,
125; information sharing, 117–18,
126–27, 161–62; initial motivation
of, 50; international outreach, 123;
interviews with protesters, 7–8, 29–
48, 91; legal assistance initiative, 98,
101; live video streams, 6, 48, 56,
74, 103, 161; logistics, management
of, 89–90; mainstream media and,
131, 138; motivations, 58, 60;
networked communities, 103, 161;
online and offline hybridity, 115,

118, 161; online in real-time, 69–70;
opinion leaders, 104; opposition
to, 105; organizing, 89–90,
92–95, 96; part-time participation,
103–7; participation, level of, 58;
Phantom Pain #maidan, 81; police
violence, 6, 52, 56, 62, 69, 76, 109,
120; recording participants' own
reactions, 47; regional networks,
57, 58, 59, 60, 122, 123; shootings,
video footage of, 82–83; social
media platforms and, 6, 11, 70, 103,
138; spread of, 57, 58; strategic
visibility in, 73–74; surveillance,
indications of, 46–47; transborder
networks/connections, 50; translation
initiatives, 123; Twitter accounts,
120; Twitter use, 119; virtual
ethnographic observation, 7–9;
visibility, 69–71. *See also* Kharkiv;
Kyiv; Odesa; Washington, DC
Euromaidan SOS, 59, 121
EuroMaydan (protest community), 59

Facebook: accounts made public during
protest, 47; activities, criticism of,
137–38; Anti-Corruption Foundation
(FBK), 148; avatars, 42, 133; bridging
ties, 101–2; civic activism, 43;
collections of Euromaidan-related
documents, 128; disinformation,
spread of, 129–30; English-language
pages, 123; Euromaidan News and
Analysis, 123; Euromaidan protest
(2013–2014), 6, 34, 40, 43–44, 54,
56, 60, 61, 82, 122, 161; Euromaidan
regional hubs, 122–23; Euromaidan
Updates in English, 123; Euromaiden
in English, 123; EuroMaydan page,
59, 121, 122; everyday use, 39, 41,
42; evidence, stored content as, 128;
fundraising, 64; Galas, 111; Kharkiv
protesters, counseling offered to,
96–97; Kyiv protesters, 41, 44, 54,
93, 125, 126; live blogging, 76;

Maidan University (public lectures), 128; Odesa participants, 100, 126; offline charity events, 64; opinion leaders, 104; police crackdown on protesters, 74; posts in *Phantom Pain #maidan*, 81; protest-themed art and slogans, 133; reasons for joining, 42; recording verbal and visual reports, 47; recruitment of Euromaidan interviewees, 31; in Russia, 143; translations, 123; transnational nature of, 51; Ukraine, usage in, 51, 119, 121; Ukrainian American networks, 65; Ukrainian community, 51; Ukrainian diaspora, 63, 64, 66; unfollowing, fallout from, 45; verification/fact-checking, 130; visual memorials, 81; warnings of riot police action, 127

Facebook Messenger, 54

FBK. *See* Anti-Corruption Foundation (FBK)

flexibility, 160, 161; of Galas, 113, 114; of social media, 158

Foursquare, 54, 55, 111

framing, 118, 119; Euromaidan and, 132, 134–38, 162; protest frames and narratives, 134–38; protest that the internet made possible frame, 135, 137–38, 139, 162; self-organized/grassroots protest frame, 135–36, 162; shift from single-issue to multiple-issue protest frame, 135, 136–37, 162; visual framing of protests, 132–34

freedom of expression, 117, 168

Freedom on the Net, 25, 26, 171

freedom of speech, 167–68; Russia and, 23, 24, 26, 27, 39; Ukraine and, 17, 168

Free Maidan University, 76

Furman, Oleksii, 84

Future Russia, 147

Galas, 11, 90, 107–14; activities, 108; crowdsourcing initiative, 107; digital tools, 111, 113; ephemerality, 107, 110, 114; Facebook page, 111; flexibility, 113, 114; founding of, 107–8; hybrid nature of, 113; information collected/disseminated, 110, 113; interactive map, 108; leaflet mapping protest locations, *112;* mobile apps, 108; online/offline work combination, 108, 110, 113; organization, 110; training of volunteers, 110, 114; volunteers, 107, 108, 110, 111, 113–14; webinars, 110; website, 108–9, *109*

Georgia, 3, 6

Gerbaudo, Paolo, 138, 162

Gezi Park, Istanbul, 120

global networks, 51

Goldstein, Joshua, 18; "Role of Digital Networked Technologies in the Ukrainian Orange Revolution, The", 16

Gongadze, Georgiy, 17–18, 20

Google Docs, 97, 111; Memo to Moderators, 96

Google News Lab, 84

Gunitsky, Seva, 16, 39, 51

hacking attacks, 130; in Russia, 151

Hall, Stuart, 119

hashtags, 59, 120; #DigitalMaidan, 124; #euromaidan, 45, 74, 120, 129

Holodomor famine, 52, 171

Hoskins, Andrew, and Ben O'Loughlin, 5

Howard, Philip N., 16

HRC Memorial, 144

Hromadske TV, 76, 131

human rights, 41, 168; digital rights and, 168, 169; organizations, 26, 153; Russia and, 12, 149, 151, 153, 168; Ukraine and, 6, 17, 50, 58, 128, 135, 136; violations, 128. *See also* freedom of speech

hybrid media system, 5, 12, 123, 162

hybrid spaces, 2, 155, 157, 167

"I Am a Drop in the Ocean", 133
ICT-enabled civic projects, 92
imagined affordances, 4–5
information and communication
    technologies (ICTs), 3, 18, 33, 44,
    72, 157
information controls, in Russia, 23,
    25–26, 142–44
information sharing: affordances of
    digital media, 144; Euromaidan
    protesters, 117–18; social media and,
    118–19, 125, 138–39, 162
Instagram, 6, 41, 54
International Telecommunications
    Union, 25
internet: affordances of, 5, 28, 43;
    anti-corruption activists, 21;
    augmented protest and, 10; civic
    activism, 42–43; cybersecurity,
    46; data localization law in Russia,
    143; democratizing potential of, 3,
    15–16; dualist nature of, 16; as new
    layer of reality, 166; role in global
    networks, 51; Russia, development
    in, 10; Russia, restrictions in, 12, 22,
    142, 142–43, 163, 167, 168; Russian
    legislation and the, 25; in Ukraine,
    10, 18, 19, 20–21, 25; VPN use, 46
Internet Archive, Wayback Machine,
    108, *109*
internet regulation, 25–27
investigative witnessing, 82–86
Isin, Engin, and Evelyn Ruppert, 168

Journalism 360 Challenge grant, 84

Karamshuk, Dmytro, et al., 136
Kendall, Lori, 38
Kharkiv, Ukraine, 31; citizen media
    coverage, 95; counseling offered to
    protesters, 96–97; decision-making,
    98; digital media skills/practices,
    130; Euromaidan interviewees, 52,
    58–61, 92, 93, 95, 96; Facebook use,
    122–23; internet use, protesters, 33,

44; media consumption patterns, 131;
    media habits, 33, 93; online coverage
    of protest events, 103; parti-time
    participation, 106, 107; police
    violence, 77; protesters' motivations,
    58; social media, 100–101; Twitter
    use, 41, 122; vicarious trauma, sense
    of, 127; workflow, decentralization,
    96
Kherson, Ukraine, 58
Kiryukhin, Denys, 17
Knight Foundation, 84
Koliska, Michael, and Jessica Roberts,
    54
Kozlovsky, Oleg, 151
Kremlin, 12, 27, 143, 147, 159
Kuchma, Leonid, 17; Ukraine Without
    Kuchma protest, 18
Kulyk, Volodymyr, 126
Kyiv, Ukraine, 7–8, 9; activists'
    motivations, 53–54; Alley of the
    Heavenly Hundred Heroes, 84,
    172; art and images in protest
    camp, 133; civic activism, 42;
    commemorative witnessing, 80;
    Euromaidan interviewees, 7–8, 10,
    30, *30*, 31, 44, 51–57, 73, 80–83,
    93–95, 125; European Square, 52;
    Facebook use, 41, 44, 54, 93, 101,
    125, 126; following users, reasons
    for, 45; illegal construction, 21,
    43; Independence Square, 49, 52,
    55, 56, 57–58, 69, 133; individual
    activity, 105; information sharing,
    125; Instytutska Street, 77, 84,
    172; internet usage of protesters,
    33–34, 44; IT-savvy volunteers,
    102; IT Tent, 92; journalists,
    protesters' engagement with, 132;
    legal assistance initiative, 101;
    LiveJournal use, 43; logistics issues,
    93, 100; management skills, 36–37;
    media habits, 31, 33, 34; medical
    supplies for protesters, 56–57;
    misinformation on social media,

129; multiple devices, use of, 46; Mykhaylivska Square, 36; networked communities, perception of, 103; old and new protesters, 35, 36, 97–98; online activity, 54; organizing the protest, 94–95, 96, 97–98; part-time participation, 106; police violence, 6, 52, 62, 69, 76, 79; recording participants' own reactions, 47; "Save Old Kyiv", 21; social media, 125, 129; social media tools, 74; visual framing of protest, 133, 134; website, information from, 125; witnessing as affective connection, 78; witnessing as participation, 75–76
Kyj, Myroslaw J., 18

Lim, C., 102
LinkedIn, 46, 63–64, 102, 143
Litreev, Alex, 152
LiveJournal, 19, 21, 39, 43
live streaming apps, 48
live streams. *See* video live streams
Livyy Bereh, 130
Lviv, Ukraine, 58
Lysenko, Volodymyr V., and Kevin C. Desouza, 152
Lyubashenko, Igor, 105–6, 138

MacKinnon, Rebecca, 16
Maidan, 172
Maidan Nezalezhnosti, 52, 172
media: Euromaidan events, framing of, 132; Euromaidan press releases/ visual content, 131; Euromaidan protesters and, 131–32; international media, 131; mainstream media, 131, 135, 138; Russia, state control of, 148
mediated witnessing, 71–73, 81
Medvedev, Dmitry, 21, 145, 148
MENA. *See* Middle East and North Africa (MENA)
microblogging, 40. *See also* Twitter

Middle East and North Africa (MENA), 3, 6
Milan, Stefania, 119, 135, 162
misinformation on social media, 129–30, 162
mobile phones, *34*, 46, 47, 61, 72, 91. *See also* smartphones
mobilization, 4, 12, 18, 19, 90, 113, 157; in mass protests, 90; in Russia, 23–24, 27; social media and, 6, 7, 120, 122, 136, 137, 162, 165; in Ukraine, 52, 59, 77, 79, 86
Morozov, Evgeny, 16
Moscow, 23, 145–49, 151, 171. *See also* Bolotnaya rallies (2011–2012)

Nagy, Peter, and Gina Neff, 4–5
Navalny, Alexey, 145–48, 150–52
Nayyem, Mustafa, 1, 117; Euromaidan protests, 1, 44, 104; Facebook and, 61–62, 104, 121
Nebesna Sotnya (Heavenly Hundred), 81
networked media, affordances of, 4, 11, 57
networked protest communities, 102–104
networked publics, 4, 7, 16, 26, 27, 67, 127, 159
networked technologies, dualist nature of, 16
new media ecology, concept of, 5
New York, 49, 65, 79, 94, 97
New York University, Social Media and Political Participation Lab, 119

Oates, Sarah, 39
Occupy movement, 3
Odesa, Ukraine, 58; commemorative witnessing, 81; Euromaidan interviewees, 52, 59, 60, 61, 74, 79, 81, 95, 100; Euromaidan protesters, *30*, 34, 36; Facebook, unfollowing, 45; Facebook use, 100, 122–23, 126; information sources, 126; opinion leaders/singular voices, 104;

organizing the protest, 95; Twitter, perception of, 41
Odnoklassniki, 25
offline: activism, 2, 166; charity events, 64; networks, 100–101
online: activism, 2, 42, 166; communities, 59; platforms, global nature of, 50; public intellectuals, 104; public sphere, in Russia, 23, 27
Onuch, Olga, 52, 58, 76
Orange Revolution (2004), 3, 6, 18–19, 52; Goldstein's report, 16; international donor support, 18; internet and, 18, 19; online platforms, 19; participants, 35; websites, role of, 18
OVD-Info, 144, 153

part-time revolutionaries, 103–7
persistence, 5; of digitally mediated information, 141–42; of social media, 134, 138, 158
Peters, John Durham, 74–75
Pirate Party, 147
Polezhaka, Serhiy, 84
police, violence in Kyiv, 6, 52, 62, 69, 74, 76, 79
political activism, 20, 34, 35, 39, 41–42, 144
political engagement, 29, 38, 41, 48, 49, 67, 166
post-protest memories, 160
post-protest witnessing, 83, 84
post-Soviet space, 3, 9, 10
post-Soviet states, 24, 39, 40, 142
pre-Euromaidan routines, 40–43
protest communities, 90–91
protest movements: affordances of digital media, 49–50, 90; horizontal, 98; social media and, 162; transnational nature of, 50
protest square, 12, 28, 113, 115, 168; in Kyiv, 10, 52–57, 67, 85–86, 137–39, 159, 160, 162; in Russia, 158–59, 163

Putin, Vladimir, 21–23
Putnam, Robert D., 101

Quan-Haase, Anabel, and Kim Martin, 113

Radio Svoboda (Radio Liberty), 76
Red Button app, 152
replicability, 57, 59, 95, 102, 129, 166
research methods, 7–9; data collection, 8; identity of researcher and, 9; virtual ethnography, 7–8, 146
revolutionaries (part-time), 103–7
revolution of dignity, 146
Rose Revolution (2003), 6
Rosgvardia, 143
Roskomnadzor, 24, 142, 171
RosKomSvoboda, 147, 171
Russia, 21–24, 141–55; anti-corruption protests, 4–8, 26, 145, 163; anti-government protests, 11–12; augmented dissent, 5, 142, 144–45, 163–65; augmented protest, 155, 158; authoritarianism, 13, 15, 16, 22, 25, 39, 141, 163, 169; Bolotnaya rallies (2011–2012), 3, 12, 171; censorship, 22, 143, 147, 148, 159; citizens' communications, state control over, 22; conspicuous security, protesters and, 12, 151–54, 164, 166; constitution, 23; counter-surveillance by protesters, 145, 147, 153, 164; Cyrillic web, 7; digital media, 7, 10, 163; digital rights activists, 147; dissent, affordances of digital media, 142; "Don't Call Him Dimon" (documentary), 145; extremism charges, 26; extremist materials, government list of, 24; fines for unsanctioned rallies, 24; freedom of speech, 23, 26, 27, 39; Future Russia party, 147; hacking of social media accounts, 151; information controls, 23, 25–26, 142–44; internet, development of,

10; internet, role of, 7; internet in social and political life, 39; internet restrictions, 12, 22, 25, 26, 143, 163, 168; interviews with Euromaidan protesters, 8–9; mass protests, 3, 143, 144; MTS mobile provider, 151; networked surveillance, 151; online public sphere, 23, 24, 27, 164; picketers, rules regulating, 144; post-Soviet, 10, 22; press freedom, 23; protest activity, reaction to, 158–59; protesters, digital media and, 2, 164; protest rallies, 142; protests, 23, 24, 26; protests, penalties, 144; Rosgvardia, 143; Roskomnadzor (telecommunications regulator), 24, 142; security services, hacking and, 151; SIM-cards, state IDs and, 143; social media networks, 25; social media regulations, 143; Soviet Union, collapse of, 21; state control, 21–23; state security issues, 22; state surveillance, 12, 23, 142, 145–48, 150–52, 164–65; strategic visibility, 146–50, 165; surveillance in digital spaces, 143, 147; United Russia party, 22; VKontakte, 51; Voters' Boycott marches, 145; VPNs, 27, 143; websites, blacklist registry of, 24, 171; websites, public opposition, 146; Wi-Fi networks, 143
Russian Constitution, 143–44
Russian legislation, 142–43, 168; amendments to the Constitution, 143–44; anti-extremist legislation, 142, 143; bloggers' law, 143; data localization law, 143, 152; Federal Law #139-FZ, 24; internet legislation, 25, 167; messenger apps/services banned, 143; surveillance-oriented, 143; Yarovaya Law, 143
Russia-Ukraine conflict, 7, 25, 27, 167

Saunders, Clare, et al., 34

Savytska, Anastasiia, and Andrey Myrhorodskiy, 81
scalability, 5, 134; of digitally mediated information, 141–42; socially mediated, 145, 164; of social media, 138, 158; strategic, 146–50
security, conspicuous security, 12, 151–54, 164, 166
Siegelbaum, Lewis H., 147
Sjøvaag, Helle, 134
Skype, 57, 60, 96
smartphones, 33, *34*, 40, 44, 46, 48. *See also* mobile phones
Sobol, Lyubov, 150
social capital, 98–102; civic participation and, 99; structural external forces and, 98–99
socially mediated visibility, 70–71, 73, 83, 85–87
social media: achievement of scale and intensity, 138; active citizen participation, 39; affordances of, 5, 43, 81, 98, 99; augmented protest and, 10, 72; avatars, 133; bots, 129; common protest language, 72; country-specific, 51; cybersecurity, 46; cyborg accounts, 129; disinformation, spread of, 129, 138; ephemerality of, 162; Euromaidan protest (2013–2014), 6, 11, 54, 70, 103, 138; following users, reasons for, 45; growth in Ukraine, 130–31; information sharing and, 118–19, 125, 138–39, 162; latest news on feeds, 41; misinformation, 129, 142; Odnoklassniki, 25; offline networks of social ties, 100–101; online coverage of protest events, 103; part-time involvement with Euromaidan, 105–7; persistence, 5, 134, 138; power of, 3; protesters' adaptations, 119; protesters' perception of, 92–93, 99; protest movements and, 162; protest networks and, 99, 100; protest use mode, 46; role in global

networks, 51; Russian networks, 25; scalability, 134, 138; spammers, 130; traditional media and, 131–32; trolls, 130; two-step authentication, 46; unfollowing, fallout from, 45; virtual stage, creation of, 72; visual framing of protest, 133. *See also* affordances of social media; Facebook; Instagram; LinkedIn; Telegram; Twitter; VKontakte

social movements: reliance on digital networks, 50; storytelling, 119

social movement theory, 118, 119

social networks, 33, 39, 42, 46, 53, 60, 66, 90, 97; affordances of, 125, 127, 128; civic engagement and, 63; connective action and, 104; online and offline interactions, 99, 122, 133; participation and, 75–76, 106; recruitment and, 102, 110; resources embedded in, 98. *See also* Facebook; Instagram; LinkedIn; social media; Telegram; Twitter; VKontakte

Soviet Union, 10, 15, 21, 22, 147

spammers, 130

Spilno.TV, 76, 77

statement movements, 72

storytelling, 72, 83, 117, 119

StrikePoster, 133

successful Kickstarter campaign, 84

surveillance, 2, 27, 28; in Russia, 12, 23, 142, 145–48, 150–52, 164–65; Soviety policy, 22; in Ukraine, 46, 71, 117

Syrian uprising, 134

Telegram, 8, 146, 151–54. *See also* Telegram messenger

Telegram messenger, 148, 151–53

temporality, 8, 48, 70, 77, 86, 108, 110, 113–14, 115; flexible, 11, 87, 90, 141

Texty.org.ua, 83, 120, 130

"Three Days in February", 83–85

Tor browser, 152

transnational protests, 50, 64

transnational services, 51

trolls, 130

Trombetta, Lorenzo, 134

trust/trustworthiness, 46, 63, 64, 65, 90, 91, 150, 154; civic engagement and, 101–2

Tufekçi, Zeynep, 72, 98, 104, 120, 162; and Christopher Wilson, 91

Twitter, 8; Anti-Corruption Foundation (FBK), 148, 153; avatars, 133; bots, manipulation by, 129, 151; buzzwords, information manipulation, 135; civic activism, 43; cyborg accounts, 129; disinformation about Euromaidan protesters, 129; Euromaidan accounts, 120; Euromaidan protests, 6, 34, 40, 54, 56, 82; everyday use, 39, 40–41; international awareness-raising efforts, 124; live blogging, 76; multilingual use, 121; perception of, 41, 120–21; public drives, 64; recording participants' own reactions, 47; recording verbal and visual reports, 47; in Russia, 143; storms (#DigitalMaidan), 124; translations, 123; transnational nature of, 51; Ukraine, spike in usage, 119, 120; Ukrainian diaspora, 63, 66. *See also* hashtags

Ukraine: anti-corruption activists, 21; anti-protest laws, 25; apps, increased use of, 48; augmented dissent, 5; citizen journalism, 18, 48, 76, 95; civic regeneration, 167; country-specific social media platform, lack of, 51; cyberwarfare concerns, 167; Cyrillic web, 7; DDoS attacks on websites, 20, 130; democracy, 17; digital media, development of, 10; digital shortcuts, 165; disinformation, 129–30, 138, 167; economic assets, privatization of, 17; election monitoring, 21; elections

(2004), 18; Euromaidan protests, 1, 3; Facebook, 51, 119, 121; free speech, 17, 168; geopolitical conflict with Russia, 7; government, 64; government, internet usage, 20; identity problems post-independence, 17; independence, 16–17; internet, development of, 10, 18, 19, 20–21; internet habits, 141; interviewees, 10; Kyiv, protest in, 7–8; legislation, 168; local maidans, 60–61; mainstream media content, 131; map of, CIA Factbook, *32;* mass protest events, 3; murder of journalist, Gongadze, 17–18; news coverage restrictions, 20; news websites, 17, 131; online journalists and bloggers, 20; online media, 20; Orange Revolution (2004), 3, 6; parliament, 117; political parties, internet usage, 20; portrayal in international media, 33; post-Euromaidan, 26–27; post-independence, 17; post-Soviet, 10; protest activity, reaction to, 158; protesters, digital media and, 2; protesters' motivations, 58; Russian social media networks blocked, 25; Russia-Ukraine conflict, 7, 25, 27, 167; "Save Old Kyiv", 21; social media, growth in popularity, 130–31; social media habits, 141; traditional media, 19; urban activism, 20–21; VKontakte, 51; walkie-talkie app, Zello, 48; websites, hacking attacks on, 130. *See also* Kharkiv; Kyiv; Odesa
Ukraine Without Kuchma protest, 18
Ukrainian diaspora, 37, 51, 52, 61–66, 79, 123–24
Ukrainians, identity and, 9
Ukrainska Pravda (*The Ukrainian Truth*), 17, 18, 81–82, 130
United Russia party, 22
urban activism, in Ukraine, 20–21
Ushahidi platform, 36, 108

Usmanov, Alisher, 148
USSR, dissolution of, 22
UStream, 48, 76

Valenzuela, Sebastián, et al., 63, 105–6, 138
Varnelis, Kazys, and Anne Friedberg, 53
Viber, 143
video live streams, 76–77, 128; Anti-Corruption Foundation (FBK), 148–49; anti-corruption protests in Russia, 148–50, 154; augmented witnessing, 76–77; drone-enabled footage, 128; Euromaidan protest (2013–2014), 6, 48, 56, 103, 161; importance as historical documents, 48; Russian anti-corruption protests, 148; usefulness of, 128; witnessing as affective connection, 78–79. *See also* UStream; YouTube
videos: Euromaidan protest (2013–2014), 6, 74, 82, 103; shootings, footage of, 82–83
virtual ethnography, 7–8, 146
virtual private networks (VPNs), 27, 46, 143, 152
visibility, 5, 11, 158; Euromaidan protest and, 69–70, 73–74, 134; hybrid protest activity, 11; socially mediated, 70–71, 73, 83, 85–86, 87, 142, 145, 154, 160, 164; strategic visibility, 73–74, 146–50, 165; versus ephemerality, 153–54
visual framing of protests, 132–34; art and images in the protest camp, 133; avatars on social media, 133; Euromaidan posters, 133; "I Am a Drop in the Ocean", 133; images as carriers of information, 134
VKontakte, 25, 41, 42, 51, 58, 105; Anti-Corruption Foundation (FBK), 148; citizen participation, 51; Euromaidan protesters use of, 40, 131; everyday use of, 40, 41; reasons

for joining, 42; tool for repression, 51; Ukrainian community, 51
Volkov, Leonid, 152
Voters' Boycott marches, 145

Wahl-Jorgensen, Karin, et al., 168
Wanenchak, Sarah, 56, 73
Washington, DC, 61–66; Basecamp (project management), 97; copywriting/analytical skills, 37; deaths of protesters, days of mourning, 133; Euromaidan protesters, 30–31, *30*, 34, 37, 44–45, 52, 80, 97; Facebook use, 61–62; fundraising, 64–65; geographical distance, effects of, 65–66, 94; internet usage of protesters, 33–34, 44–45; LinkedIn, assessment of professionals, 46; media habits of protesters, 31, 33, 34; media relations wing of protest network, 132; opposition to Euromaidan protest, 105; part-time participation, 106, 107; protest at Ukrainian Embassy, 62–63; real-time coverage, 77; social capital, 99–100; Ukrainian diaspora, 52, 61–66, 79, 123–24; witnessing as affective connection, 78–80
Washington interviewees, 61–63
Wayback Machine, 108, *109*
websites: Galas, 108; hacking attacks, 130; Orange Revolution, role in, 18; Russian blacklist registry, 24, 152, 171; Russian opposition websites, 146; Ukrainian news websites,

17, 131; *Ukrainska Pravda* (*The Ukrainian Truth*), 17, 18, 81–82, 130
WeChat, 51
Western Europe, protest events, 6
Western protest events, 3; anti-Trump movement, 3; Occupy movement, 3
Wi-Fi, 114, 143
Wilson, Andrew, 16–17, 90–91, 136
witnessing, 11, 67, 73–74, 160; as affective connection, 78–80; augmented, 74–75, 83–86, 87; commemorative, 80–82; investigative, 82–85, 86; as key affordance of social media, 47; mediated, 71–73, 81; media-witnessing devices, 72; mindfulness of, 86; as participation, 75–78; post-protest, 83, 84; traditional modalities of, 74–75

Yanukovych, Viktor, 1, 18, 19–20, 25, 117, 131; EU Association Agreement and, 1, 6, 43, 52, 58, 61
Yeltsin, Boris, 21
YouTube, 82; Anti-Corruption Foundation (FBK), 148; "The Cloud", 152; "Don't Call Him Dimon", 145, 148; Euromaidan protests, 8, 79; Navalny LIVE, 146, 152; tribute videos, 82
Yushchenko, Viktor, 18, 19

Zdolnikov, Vladislav, 152
Zelinska, Olga, 60
Zello (walkie-talkie app), 48

About the Author

Tetyana Lokot is an associate professor at the School of Communications at Dublin City University. She researches protest and digital media in Ukraine and Russia, as well as internet freedom, internet governance, and urban media practices in Eastern Europe. She completed her PhD at the Philip Merrill College of Journalism at the University of Maryland.

Her research has been published in *Information, Communication & Society*; *Digital Journalism; Surveillance & Society*; *Irish Studies in International Affairs*; and *Social Media + Society*. Her work has appeared in the edited collections *Gender Hate Online* and *The Routledge Companion to Urban Media and Communication*. She has contributed to Freedom House's *Freedom on the Net* report, and she currently contributes research to the Ranking Digital Rights *Corporate Accountability Index*. Her writing has also appeared in *The Guardian*, *The Washington Post*, *The Moscow Times*, *Point & Counter Point*, and *RTÉ Brainstorm*.

From 2014 to 2016 Lokot was contributing editor for the *RuNet Echo* project at *Global Voices*. She is a member of the conference committee for the *Theorizing the Web* conference and chair of the Media, Cities, and Space section of the European Communication Research and Education Association. Before stepping into academia, she worked as a journalist, nonprofit consultant, and media trainer in Ukraine, Belarus, and Georgia. She is equally happy speaking English, Ukrainian, and Russian.